Light railways

in England and Wales

Light railways

in England and Wales

Peter Bosley

Manchester University Press
Manchester and New York
Distributed exclusively in the USA and Canada by St. Martin's Press

Copyright © Peter Bosley 1990

Published by Manchester University Press
Oxford Road, Manchester M13 9PL, UK
and Room 400, 175 Fifth Avenue,
New York, NY 10010, USA

Distributed exclusively in the USA and Canada
by St. Martin's Press, Inc.,
175 Fifth Avenue, New York, NY 10010, USA

British Library cataloging in publication data
Bosley, Peter
  Light railways in England and Wales.
  1. England. Light railway services
  I. Title
  385'.5'0942

Library of Congress cataloging in publication data
Bosley, Peter. 1944–
    Light railways in England and Wales/Peter Bosley.
      p.   cm.
    Includes bibliographical references.
    ISBN 0-7190-1758-0
    1. Railroads. Local and light—England.   2. Railroads, Local and
  light—Wales.   I. Title.
  TF57.B597 1990
  385'.0942—dc20   89-13335

ISBN 0 7190 1758 0

Typeset in Great Britain
by Megaron, Cardiff

Printed in Great Britain
by Billings Ltd., Worcester

Contents

Figures and tables

Acknowledgements

This book is a revised version of a thesis accepted by the University of Reading for the degree of M. Phil. I should like to thank Dr Sadie Ward for her help during the initial stages of its academic career. In its present form it owes much to the constructive criticism of Dr Jonathan Brown who has given generously both of his time and his detailed knowledge of the more remote branches of the subject.

Mr Gordon Brown has proved to be a most accurate and expeditious typist.

It is right that I record my indebtedness to my wife and two daughters, who, seven years ago, knew nothing of light railways but who have now holidayed by, walked over and even travelled on them.

Finally, lest it not now emerge from the text, it must be accepted that my initial interest in railways derived from a fascination with steam locomotives. This for a historian may be considered too nostalgic or even maudlin; the true inspiration for this work must be acknowledged, however.

P. B.

That Tight Little, Light Little . . .

You farmers who lately
Have suffered so greatly
   From agricultural depression
Shake off gloom and sorrow
A brighter tomorrow
   Will dawn in the course of the session.

By no relaxation
Of rates or taxation
   By a certain sure-never-to-fail way
Through government's pleasure
To bring in a measure
   For giving some districts a railway:
   A tight little, light little, railway,
     A nice little, light little, railway.
O think of the joy
Of that exquisite toy
   A tight little, light little, railway.

Your wheat may grow cheaper,
The pay of your reaper
   May rise to a figure outrageous;
The weather may lay all
Your crops, and your hay all
   be ruined by tempests rampageous;
Your stock mayn't grow fatter,
But that does not matter,
   Except in a bargain and sale way:
What are these to the blessing
Of really possessing
   A tight little, light little, railway.

                     (Chorus)

You may not have a fraction
Of produce for traction,
  Not a stone's weight to put in a wagon,
Not a horse in your stable,
No bread on your table,
  Not a shoe to your foot, not a rag on:
All this would be frightful
Were it not so delightful
  to see in a slow as a snail way
The trucks all go gliding
From track into siding,
  From siding to track on your railway.
                                                 (Chorus)

Then, oh *fortunati*
Agricola, wait, aye
  Wait, for the clouds to roll by you:
Your troubles are over;
To-morrow, in clover,
  You'll laugh at the ills that now try you.
'*Ex machina Deus*
Is coming to free us,
  Not in the old-fashioned or stale way.'
Let this be your chorus
  'A future's before us;
  Three cheers for the light little railway!'
                                                 (Chorus)

A contemporary response to the Light Railway Act expressed in a
London evening newspaper. Quoted by Sir Arthur Heywood, *Minimum
Gauge Railways*, pp. 57–9.

Introduction

Despite the number of books on railways published in recent years, and they include many chronicles of individual light railway companies, there has been little serious analysis of the development of light railway legislation in the light of the economic and political factors which brought it into being. In the last thirty years only W. J. K. Davies's *Light Railways* has tackled this problem, but this valuable work, by providing comparison with overseas practice, necessarily does not take the discussion of events in England and Wales far enough. Apart from this work, railway history in the main is still bedevilled by the pictorial, the anecdotal and the nostalgic bemoaned by H. W. Parris in 1954[1] and J. R. Kellett in 1969.[2] Light railways have inspired few exceptions.[3]

The purpose of this study is to survey the political and economic history of light railways from their first official appearance in 1868 to the Light Railways Act of 1896, and the achievements of the Act up to 1914. The book concludes with a review of light railways in decline: if light railways constituted the last serious expansion of the railway network in Britain, many were among the first railway lines to be closed in the face of road competition.

It is a feature of this subject that the historian suffers — or enjoys — both too much and too little source material. There is an abundance of material, from official reports to company archives, from which the history of railways can be constructed. Yet for some questions to which the historian would most like answers — the business management of light railways, the details of traffic, for example — there is remarkably little. This was the problem encountered when attempting to subject a number of light railways to close scrutiny. For some companies, such as the North Sunderland Railway, there is a solid body of evidence from directors' minutes, correspondence, external reports from the London &

North Eastern Railway and from newspapers; but for other light railway companies there is virtually nothing. However, even when a significant body of material is available, it is rare to find the detailed statistical material that one would like, or at least in a form appropriate for the purpose of comparison. Figures for passenger travel rarely show destination on or off a line, livestock figures are rarely broken down and information as to the nature of general merchandise or parcels is hard to come by. The details of rolling stock, diagrams of track layouts, dates of sod-cutting ceremonies, costs of locomotives are readily available, whereas precisely what the railway carried is shrouded in mystery. It is with a strict consciousness of such limitations that this work attempts to evaluate the part played by light railways in the rural community.

Any study of light railways immediately raises the question, what is a light railway? This study takes as its basis light railways as legally defined in a series of acts of Parliament passed between 1864 and 1896 which permitted railway companies, on authorisation from the Board of Trade, to dispense with some of the most stringent safety requirements in return for certain restrictions, notably on speed and the axle load of locomotives. As will be seen, this was a definition which did not entirely satisfy contemporary experts; nor, indeed, some recent historians, such as C. R. Clinker, who declared that 'the term light railway has not been defined in any Act or Order', and W. J. K. Davies, who decided that 'the best definition is a railway below the standard of a country's mainline railways'.[4] There is justification for their views for it can be seen that there were railways, many built after 1864 and 1896, which were operated in no way differently from those that were styled 'light railway', but which were authorised by private Act of Parliament. One of the most often-quoted examples of these railways is the Lynton & Barnstaple. However, while it is not appropriate to consider light railways as isolated phenomena, so that the Lynton & Barnstaple and others do receive honourable mention, it is with those railways that sought authority under those general Acts of Parliament (even if, like the Easingwold, it was done somewhat belatedly) that this book is really concerned.

Even taking this legalistic definition, it will be seen that light railways were immensely varied, built to serve a variety of purposes and places, from waterworks, to docks, to remote country districts. The primary purpose of light railway legislation was to promote the expansion of transport in rural areas to help alleviate the depression in agriculture of the last quarter of the nineteenth century. Most proposed and constructed light railways were, in fact, attempts to improve rural transport, and in the discussion that follows in this book the results of those attempts will be a major consideration. However, this is no more than an introduction to a subject about which it is to be hoped more will be learned as time goes on.

This work, for practical purposes, has accepted as a light railway anything which was regarded as such by the Light Railway Commissioners, or any such line that was already in existence. Within such a definition this study has concentrated on rural light railways and thus a substantial group of largely mineral lines has been deemed beyond its scope; similarly, private industrial railways have been left to other historians.

Notes

1 H. W. Parris, '_Railways in the Northern Pennines_ to 1880', M.A. thesis, University of Leeds, 1954.

2 J. R. Kellett, 'Writing on Victorian railways, essay in nostalgia', _Victorian Studies_, XIII (1969), pp. 90–6.

3 W. J. K. Davies, _Light Railways_, 1964, is worthy of close attention but little else goes beyond the purely descriptive. Only two small companies have received satisfactory treatment in published works: the Golden Valley Railway and the Wissington Railway.

4 C. R. Clinker, _Light Railway Orders_, 1977, p. 2; Davies, _Light Railways_, p. 10.

1

Why light railways?

Light railways were railways built to a lower standard than ordinary railways because expected traffic would not justify a conventional railway. Many light railways thus came into being to serve the needs of mineral producing areas where not only might traffic be relatively slight but the absence of a passenger service would remove the need for speed to be a consideration. It was in rural areas, however, where freight traffic was often light and seasonal and passengers few, that light railways were expected to come into their own.

To identify light railways as of 'a lower standard', carrying traffic which was 'less' is to indicate a comparison with ordinary railways, and as light railways can be understood only in this relationship it is necessary to present them in relation to their larger scale brethren. One of the characteristics of public railways built under private Act of Parliament from 1825 onwards was their high costs and capital. Initially traffic justified such expenditure on major routes, but even by the 1850s lines of a local and rural nature were facing difficulties. The Northallerton to Hawes branch was 'crushed by the several burdens of working expenses, lack of capital, and interest on debts'.[1] In West Wales the Mid Wales Railway, the Carmarthen & Cardigan Railway and the Manchester & Milford Railway all experienced financial crises; the latter company survived the financial crisis of 1867 only because of the capital resources of the contractor David Davies, while all three companies spent years in the hands of receivers.[2] The Golden Valley Railway in Herefordshire was dogged by difficulties and experienced ignominious closure before being bought by the Great Western Railway (GWR).

One of the problems facing railway promoters from the outset had been high capital costs. Railway companies delighted in building on a grand scale but for most railways it was the cost of land and of obtaining parliamentary authority that significantly affected capitalisation. The legacy of this afflicted later railways, even those whose ambitions were at most parochial.

At the end of 1884 costs per mile were estimated as £42,486 compared with £21,236 in Germany and £11,000 in the USA.[3] The price of land was a major factor. The London & Brimingham Railway acquired land valued at £250,000 for three times that amount while the GWR had paid £6,696 per mile and the London to Brighton railway up to £8,000 per mile for land and even then faced heavy engineering works. In a technical sense many of the railways' engineering problems had been solved by the canal companies, but far more than the canals the railways sought directness, so cuttings, embankments and tunnels were more numerous and on a grander scale, inevitably adding to costs. Such costs were not reduced by the scale and solidity of construction: elegant tunnel mouths, decorated arches and grand or eccentric station buildings.

Another major expense for railway companies was the obtaining of parliamentary approval. The method in operation was time-consuming as far as Parliament was concerned, giving scope for minute and detailed objections by a company's rivals, and being correspondingly expensive for the companies. E. D. Chattaway, a director of the North British Railway, estimated that each mile of railway cost about £1,000 in parliamentary and legal expenses.[4] To have its first bill approved by Parliament cost the GWR £87,197, while the Great Northern Railway (GNR) spent £433,000 on its Acts in 1845–46, and its legal and parliamentary expenses had risen to £1·4 million by 1858, out of an authorised capital of £9·6 million.[5]

Land and parliamentary costs at 16 per cent were, as P. S. Bagwell points out, a significant part of the total investment on British railways.[6]: the significance of such costs becomes even greater when related to the building of minor railways in rural areas in the second half of the nineteenth century. Some railway companies never fully recovered from a combination of a heavy capital burden, excessive legal and parliamentary charges, and dubious financing, especially if traffic was too sparse to provide adequate revenue.[7]

Light railways

Light railways were seen as a solution to the problems associated with high capital cost. They would be constructed cheaply and operated economically; above all they would be flexible. Not only would they reach out to every village but spurs or sidings could be thrown off to every farm or even every field. For passengers there would be few stations but trains would stop where requested. Some commentators envisaged an extended network of such lines reaching out to all parts of the country. One such was William Bridges Adams, whose proposal was to lay rails along turnpikes flush with the road surface covering some 22,000 miles of highway. He also pointed out the advantages of rails laid into farmyards and movable rails laid into fields. Locomotives would be equally flexible, for lifted from the rails their wheels could be used to drive threshing machines, turnip and chaff-cutters or small saw benches.[8] 'But it was Adams's fate, as a prophet, to be ignored',[9] such opinions came not only from those with a professional interest such as E. R. Calthorp or W. M. Acworth but also from the altruistic. The Bishop of Chester, writing in the 1890s, bewailed the backwardness of his 'benighted country' and supported the construction of light railways as a remedy for this.[10] Such concern was not restricted to the episcopate. The Reverend R. Isherwood of Stoke Row in Oxfordshire had as his concern his parish rather than his country. He saw a light railway as the *sine qua non* of opening up his locality — it would provide employment for labourers and would prevent the depopulation of the countryside. The farmer, fruit-grower, poultry-breeder and wood-turner were all hampered by distance from a railway and 'every little man . . . [was] . . . obliged to have his pony and trap to carry his produce into market'.[11]

Railways and the rural community

The need for good transport for agriculture had long been recognised: seed, manure and feedstuffs for livestock had to be brought in to the farm and all forms of produce had to be dispatched. In 1815 the Reverend Walter Davies, noticing obstacles to the improvement of agriculture in Wales, listed the following: 'soil, climate and the quantity of clouds; the local situation which rendered impossible the transportation of lime and coal in requisite quantities; bad roads; open wastes; intermixture of properties; some bad landlords; the system of land agency; vermin (including foxes, foxhounds, and foxhunters)'.[12] In particular much was made of the cost of transporting lime and the associated burden of the system of toll roads, avoidance of which contributed to the destruction of many parish roads.[13] Railways offered the chance to overcome the problems of poor transport in rural areas, and it is not surprising that they were soon being promoted to serve country districts. Local landowners were often prominent supporters of such schemes, just as in the previous century they had been backers of turnpike trusts and canals, for they were interested in improvements to transport that would enhance the value of their estates. They were joined by the business and professional people of the market towns — the grain merchants, brewers, coal merchants, bankers — who at the very least regarded railways as a means of expanding existing business, and at their more optimistic thought in terms of those at Salisbury who declared that railways would make their city 'the Manchester of the south'.

Local newspapers carried verbatim accounts of meetings held to promote new railways when a succession of speakers would underline the advantages to be derived from the venture. One such meeting was held in Cirencester in March 1881 to promote the Swindon & Cheltenham Railway (later part of the Midland & South Western Junction Railway).[14] A point of some significance is that Cirencester was already served by a GWR branch line for this enabled speakers to attack the established company's rates as they outlined the benefits which would follow from the new line. Landowners and traders joined to emphasise reductions in their costs and to affirm their expectation of the new age which would dawn for Cirencester once the GWR's monopoly had been broken.

To a considerable extent the expectations of landowners and farmers were met by the rural railway. Coal and lime were cheaper and farm produce was more easily transported, often reaching a wider market. One of the most immediate consequences of the extension of the railway system was the elimination of long distance droving, with a consequent potential improvement in prices for the farmer. Variation in costs dependent on the weather were ironed out, as flooding in winter no longer meant delays at river crossings which might have meant missing a fair or a market, while drought in summer pushed up a drover's costs by obliging him to buy in feed. Furthermore, drovers had been encountering increasing difficulty in securing accommodation for their herds, a problem which became more acute after the plague epidemic of 1865–66 made farmers less willing to provide accommodation fields, thus inflating forage costs. The most striking advantage attendant upon the shift from droving animals to 'trucking' was the avoidance of weight loss and deterioration of the post slaughter quality of the meat. Fat cattle from Norfolk may have taken five days to walk to Smithfield; by rail, at perhaps a slightly higher cost, the journey was accomplished in one day, and reduced weight loss and improved carcass quality may have achieved a price advantage of £1 per head.[15] Lean store cattle from Wales would have deteriorated less but driven flocks of sheep were more likely to suffer a decline in value: perhaps fifty would die from a flock of 2,000 on the drove road from Wales to England, in 1865 a loss of approximately £25.[16]

The coming of the railway effected a significant change in traditional marketing practices. The farmer could dispatch his produce as livestock direct to an industrial centre; he could visit larger fairs and markets personally to sell or buy in equipment and materials. The labourer, too, particularly if he and his family operated a smallholding or an allotment, could sell his produce in fairs and markets in larger centres. Here he could also buy, at a cheaper price and from a wider range of goods. Beyond the purely personal element the growth of town and villages was influenced by being on a railway: fairs and markets in settlements away from railways declined in number, frequency and importance. Even among railway-served towns those on main lines or junctions benefited at the expense of others which were more remote.[17] In *Memoirs of a Station Master* Ernest J. Simmons noted: 'Railways feed large towns and drain small ones.'[18] His experience on the GWR in Berkshire and Oxfordshire holds true elsewhere. In west Wales the incidence of fairs increased along the routes of railways: thus, the number of fairs doubled at Carmarthen, Lampeter and Llandovery, quadrupled at Newcastle Emlyn, while at Llandilo Fawr and Crymmych, where there had been no fairs in 1792, there were ten and twelve respectively in 1888.[19]

But it was perhaps in respect of dairy produce that railways participated most significantly in the changes that occurred in British farming.[20] The acceptability of railway milk was not immediate: suspect quality as a result of the journey and adulteration led many people to prefer 'town' milk despite the fact that railway milk was cheaper, but with growing restrictions on urban milk suppliers and the development of special vehicles the railways' advantages of speed and cheapness came to the fore. In the early years the railway companies had used open wagons or even fish vans to carry milk, with obvious risks of contamination. In the 1880s vans with white painted roofs and ventilated sides became the standard. The churn, however, remained in common use until 1927 when United Dairies introduced a fleet of fifty railway tankers.

The Great Eastern Railway (GER) had the greatest business in milk up to 1865. The shortage of urban milk in that year because of the outbreak of cattle plague meant that it became profitable to carry milk over longer distances; indeed 1866 saw a 100 per cent increase in the quantity of railway milk compared with 1865. The GWR became more significant with the longer distance milk trade, its milk traffic trebling between 1870 and 1874. The company found that it was moving sufficient milk for special milk platforms to be built at Paddington and a milk station to be built at Wootton Bassett near Swindon. Special milk trains, reluctantly adopted by all the companies, came to the GWR in 1890.

For tenant farmers, as well as the opportunity to diversify into new areas of agriculture and the direct reduction in the cost of their purchases and produce, there was the prospect of a reduction in the number of horses they were obliged to keep. A Scottish farmer claimed before the 1896 Royal Commission on Agriculture that a farm employing ten horses and being 5 miles distant from a railway station would be able to dispense with 1½ horses and save £140 per annum if a railway were to pass his gate.[22]

Landlords also looked to the railways for financial benefits. The coming of the railway would bring, or so it was believed, a definite increase in the value of the land. Depending on the distance from stations and the previous means of transport, increases of 10–15 per cent could be expected. In Scotland a witness before the 1896 Royal Commission suggested that a farm adjacent to a light railway would be subject to an increase of 5s an acre.[23] D. W. Howell emphasises that in Wales rent increases in the third quarter of the nineteenth century were to a large extent due to improved communications rather than the avariciousness of landlords.[24] A note of caution is sounded by Professor J. Simmons, who remarks that the benefits derived from a railway were centred upon stations which even in 1914 were on average 4 miles apart on trunk lines and that 'farm sidings were rare, prizes to be secured as a rule only by great pertinacity'.[25]

However, the provision of a railway offered advantages to the rural community; the difficulty was that such advantages were not enough to stimulate rural railway building in all areas of the country. In the 1880s quite large areas of the country remained poorly served by railways. These were areas hit by the depression in agriculture and distant from the large centres of population: parts of East Anglia, the West Country and Wales. Cardiganshire provides good examples of lines which were constructed but failed to prosper and of lines which were projected but which were not built. A scheme to extend the railway system to Newquay on the Cardiganshire coast was proposed in 1885 and 1895.[26] The line was reckoned to be capable of generating traffic worth £70 per week, which, after expenses of 55 per cent, would leave a net income of £1,638 per annum, or 4·5 per cent on the capital of £36,000. This line was seriously canvassed in a locality sprinkled with other schemes which had failed to get off the ground, while those which had been completed provided clear evidence of a heavy burden of capital debt, revenue which was inadequate to finance essential repairs and renewals, and operating costs which despite economies were high in relation to traffic. Many neighbouring lines were, or had been, in the hands of the receiver, while others were supported as an act of charity by wealthy local families.

Farmers many miles from the nearest station were, therefore, still unable to benefit fully from reduced costs of transport. The answer, the farming interest said, was to build more railways to fill the gaps in the maps. It was an argument which gained force from the state of the agricultural economy in the final quarter of the nineteenth century. The twenty years before the Light Railways Act of 1896 saw farming move through a period of deepening depression. The price of staple farm products had all fallen considerably since 1875 and as prices fell so, too, did farmers' profits. Foreign competition, first in the form of cheap grain and later in the form of frozen meat, overwhelmed farmers. There were many bankruptcies and many others got out of farming before matters reached that extreme, leaving farms unlet and in the hands of landlords.

With British governments committed to free trade and cheap food a tariff on imported agricultural produce was unthinkable. An alternative method of assisting farmers was to improve transport facilities at their disposal. This might help in two ways: improved transport would make them more competitive; and it would enable them to move into different types of farming such as liquid milk, fruit, vegetables or flowers. Not only was this produce perishable, and so less susceptible to foreign competition, but also it was increasingly what the public wanted. However, success with these new lines of farming would depend upon good access to markets. In practice, in the late nineteenth century, this meant that any farmer more than about 3 miles from a railway station should forget dairying and fruit. Even those who wished to extend their potato crop were affected for although not perishable potatoes were bulky, making long trips in farm carts expensive, while the heavy manuring on which the crop depended demanded effective transport if city stable manure was to be used.

In the eyes of many in the agricultural community light railways fitted the bill for the improvement of transport. The light railway publicists presented them as cheap and flexible which would enable them to reach out to the Reverend Isherwood's Stoke Row and the Bishop of Chester's Newquay, which other railways had been unable to accomplish. However, there was a strong body of opinion which argued that light railways as they existed through the 1880s and early 1890s were right in principle but not in practice, and that if they were to solve the problems of agriculture new legislation and a higher public profile was necessary. The first of the two Royal Commissions which reported on the condition of agriculture during the period of depression published its findings in the 1880s and contained no references to light railways. The Royal Commission of 1893 published its reports during the following four years, coinciding with the agitation for the Light Railways Act, and heard frequent demands for light railways. Such railways would 'open up the rural parts . . . and expedite and cheapen the transit of produce';[27] light railways would 'do more good for agriculture than almost anything we have'.[28] Thus, railway provision was clearly in the minds of agriculturalists and even though complaints about them were to the fore, the attention given to light railways was an indication of the farmers' awareness of the cost and convenience of transport provided by railways in general and light railways in particular.

Notes

1   H. W. Parris, 'Northallerton to Hawes: a study in branch line history', *Journal of Transport History*, IV, 2 (1976), pp. 235–48.

2   P. Bosley, '*The* Manchester *and* Milford *Railway 1860–1906*', MA thesis, University of Wales, 1977, pp. 113–14.

3   P. Bagwell, *The Transport Revolution from 1770*, p.99.

4   H. J. Dyos and D. N. Aldcroft, *British Transport*, p. 207.

5   *Ibid.*

6   Bagwell, *op. cit.*, pp. 101–2.

7   For consideration of one such line see Bosley, *op. cit.*

8   W. Bridges Adams, *Roads and Rails*, pp. 206–7.

9   J. Simmons, *The Railway in Town and Country 1830–1914*, p.318.

10   *The Times*, 7 September 1895.

11   *The Berkshire Mercury*, 9 February 1895.

12   W. Davies, *General view of the Agriculture of South Wales 1815*, ch. 16.

13   D. Williams, *Rebecca Riots*, p. 176; Sir J. Lloyd, *History of Carmarthenshire*, II, p. 353.

14   Supplement to the *Wilts and Gloucestershire Standard*, 12 March 1881.

15   R. J. Colyer, *The Welsh Cattle Drovers*, pp. 81–2.

16   J. Llefelys Davies, 'The livestock trade in west Wales', *Aberystwyth Studies*, XIV (1936), p. 107.

17   J. Eurfyl J. Jones, 'Fairs in Cardiganshire', *Transactions of the Cardiganshire Antiquarian Society*, 1930, p. 100.

18   Ernest J. Simmons, *Memoirs of a Station Master*, p.103.

19 Colyer, *op. cit.*, pp. 83–5.

20 P.J. Atkins, 'The Milk Trade of London', Ph.D. thesis, University of Cambridge, 1977.

21 The year 1865–66 was the time of the cattle plague, a combination of rinderpest, pleuro-pneumonia and foot and mouth disease which inflicted heavy losses on urban dairies and thus created an extraordinary demand for new sources of milk. E. H. Wetham, 'The London milk trade 1860–1900', EHR, XVII (1964), pp. 369–80.

22 Royal Commission on Agriculture, 1896, Q 55054.

23 *Ibid.*, Q 55123.

24 D. W. Howell, 'Impact of railways on agricultural development in nineteenth century Wales', *Welsh Historical Review*, VII, 1 (1974), p.59. 'Rents have of course been raised in the last fifty years as fifty years ago this part of the world [Cardiganshire] had no railways, very few roads, and the country itself was swampy and undrained', J. C. Harford, Royal Commission on Land Use in Wales and Monmouthshire, Q 46181.

25 Simmons, *op. cit.*, p.324.

26 Royal Commission (RC) on Land Use in Wales and Monmouthshire, Appendix: Case presented by A. C. Humphreys-Owen MP in answer to Q 47981.

27 RC 1896, Q 33403.

28 *Ibid.*, Q 55040.

2

The Light Railways Act

The most prominent piece of legislation governing light railways was the Light Railways Act, passed in 1896. It was passed in response to a prolonged period of argument and representation that the construction and regulation of light railways should be simplified. The impetus for new legislation was provided by the depressed state of agriculture, which had induced governments to appoint two Royal Commissions of inquiry, and to introduce a number of new measures, including tenant farmers' compensation for unexhausted improvements, the partial derating of agricultural land. Light railways were a lesser issue in agricultural affairs, little discussed in the early years of depression in the 1880s, but by the 1890s it was more commonly being argued that new legislation was needed to promote light railways in country areas.

In some respects the new Act may seem superfluous, as earlier legislation had already laid down the basic conditions under which light railways could be operated, settling such matters as weight and speed limits. In 1864 the Railway Construction Facilities Act mentioned light railways, while the Improvement of Land Act of the same year attempted, among other matters, to assist land improvement by facilitating the making of 'permanent farm roads . . . tramways and railways'. However, the light railway movement in Britain more effectively dates from the Regulation of Railways Act of 1868. Section V of this Act empowered the Board of Trade to license companies to construct or work a light railway. Two conditions were imposed: first, that the maximum axle loading should be 8 tons; and second, that trains should not exceed 25 m.p.h. With few advantages deriving from the Act to compensate for these limitations, together with the need for landowners' consent to the building of a light railway, it is not surprising that the measure was not responsible for a rash of light railways appearing throughout the country. Only a handful of railways was authorised under these Acts, among them the Southwold Railway and the Lee on Solent Railway.

Two years later, in 1870, came the Tramways Act; it enabled lines to be authorised with rails laid along the public highway. Passed with urban passenger tramways in mind, it was nevertheless used to promote a number of rural lines, such as the Wantage Tramway, the Wisbech & Upwell, and the Glyn Valley Tramway. In operation they were more akin to light railways; they carried goods as well as passengers, on some the goods being the more important traffic; they ran trains rather than tramcars. At least one, the Wotton Tramway, was also known as the Wotton Light Railway, and generally these few lines were often quoted later as exemplars of the type of railway the Act of 1896 was supposed to produce. The major advantage of this Act was that tramway promoters did not have to obtain a private Act in respect of each new line they wished to construct, but could instead apply to the Board of Trade for a Provisional Order, thus simplifying and cheapening the process of authorisation. There was a number of severe restrictions relating almost entirely to urban tramways: promoters were not granted compulsory purchase for street widening; there could be no Provisional Order if the local authorities for two-thirds of the route objected; and perhaps the most celebrated clause was that the franchise was not permanent, and the tramway undertaking could be bought by the local authority after a period of twenty-one years.[1] This last was held to be responsible for a number of problems in later years as tramway companies deferred electrification for fear that their investment in modernisation would not be recouped by the local authority's purchase price.[2] For the Tramways Act did not anticipate such developments; indeed, it was not until an amendment of 1875 that steam engines could be used instead of horses on lines authorised by the Act. The locomotives had to comply with stringent restrictions, including the provision of a speed indicator, a maximum speed of 8 m.p.h. and the concealment of the motion of the engine from public view.

It was under these regulations that the few out-of-town tramways operated. The Wantage Tramway filled the 4 mile gap between the country town of Wantage and the Great Western main line passing to the north, and ran for much of the way alongside the public road. The Wisbech & Upwell was a purely rural line operated by the GER in Cambridgeshire and conveyed agricultural goods as much as passengers. But, while lightly constructed lines running alongside country roads were becoming common on the continent, they remained rare in this country.

The under use of the existing powers lent weight to the argument in the 1880s and 1890s that something more was needed to encourage the promotion of light railways. For it seemed that the existing legislation did little more than replace one set of restrictions with another. What extension there was to the network was largely in the form of railways promoted and constructed in the conventional manner. There was, however, a vocal and growing lobby of those who favoured positive encouragement of light railways, sweeping away Board of Trade restrictions and supplementing local finance with Treasury grants. Initially this group comprised mainly engineers with practical experience of light railways overseas such as A. C. Pain and E. R. Calthorp, but as the agricultural depression deepened farmers, land agents and landlords became converts. There were dissenting voices. At the height of the parliamentary debate one individualist was heard to say 'to run light railways here and there without due cause shown may leave the state of things seven times worse'.[3] Another, prophetic, opinion was that the unrestricted use of traction engines would be of far greater use to agriculture than money spent on light railways.[4] But these were a minority and light railways provided a useful rallying cry for a particularly disparate group.

An early target was the Board of Trade and its hostility to any relaxation of its provisions for railway operation, although W. M. Acworth emphasised that the Board itself was the wrong target of criticism, for it acted merely as a mouthpiece of a practically unanimous public opinion, excited by a series of particularly bad railway accidents into a heightened awareness of the need to maintain safety standards.[1] It was the Board of Trade's task to see that standards were maintained and that the most up-to-date methods, which at this time included the introduction of block working, the interlocking of points and signals, and the fitting of continuous automatic brakes throughout passenger trains, were being applied.

No one could grumble at that, but where the protagonists of rural development and light railways did take issue with the Board was on the grounds that it seemed unable or unwilling to differentiate between the safety requirements of a main line running express passenger trains and long-distance coal trains, and the country branch line along which the train of a couple of coaches and a wagon trundled at no more than 25 m.p.h. Would the Little Pedlington Highway Board, Acworth wondered, 'think of paving its parish roads with jarrah wood blocks laid on six inches of concrete because that had been found most suitable for the traffic of Piccadilly?'[6] Yet that was precisely the principle applied by the Board of Trade when it expected the Cambrian Railways, with receipts of £21 per mile per week, to install exactly the same types of safety measures and equipment as the busy London & North Western Railway, which had an income of £119 per mile per week.[7] This was despite the fact that the Regulation of Railways Act of 1889 appeared to give the Board of Trade powers of discretion in requiring railway companies to adopt such things as continuous brakes and interlocking of points and signals. The Board of Trade was also hostile to mixed trains of passenger and goods vehicles, which were a common feature of light railway operation. Single-track railways were disliked, irrespective of traffic, but as E. R. Calthorp remarked, 'this may be magnificent, but it is not business'.[8]

Cheaply constructed and operated light railways were felt to be an impossibility in the face of such rigidities. Consequently, their promoters felt it was time for new legislation which would state quite clearly that there was such a thing as a light railway that could be operated in a way different from conventional railways. Only thus, it was felt, would come a significant change of policy from government and the Board of Trade, reflecting a shift in the attitude of the railways' customers. Before 1896 it could be said with some confidence, 'when it is being built every man's hand is against the railway, and when it is completed every form of rating and taxation is sought to be imposed upon its property'.[9]

If the Board of Trade was one obstacle in the way of light railway expansion in rural areas, the established railway companies were another. The railway companies' relationship with farmers was a particularly unhappy one by the 1890s. The principle bone of contention was the rates charged by the railway companies, regarded by farmers everywhere as excessive. In this the farmers found common cause with commercial and industrial interests during the 1870s and 1880s, and this coalition ultimately forced the government to pass the Railway and Canal Traffic Act of 1888, which severely restricted the railway companies' powers to increase charges.[10] Farmers, however, felt their case had still not been answered in full when they saw trains leaving Liverpool docks loaded with American wheat on which the carriage was less per ton than that charged on English grain.

Farmers found the railway companies convenient scapegoats for depression in that their rates were high in both absolute and relative terms. The railway companies, on the other hand, challenged the farmers to improve their efficiency, by means of co-operation and combination, which would enable them to take full advantage of specially reduced rates for bulk loads, competing on equal terms with foreign shipments. The main line railway companies organised conferences to carry this message to the farmers, but they remained largely unconvinced, inclined to see their salvation as far as transport was concerned in an extended system of light railways.[11] The relationship between farmers and the railways remained one of mutual suspicion and recrimination, and it is not, therefore, surprising to find that the existing railway companies were not keen on the idea of light railways and could see little reason to help farmers who had failed to take advantage of the offers already open to them.

For the established companies light railways meant expanding the railway network into areas where the potential traffic was small, and this would constitute a dangerous over-extension of their resources. The Basingstoke & Alton Railway, promoted by the London & South Western, was one of the few light railways initiated by an established company, and even that line owed its existence to inter-company rivalry; in this case the need to prevent the GWR from penetrating further into Hampshire.

The railways already had trouble enough as it was.[12] The extension of the railway network into remote areas of the country, in so far as it had already taken place, rarely tapped lucrative traffic, while at the other end of the scale increased commuter traffic intensified problems of excess capacity. Secondly, the travelling public and those who used the railway as a carrier expected an increasingly higher standard of service: both expected faster and more frequent services; the passenger looked for greater comfort both in travelling and waiting, and the trader sent small consignments, expected the use of wagons for storage, queried the station charges, and expected free collection and delivery.[13] Coinciding with a certain disenchantment on the part of its customers, the railway industry found itself increasingly constrained by government criticism and concern with legislation imposing minimum safety standards and maximum hours for employees, and above all limitation on the companies' freedom to alter charges.[14] In the face of such difficulties, partly as a result of them, the railway industry experienced a decline in profitability. Between 1870 and 1912 gross receipts increased nearly threefold but working expenses went up nearly four times. The relationship between costs and revenue is expressed as an operating ratio which is widely accepted as an indication of the financial well-being of the railways.

We need not consider here whether the problem was caused primarily by over-capitalisation, unchecked inter-company rivalry, diminishing

Table 2·1   Operating ratio, 1870–1912[15]

Year	Operating ratio (%)
1870	48
1880	51
1890	54
1900	62
1910	62
1912	63

returns typical of a maturing industry, government restrictions or rising prices. By 1896 it seemed pointless to the main line companies to take on yet more rural branch lines. Yet these same arguments, lavish expenditure, expectation of high profits, reduction in rates, strengthened the case for light railways in the eyes of many farmers and pundits of transport. Rural transport problems would be met best by low-cost railway provision with minimal facilities and maximum flexibility.

By the mid-1890s the arguments in favour of new legislation on light railways fell into two main categories. The first was that something should be done to make country areas more accessible to provide better means of transport for farmers, this being one way to help agriculture become profitable again. The second was the need to overcome the obstacles caused by the Board of Trade's reluctance to moderate its strict line with regard to safety and by the attitudes of the main line railway companies, which had largely nullified the legislation of the 1860s. Indeed, these obstacles had contributed to the inaccessibility of rural areas. The existing railway companies, troubled by declining profitability and subject to vociferous attack on the issue of rates, most notably from farmers, were unwilling to expand further into rural areas where traffic would not justify the capital expenditure on lines that met the Board of Trade's demands.[16] The main line companies also operated agreements, frequently tacit, which provided mutual protection from third parties and which left some areas of the country without railway provision.[17]

The plight of agriculture was widely publicised, and cheap flexible railways were assiduously promoted in newspapers, journals and pamphlets. One of the earliest members of the group that produced these articles was John Bailey Denton, who, in a paper presented to the Institution of Surveyors in 1869, reviewed the problems railways faced with regard to land and legal costs, and drew attention to the light railway implications of the legislation of 1864 and 1868.[18] A. C. Pain, engineer of the Southwold and Culm Valley Railways, was another leading advocate of light railways, but it was a barrister, William Acworth, whose arguments and ubiquity seem to have had most influence. Acworth was a member of the committee set up following a conference at the Board of Trade in 1894 to investigate light railways; he was a member of the Light Railways Association, founded in 1895, and his views on railways and agriculture were stated at length in an article in the *Journal of the Royal Agricultural Society* and as a key witness before the 1893 Royal Commission investigating the condition of agriculture.[19]

The first step in the sequence of events which led to the Light Railway Act of 1896 appears to have been the introduction of a bill by Major Rasch in 1894, the purpose of which was to assimilate the laws of England with those of Ireland on the subject of light railways.[20] The bill was an attempt to secure local authority financial guarantees for expenditure on light railways: county councils would guarantee railway promoters a return of 3 per cent on loans and they would meet any operating deficit.

Subsequent action by the Board of Trade probably owes nothing to Major Rasch's initiative, but three months later it was circularising chambers of commerce, chambers of agriculture, the Railway Companies' Association, the Institute of Civil Engineers, municipal corporations and the Association of County Councils, informing them of a conference on Light Railways to be held under the auspices of the Board.[21] These bodies were invited to consider the effects of relaxing the existing Board of Trade rules and also the implications of providing additional legal facilities for obtaining powers. The conference took place on 6 December 1894, and a subsequent committee's deliberations were to be presented before the end of January 1895.[22]

The committee's report[23] indicated that particular consideration had been given to light railways in agricultural districts, and both urban and rural tramroads and tramways had been investigated. Lines where 'the traffic may be expected to be of good volume' were considered to be outside the committee's scope. Information had been obtained from the relevant Acts of Parliament, officers of the Board of Trade, committee members with special knowledge, the railway companies and the Foreign Office.[24] The committee felt that the reasons for the failure of the Acts of 1864 and 1868 to stimulate light railway construction were the opposition of landowners and canal companies and the want of latitude left to the Board of Trade by law and by the Board's conception of its duty to the public. The committee concluded that safety standards could be relaxed on lightly used lines, that matters such as gauge, fencing, level crossings, signals and continuous brakes could differ in various parts of the country, depending upon local needs, and that some means should exist to avoid recourse to Parliament. On this question it drew attention to the 'recent creation of popular local authorities' which might be given powers to authorise railways of local significance. In any dispute about what constituted a light railway the question would be determined by the Board of Trade. On the subject of finance, the committee doubted whether it was within its terms of reference and refrained from voicing an opinion as to whether local authorities should be empowered to involve themselves. The report was signed by the twenty-four members of the committee, but nine of those signing did so subject to one or more appended memoranda, which totalled eight in number. The memoranda, quoted in full by J. C. Mackay, suggest certain divisions among members of the committee, particularly on the subject of lowering safety standards, the failure to define a light railway, the association with tramways and the degree of involvement of the County Councils.[25]

The committee's report was received with scorn by *Herapath's Journal*, which condemned it as a 'hotchpotch' due to the conflicting interests of the 'selected or self-elected' members of the committee.[26] The majority report was condemned for its failure to grasp the nettle of local authority subscription and the 'minority' report was accorded grudging praise for suggesting, among other things, that no deposit should be required, that landowners should not be able to block sound schemes and that local authorities should be able to engage in the construction of light railways. But the overall criticism was that the report and its appended memoranda merely 'reflected the view of faddists'.[27] One member of the committee, R. Melville Beachcroft, it was claimed, favoured tramways as a means of relieving population congestion in urban areas, but he had overlooked the objective of the moment as outlined in the Queen's Speech which was the relief of rural districts. Mr Channing favoured municipalisation, but that was to be expected of a socialist; Sir Alfred Hickman was particularly concerned to have the value of the land fixed by a Board of Trade Arbitrator; Earl Cathcart representing the Royal Agricultural Society said that light railways would not aid the fight against depression. *Herapath* admitted the likelihood of the last point but noted that if the measures tended towards relief the attempt was surely worth while.

In February 1895 Mr A. C. Pain of the Southwold Railway proposed at the Surveyors' Institute certain modifications of parliamentary procedure.[28] He suggested that notice should be published in a London daily paper and in a local paper; not in the *London Gazette* for no one read that. The parliamentary deposit should be reduced to 2·5 per cent of construction costs rather than the existing 5 per cent, while the scale of fees for putting bills through Parliament should also be reduced, by 50 per cent. He felt that the Customs and Inland Revenue Act of 1889 (Goschen's Act) should be scrapped: up to that time railway companies were charged 2s per cent on authorised capital on obtaining their authorisations. Light railways were also to be able to issue shares at a 10 per cent discount, pay interest out of capital if required (at no more than 3 per cent) and issue up to 50 per cent of the ordinary share capital. Moreover, Pain argued that light railway companies should have the power to compel parishes to levy a rate on all property to be equal to one moiety of the improved annual value, which improvement would derive from the existence of the railway. Such a rate levy could be carried out only when the railway had been completed. He felt, too, that compulsory purchase should be eased, that the company should be able to pay a rent charge rather than compensation where the value of the land purchased was fixed at more than £100 and that passenger duty should be abolished for light railways. Finally, he maintained that light railways should not be burdened with the obligation to fit continuous brakes, and that mixed train operation should be encouraged as should the use of good quality second-hand equipment.

Pain's views, coming as they do between the rather tentative consensus of the Light Railway Conference Committee and the bill introduced in 1895 by James Bryce, represent a strong argument for easing the legislative burden on potential railway promoters. Pain was particularly concerned to cut the cost of parliamentary approval; James Bryce, President of the Board of Trade in 1895, tried to meet requests such as this by transferring from Parliament to local authorities the power to investigate and authorise railway schemes.[29] Sections 1, 2 and 3 of the bill established the machinery by which county councils were to investigate the plans of railway promoters, satisfying 'themselves that the applicants have taken all reasonable steps for ascertaining the views of the local authorities, including the road authorities, through whose areas the railway is intended to pass, and of the owners whose land it is intended to take, and for giving public notice of their applicants and if they are satisfied . . . shall proceed to make enquiry into all such matters as they may consider material'. The investigating committee would consist of council members by themselves or with others co-opted and its investigations would be in public. The council's authorisation would be placed before the Board of Trade for confirmation.

Section 4 of the bill dealt with the Board of Trade's responsibilities. It was to provide specialist advice to the councils, act as an appeal body in the event of disputes over the compulsory purchase of land and ensure that the safety of the public was not endangered. Further, it was to dispatch to Parliament any scheme which in its view was beyond the scope of the Light Railways legislation. This section also provided that if a Light Railway Order proposed by the county councils was confirmed by the Board of Trade it would then be passed to Parliament and a bill introduced for its confirmation.

The bill provoked a mixed reception in the press and in Parliament. In a leader the *Railway Times* noted that the bill aimed to achieve a cheapening of the cost of obtaining powers and a relaxation of safety regulations, and with these objectives in mind the bill must be considered 'an honest attempt'.[30] The formulators of the bill were congratulated for having steered 'clear of the temptation to devise heroic schemes for the creation of a Light Railway system at the expense of the taxpayer. No more fatuous method of assisting our languishing agriculture could be invented.' It was considered to be a practical, limited, scheme and as such was worthy of whatever support the *Railway Times* could offer it.

Several Members of Parliament, however, felt that its provisions were inadequate. Mr Chaplin, MP for Sleaford and at one time President of the Board of Agriculture, condemned it for not doing enough for agriculture and, while pleased that the ratepayers were not going to have to pay, believed that the central Treasury must give grants. Colonel Kenyon Slaney considered that the bill was a poor and paltry measure.[31] The President of the Board of Trade, he commented, had appealed to landlords to give their land but in the last session the Chancellor of the Exchequer had tried his best to ruin landlords. He felt that there would have to be central Treasury assistance, after all, the main line railway companies 'were not philanthropic institutions'. After the experience of the last session when the government 'dealt agriculture a blow from which its life blood was now flowing it was almost a mockery and an absurdity to try to heal that wound with the ridiculous sticking plaster called the Light Railway Bill'. Sir Michael Hicks-Beach thought that the proposed legislation would be a useful addition to the law but hoped that no more would be heard of the proposal as a remedy for agricultural depression. Generally, it was believed that agricultural MPs were opposed to Bryce's Bill because they feared that it would make county authorities responsible for losses incurred by English Light Railways. *Herapath's Journal* concentrated on what it considered to be the financial weaknesses of the bill, questioning how it could be expected that railway lines were to be built without cash.[32] The proposals did not authorise local authorities to contribute; hope had been expressed that the main line companies would finance light railways but, asked *Herapath's*, why should they be expected to do so in view of their recent treatment by Parliament and the public? The railway companies might possibly finance those light railways which looked profitable, but those which were never likely to make a profit were as important if the bill's objectives of improving rural transport, reducing depopulation and establishing new industries in rural areas were to be accomplished. Finally, the bill's attempt to reduce the cost of obtaining powers by delegating such authority to local authorities was questioned. Was there any reason to suppose that local enquiries would be cheaper than parliamentary ones?[33]

Criticisms of the bill mounted as it reached its second reading. Its failure to provide some form of central Treasury assistance was considered especially reprehensible particularly when similar light railways in Ireland which were used to help transport agricultural produce to England had received government subsides.[34] The Bill had avoided the problem of defining what constituted a light railway. Its critics now pointed out that under its terms promoters might go to the trouble and expense of a local authority investigative committee only to find that when the scheme was passed on to the Board of Trade for confirmation it was considered that the scheme was not a light railway and that it would have to start anew by applying direct to Parliament for its powers. Finally, it was pointed out that, in the absence of state aid, the fact would have to be faced that many light railway companies would have to charge higher rates than those of the main line companies if they were to meet their costs. Inevitably the larger main line companies would be able to operate more economically, so Parliament and the public would have to accept the imposition of rates higher than those about which there were now bitter complaints. The strength of opposition, and ultimately the change of government, meant that Bryce's Bill did not proceed.

The Light Railway Bill, 1896

In November the formation on two successive days of associations to provide light railways represents the beginning of a new initiative. On 27 November 1895 the Light Railways Association, supported by W. J.

Carruthers Wain, W. Acworth and Major-General Webber,[35] was established to bring together all those interested in light railway construction. It was felt that parish and county councils were not the best organisations to promote light railways; they might have the best intentions but they lacked the knowledge to put their ideas into practice and the association hoped to provide appropriate guidance. The following day the Light Railways Association of Great Britain was formed with the purpose of representing the local councils and the intention of working closely with its sister association.[36] The Light Railways Association of Great Britain, led by Sir A. K. Rollitt and Major Rasch, formed itself into a conference with the purpose of formulating and advancing legislation. They wanted a 'complete reform of railway procedure', while Major Rasch moved a resolution that the conference supported light railways with improved parliamentary facilities and state and local aid.[37] The conference sent a circular to all county councils inviting them to send delegates to a further session in February 1896.[38] Presumably as a result of this second session of the conference, a deputation from the association met Mr Ritchie, the new Conservative President of the Board of Trade, in February 1896 to ask for improved facilities for light railways. Ritchie promised better legislation than the 'invertebrate scheme of Mr Bryce'.[39] *Herapath's Journal* continued its article: 'We only wish to guard against illusion especially when we find men like Major Rasch declaring that Essex farmers would have no objection to using the railways provided that other people paid for them.' Evidently a claim on the rates was in Mr Ritchie's mind.[40]

When the bill was presented to Parliament *Herapath's Journal* noted with relief that it was 'a moderate, practical measure which should excite little opposition' and should certainly help light railways in those areas where people were prepared to help themselves.[41] The major defect in the bill was the absence of any machinery for securing the co-operation of the existing railway companies, without whom the majority of light railway schemes must be a failure. The main line companies could not be expected to have an interest in schemes about which they had not been consulted.[42]

At the beginning of March the bill was read for the second time. The *Railway Times*, unlike *Herapath's Journal*, could see few things in its favour apart from the fatuity of its opponents' speeches.[43] The bill's reference to the involvement of the Treasury was praiseworthy, but the *Railway Times* followed a Mr Lough, Liberal MP for West Islington, in his criticism of the proposed Light Railway Commission of three for being too small in number and too ill paid to function properly. In other respects the *Railway*

Times could find little merit in the bill but poured scorn on its critics. Mr Perks, MP for Louth, opposed the bill on the 'novel grounds that it would be prejudicial to the interests of village shopkeepers'.[44] James Bryce attacked his successor's bill on the rather more serious grounds that the £1 million available from the Treasury by the terms of the bill would whet the appetite of the rural and fishing districts and would raise expectations which Parliament would be unable to fulfil.[45] Bryce's opposition, however, was decried by *Herapath's Journal* and he was accused of attempting to strangle the bill merely because it was not his own.[46] Other critics were also ridiculed: Sir John Lubbock for referring to the proposals as a hybrid example of state or municipal socialism and Mr Mundella, ex-President of the Board of Trade, who sneered at existing railway companies and felt they should have no part in rural railways. A fruitless effort was made to raise the salary of the paid official of the commission beyond £1,000 per annum to attract a really competent man, but after pressure was applied the interest to be charged on any Treasury loans was lowered from $3\frac{1}{2}$ per cent to $3\frac{1}{8}$ per cent.

By the beginning of May two further amendments had been carried in committee.[47] By a majority of nineteen votes light railways were to be exempt from passenger duty. The Chancellor of the Exchequer complained that this weakened his position with regard to passenger duty as a whole, earning the caustic comment from the *Journal* that it was to be hoped that the logic of this would not escape him when the next Budget came. By the second amendment, carried only by means of the chairman's casting vote, landlords were not allowed to claim compensation for disturbance in compulsory purchase cases.

In June the bill was once again before the Commons. Mr J. Lowther deprecated any powers given to local authorities to speculate in railway enterprises with ratepayers' money. He claimed not to speak on behalf of the new motor cars but believed that a new age for road transport was imminent and thus it was not an appropriate time for making changes in the railway system. Indeed, the construction of 'little paltry tramways' in various parts of the country was a retrograde step.[48] Ritchie defended his bill, claiming that the Central Chamber of Agriculture and many rating authorities favoured it. Mr Mundella feared that if local authorities were not given powers to construct light railways themselves then the public would be at the mercy of the railway companies. A similar fear of the main line companies inspired an amendment to the effect that no Treasury grant should go to an existing company proposing to build a light railway if the parent company's rates were considered unfair or oppressive by the Board of Trade. The amendment was defeated.[49]

The Light Railways Bill became law on 14 August 1896.[50] It established a commission of three members to consider proposals for light railways, the attendance of two of them being sufficient to act. The first commissioners were the Earl of Jersey, G. A. Fitzgerald, a barrister, and Colonel G. Boughey R.E., their term of office to be five years. The Act simplified procedures by which authority to construct railways could be granted. Promoters put their case before the Light Railways Commissioners, who, after enquiry and if the application was considered acceptable, granted a provisional Order, confirmation of which came from the Board of Trade. If the Commissioners rejected the scheme an appeal to the Board of Trade was possible, although this never actually occurred. Local authorities (county, borough and district) were encouraged to take a positive interest and were empowered to promote or work a light railway themselves or in collaboration with private enterprise. The local authorities were also able to help finance privately promoted light railways either by loans or by buying shares. In the event of local authorities lending money to a light railway company, the Treasury was also empowered to lend to the railway up to the amount lent by the local authority, and provided that the Treasury did not exceed one-quarter of the total amount required for the purposes of the light railway; the Treasury loan or a free grant could represent one-half of the cost of the railway provided that the Board of Agriculture certified that the railway 'would benefit agriculture', or the Board of Trade certified that 'by the making of such a railway a necessary means of communication would be established between a fishing village and a harbour'. The sum of £1 million pounds was set aside for the purpose of the Treasury loans and grants. The Act also specified that light railways, if they were considered not to be a railway within the meaning of the Railway Passenger Duty Act of 1842, were exempt from the payment of passenger duty. The burden of compensation was eased slightly as it was established that arbitrators would have to consider the improved value of the land following the construction of the railway.

Notes

1   H. J. Dyos and D. H. Aldcroft, *British Transport*, p. 235; H. Vesey Knox, *Light Railway and Tramway Journal*, October 1901.

2   E. A. Pratt, *History of Inland Transport and Communications*, p.456.

3   *Engineer*, 11 January 1895.

4   *Ibid.*, 24 May 1894.

5   W. M. Acworth, 'Light railways', *JRASE*, V (1894), pp.647–67.

6   *Ibid.*

7   Dyos and Aldcroft, *British Transport*, p.235.

8   E. R. Calthorp, *The Economics of Light Railway Construction*, 1896.

9   E. R. Calthorp, 'On some aspects of the light railway problem', *The Land Agents' Record*, 16 March 1895.

10   P. J. Cain, 'The British railways rates problem 1894–1913', *Business History Review* XX (1978), pp. 87–99 and elsewhere.

11   PRO, RAIL, 1057–3007.

12   The cause of the railways' crisis of confidence is discussed by, among others, D. H. Aldcroft, *British Railways in Transition*, 1968; H. Pollins, *British Railways, An Industrial History*, 1971; R. J. Irving, *The North Eastern Railway 1870 to 1914*, 1976; and T. R. Gourvish, *Railways and the British Economy 1830 to 1914*, 1980.

13   Faster services, criticised by Sir George Paish, *The British Railway Position*, pp. 144–5, demanded improved signalling services, more powerful locomotives and shorter stays in stations, which in turn required more station staff. All added to costs.

14   Large companies which were involved in a continuous renewal programme were less severely hit by the legislation than smaller, impecunious companies. In 1893 only eight of the Manchester & Milford Railway's fifteen coaches were fit for the addition of continuous brakes. With profits averaging only £125 per annum upgrading the rolling stock would have taken four years. PRO, RAIL, 456–1, 28 February 1893.

15   H. Pollins, *British Railways*, p.92.

16   An increasingly businesslike attitude is evident on the part of the main line companies with regard to the viability of projected rural branch lines. The GWR, for example, showed considerable intransigence in its dealings with the proposed Witney Burford & Andoversford railway. PRO, RAIL, 258–309, 25 April 1901. Equally, all the main line companies were aware of the benefits they derived from the 'added value' of traffic which passed over their systems to and from the branch line or light railway.

17   The division of Cornwall between the GWR and LSWR meant that the GWR abandoned its proposed involvement in a Saltash to Callington railway in return for the LSWR not promoting a line between Padstow and Newquay. PRO, RAIL, 258–309.

18   J. B. Denton, 'The future extension of the railway system with special reference to the influence of railways on landed property and agriculture', *Institution of Surveyors*, 8 February 1869. Denton was surveyor to a number of railway companies including the Kettering Thrapston & Huntingdon Railway.

19   W. M. Acworth, 1850–1925, was one of the most informed writers and lecturers on railway affairs, particularly railway economics. Changes in railway accounting methods owe much to his influence and he was the author of a seminal

work on railway economics, *The Elements of Railway Economics*, first published in 1905. He was a director of the Midland & South Western Junction Railway and promoter of railway projects in Devon including the Plymouth & North Devon Direct Railway. PRO, RAIL, 523–6.

20 *Herapath's Journal*, 31 August 1894. Major F. C. Rasch had been Conservative MP for South East Essex since 1886.

21 *Ibid.*, 2 November 1894.

22 Those attending the conference included James Bryce, President of the Board of Trade in the Liberal government; Sir Michael Hicks-Beach, Conservative MP for East Gloucestershire and later West Bristol, Chancellor of the Exchequer 1896; Lord Claud Hamilton; Sir Courtney Boyle and Messrs Hopwood, Humphries-Owen, Channing, Acworth and Sellon.

23 Quoted in full with appendices by Mackay, *op. cit.*, pp.247–54.

24 Consulates in various countries were asked to supply information on local light railway operation. It was unfortunate that the one reply to carry weight was that from R. Stovin Warburton of the Consulate at La Rochelle. He drew attention to the extent of state financial guarantees and rather damned the whole concept with faint praise: 'There may be some lines of tramways which are exceptions to the general rule and have proved a success . . . but this will be owing to exceptional circumstances.' Quoted by Davies, *Light Railways*, Appendix B, p. 268.

25 Mackay, *op. cit.*, p.254.

26 *Herapath's Journal*, 8 February 1895.

27 *Ibid.*

28 Quoted by Mackay, *op. cit.*, pp.85–6.

29 *Railway Times*, 27 April 1895.

30 *Ibid.*

31 Colonel Kenyon-Slaney, Conservative MP for Newport, Shropshire, was a frequent speaker on agriculture and was regarded as a model landlord.

32 *Herapath's Journal*, 3 May 1895.

33 *Ibid.*

34 *Railway Times*, 15 June 1895.

35 Major-General Webber R.E. was Managing Director of the Anglo-American Brush Electric Light Company.

36 *Railway Times*, 31 November 1895.

37 *Herapath's Journal*, 29 November 1895.

38 *Ibid.*, 6 December 1895.

39 *Ibid.*, 14 February 1896.

40 *Ibid.*

41 *Ibid.*, 28 February 1896.

42 *Ibid.*

43 *Railway Times*, 7 March 1896.

44 *Ibid.*

45 In the event his suspicion proved to be entirely unfounded. Rather than being unable to satisfy the demand aroused, Parliament was to find the rural and fishing appetite was not at all titillated by the proposed £1 million.

46   *Herapath's Journal*, 24 April 1896.
47   *Ibid.*, 1 May 1896.
48   *Ibid.*, 5 June 1896.
49   *Ibid.*
50   For the text of the Light Railways Act see Davies, *op. cit.*

3
Light railways in theory

The discussions that preceded the passing of the Light Railways Act were dominated by those who were very much in favour of light railways. There were few who troubled to suggest that such railways had no merit at all. Instead, it was the arguments as to their advantages, especially their benefits to agriculture, and rural areas generally, that were continually canvassed. Light railways would serve the interests of the local community in various ways. The farmer hitherto distant from a railway station would benefit through reduced costs of seed potatoes and manure, and his produce would not only be cheaper but would be more varied and could reach a wider market. The landlord would be heartened to see agriculture revive, his farms would be less likely to remain unlet and rents would, perhaps, be no longer subject to rebates and reductions. Country people at large would benefit from improved communications.

However, heated discussion did occur as to the form that light railways should take, and the failure to achieve unanimity which produced railways in many shapes and forms contributed to the early decline of light railways. In Britain there was no network of light railways with a uniform gauge to benefit from economies of scale in purchasing or operations. Comparison is often made with Continental experience where, operating in an entirely different political and social environment, considerable uniformity was obtained and networks did emerge. In England and Wales light railways were planned in an entirely *ad hoc* fashion to suit often parochial needs, geographical contiguity was rarely achieved or even contemplated and the only real attempt at integration was that made by Colonel Stephens, and that in a somewhat eccentric fashion.[1]

There was even disagreement as to what should constitute a light railway. The Regulation of Railways Act of 1868 had given clear indication:

A light railway shall be constructed and worked subject to such conditions and regulations as the Board of Trade may from time to time impose or make; Provided that (*1*) the regulations respecting the weight of locomotive engines, carriages and vehicles to be used on such railway shall not authorise a greater weight than eight tons to be brought upon the rails by any one pair of wheels; (*2*) the regulations respecting the speed of trains shall not authorise a rate of speed exceeding at any time 25 miles per hour.

This definition was clear, although expressed in negative terms, and Parliament in 1896 felt no need to re-enact it, or to incorporate a new definition in the Light Railways Act. In practice it was always understood that light railways authorised under the 1896 Act were bound by the terms of 1868. None of this, however, seemed to satisfy the contro-versialists of the 1890s and later who agonised over how a light railway should be defined, and after 1896 criticised the new Act for lacking a definition.

In 1894 W. M. Acworth declared that definition of a light railway was impossible: ' . . . you can only define a light railway be reference to railways which are not light'; and ' . . . a light railway may be said to be a railway of second or third class standard'; or again 'A light railway is . . . inferior to the ordinary railway.'[2] The following year he provided more details, but still put fundamentally negatively: 'Light railways would be narrow gauge if long and standard gauge if short. They would have lighter permanent way. There would be no houses at level crossings, no station staff, but there would be mixed trains and easier means of obtaining Parliamentary approval.'[3]

In 1896 he further stated that he saw light railways as cheaply constructed extensions of the main line.[4] This approach was echoed in 1896 by Sir Arthur Heywood, who tried to ease the problem of definition by identifying additional categories of non-standard railways. Referring to light railways, he observed that ' . . . the term "light railway" is properly applicable and should be confined to a line of standard gauge, of which the entire construction is lighter, cheaper, and simpler, than is obligatory where weighty engines, heavy traffic, and high speeds are dealt with. Any line of less than the standard gauge is correctly described as a "narrow gauge railway" . . .'[5]

In the opinion of J. C. Mackay 'many people jumped to the conclusion that light railways must be identified with narrow gauge. In reality light railways were railways constructed to a lighter standard than the main line system, worked at a slower speed, with less accommodation for passengers and goods, and capable of taking mainline rolling stock but not locomotives.'[6] The comparison with main line practice was reflected the following year by Sir John Wolfe-Barry, who argued that 'so far as works are concerned light railways should be slightly superior to contractor's lines'.[7] Light railway passengers should not expect station buildings, platforms, frequent services or an army of porters, guards, ticket collectors or station masters. But three years later, in 1899, W. H. Cole was unable to write so confidently. Light and standard railways, he thought, 'only differ from each other in degree and no sharp line can be drawn between them. We are all feeling our way in the matter of light railways . . . a subject which is more or less unformed and undefined.'[8]

A slight note of desperation is evident in comments by J. Tatlow of the Midland Great Western Railway of Ireland in 1900.[9] He pointed out that as the Light Railways Act of 1896 had failed to define what constituted a light railway, the responsibility was placed on the three Light Railway Commissioners, who were expected to judge each case before them on its merits. In 1915 Harrison Veevers, Parliamentary Assistant to the chief engineer of the Lancashire and Yorkshire Railway, was obliged to resort to a circular argument:

It is difficult to say in so many words what constitutes a light railway. They are really undertakings whose special incidents and characteristics are determined by the Light Railway Acts of 1896 and 1912 . . . There is no definition in the Acts of the expression 'light railways' and a light railway is therefore distinguishable from an ordinary railway mainly by reason of its being constructed under the powers of a Board of Trade Order.[10]

The technical debate

The disagreement over the nature of light railways made it unlikely that there would be unanimity of opinion over the form that they should take. There was even a divergence on the issue of motive power. The majority of promoters and engineers favoured the steam locomotive operating on fixed rails, but other forms of motive power had supporters.[11] The horse was still considered a possibility in 1873 for short hauls,[12] while electricity was favoured for urban tramways, stationary steam engines for aerial ropeways and manpower for 'railed wheel barrows'.

It will be apparent from some of the opinions already quoted that gauge was the major cause of dissension. Debate did not merely centre on standard or narrow gauge, but how narrow 'narrow gauge' might be. The supporters of narrow gauge — and they include R. B. Grantham (1873), J. K. Rodwell (1884), E. R. Calthorp (1904) and J. C. Mackay (1896) —

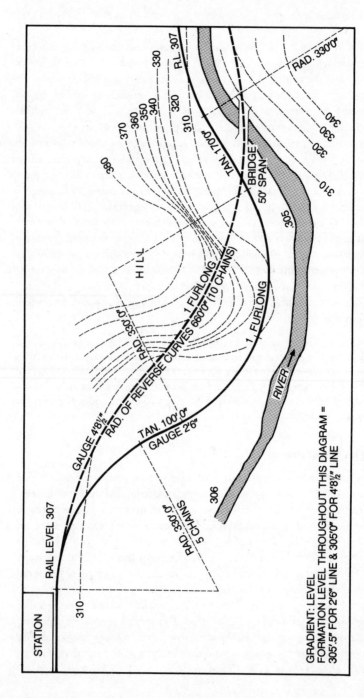

Fig. 3.1 Typical diagram showing saving of expense in construction by use of 2ft.6in. gauge in place of 4ft.8½in. gauge

pointed to savings in construction costs with the ability to follow contours, thus reducing the need for expensive civil engineering works, especially significant in mountainous territory or when laid at the side of roads (see Tables 3·1, 3·2 and Figure 3·1).[13]

This group favoured the use of narrow gauge as a means of clearly distinguishing light railways from the main line system: 'the break of gauge would give to all concerned notice in the most conspicuous manner possible that the new light lines had finally broken with the extravagant traditions of our English railway past'.[17] Naturally, the supporters of narrow gauge discounted the problems associated with the break of gauge. Costs incurred were considered minimal. Mackay argued that transhipment costs would range between $1\frac{1}{2}d$ and $3d$ per ton and he took as an example a 12-mile line producing 24,000 tons of goods to be transhipped at $3d$ per ton, a total annual cost of £300. This he believed

Table 3·1 Minimum radius of curves[14]

Gauge	Chains
4 ft 8½ in.	8
3 ft 6 in.	5
2 ft 6 in.	1½

Table 3·2 Estimated construction costs[15] (excluding land and fencing)

Gauge	2 ft 0 in	2 ft 6 in	3 ft 6 in	3 ft 6 in
Weight of rail lbs/yd	20	30	30	50
	*	*	*	*
	£	£	£	£
Survey	25	25	25	25
Engineering and supervision	125	125	125	125
Earthworks	200	250	350	400
Bridges and culverts	200	250	350	500
Permanent way and ballasting	500	730	864	1,385
Stations and buildings	50	50	60	70
Rolling stock	250	300	350	400
Temporary works and sundries	100	100	100	150
Total probable costs per mile	1,450	1,830	2,224	3,055

would be more than matched by the reduction in construction costs derived from the use of narrow gauge.[18] The problems of transhipment could be eased by the construction of split-level loading bays or by the use of transporter wagons to carry standard gauge rolling stock, such as those designed by E. R. Calthorp for the Leek & Manifold Railway.[19] The apparent economy of using larger wagons was diminished, it was argued, by the fact that standard gauge wagons were often run half empty; indeed, the smaller capacity of narrow gauge stock would ideally suit agricultural traffic. A. C. Pain had earlier pointed to the fact that the light traffic expected on such lines would in itself reduce the problems of transhipment. As engineer of both narrow and standard gauge light railways, he believed that 'No rule can be laid down as to what should be the gauge of a light railway . . . it will depend entirely on the district to be served and the traffic to be carried.'[20]

The proponents of standard gauge included T. S. Sellon (1888), W. H. Cole (1899) and, less unequivocally, the authors of the 'Technical Correspondence Agency'. In the final analysis most promoters of light railways came to favour standard gauge. No doubt inertia played a part in such decisions, but it was argued that standard gauge did not require the purchase of significantly more land and that sharp curves were more a product of short wheelbases than narrow gauge.[21] Transhipment costs could not be dismissed and with short lines (many light railways were significantly shorter than the 12 miles postulated by Mackay in his defence of transhipment) the burden of break of gauge would be correspondingly greater. W. M. Acworth pointed out in his evidence to the Royal Commission on Agriculture in 1896 that, although most Continental light railways were narrow gauge, transhipment costs were eased because wage rates in Europe were lower than in Britain.[22] Furthermore, with transhipment there would be delays and the possibility of damage. J. Sadler, Secretary of the Cheshire Chamber of Agriculture and the Cheshire Milk Producers' Association, believed that the delays and damage inflicted by transferring goods from one train to another would mean that 'The farmer does not know his own cheese when it gets to the end of the railway journey.'[23] The recent history of the GWR's conversion to standard gauge also militated against introducing further breaks. Undoubtedly the supporters of standard gauge anticipated the through running of wagons and the possibility of hiring rolling stock from main line companies on those occasions when traffic demanded it. There was always the prospect of buying second-hand equipment as a cheap means of equipping or re-equipping a light railway. Finally, a rather seductive consideration which may have weighed heavily on the minds of some promoters was that standard gauge lines were more likely to become through lines. There were speculators amongst promoters of rural railways who hoped to make their line an attractive proposition to be swallowed by a main line company. Such ambitions bedevilled many rural lines, including the Golden Valley Railway and the Lambourn Valley Railway.

The Light Railway Commissioners were happy to see the narrow gauge network extended, especially where the terrain was inimical to standard gauge. Indeed, they occasionally expressed a preference for narrow gauge. Their report on the proposed branch line to Newquay in Cardiganshire concluded that it was a 'pity that the Manchester & Milford Railway and all these branches cannot be on the 2 ft 6 in. gauge which is far more suited to this difficult country than the standard gauge, but this is past hoping for now'. The report on the associated Lampeter & Llandilo Railway also commented on the benefits of the narrow gauge, but accepted that as the line had to link standard gauge lines at each end 'there is no help for it'.[24]

It is interesting, if ultimately fruitless, to reflect on the changes that might have occurred if certain narrow gauge lines had instead been built or converted to standard gauge. The Southwold Railway, which could not be said to have owed its narrow gauge to difficult terrain, might have survived because of the greater likelihood of an extension to Lowestoft. Would increased costs of construction have outweighed the transhipment costs on the Welshpool & Llanfair Railway? Perhaps the only certainty was that a break of gauge was better than no railway at all.[25]

A difference of opinion arose as to whether or not light railways should follow the roads, largely as a means of saving on the cost of land. This was by no means so contentious an issue, despite the fact that battle lines were drawn loosely as in the gauge dispute. Narrow gauge supporters claimed not only a cost advantage but also greater flexibility, a greater freedom to run from the farmer's field direct to the merchant's storeroom. Only narrow gauge could compete with the roads in respect of immediacy and completeness as a medium of transport. A railway line that ran beside or along the road was unlikely to be so distant from villages. This was a problem frequently aired, since so many country stations were a mile or more from the village they were intended to serve. A calculation in 1894 assumed that agricultural produce in Britain had an average journey of 10 miles to a railway at a cost of some 10s a ton, a figure doubled when terminal and other charges were included.[26] Ten years earlier it had been stated that areas as little as 3 or 4 miles from a railway were, to all intents, 'commercially considered, lost parts of the country'.[27]

To many, roadside tramways running through every village and settlement appeared to be the answer. One such was W. H. Delano. Writing in the *Journal of the Royal Agricultural Society* in 1881, he envisaged a system of narrow gauge lines laid on roads with sidings to each farm. This, he believed, would stimulate production by reducing transport costs; equalise the price of produce in outlying areas, making them more competitive; and numerous villages would awake 'from the torpid condition to which they were reduced by railway construction and the diversion of traffic'. Delano also advocated the extensive use by farmers of a portable trackway system which could be laid on hard or soft ground by farm labourers. Such a system had been exhibited at the Royal Agricultural Society show at Leeds in 1861 but had attracted little interest in England although used extensively in France. The agricultural engineers Fowler's of Leeds had demonstrated such a system at the Royal show at Kilburn in 1879. Their portable railway had provided frequent trains in the showground which had not only been of great convenience to the visitors but had also provided proof of the practicality of the system. Although the extremely soft ground caused the rails to move up and down, the gauge had been maintained and the trains never derailed, although often, it was suggested, looking like ships at sea.[28]

There was, however, a reluctance to build on or alongside roads: in many cases the engineering difficulties would have been enormous, for rural roads frequently turn at right angles and traverse steep inclines, neither of which even narrow gauge railways could manage. Furthermore, in many cases the roads were not wide enough to accommodate railway tracks, while the questions of fencing and disruption of traffic raised further problems. Not only was there the danger that livestock might take fright at the proximity of a train but in narrow streets when tramways entered a town there was a likelihood of congestion.

Paradoxically, roads were too indirect. Railway promoters may well have looked to tap rural traffic but shareholders required a direct and economical line: an indirect route, heavy engineering works and slow speeds were simply unacceptable.[29] Ultimately, few roadside tramways were built, even those lines built under the Tramways Act largely avoided the roads. None of them was narrow gauge, although the Welshpool & Llanfair Railway did run on roads in Welshpool. The only two notable standard gauge rural tramways were the Wisbech & Upwell Tramway and the Wantage Tramway.

Finance

One of the most controversial aspects of light railway agitation was their financing. Traditionally any suggestion that domestic railways should receive national or local government aid was treated with scant respect. In 1859 the *Railway Times* dealt scathingly with an extraordinary device proposed by the incipient Manchester & Milford Railway: 'The forthcoming Bill, if it is to come forth, will purport to enable, if not to compel, owners or lessees of land as well as ratepayers and their vestries to contribute towards expenses of construction.'[30] Fifty years later the caution expressed here was substantiated in the reaction to the proposed county council financing of other railways in Cardiganshire (see Chapter 5). Central government participation was viewed with equal suspicion: the provision built into the Tramways Act of 1870 that tramway operators could be bought out by the government after a period of twenty-one years was a serious inhibition and accords well with the railway industry's suspicions of government intentions. Yet it was quite clear that some sort of financial aid was necessary if railways were to be built in what was likely to be unprofitable country. Government assistance was provided for in the Light Railways Act, but by far the greatest single source of support for light railway undertakings, both before and after the passing of the Act, was one or more of the main line companies.

Again, the relationship with a main line company was a bone of contention amongst the light railway theorists. For some, the financial strength and operating expertise of the established railway companies were essential elements in the successful promotion of rural railways. For others, the major companies typified everything that was wrong with rural transport: they were over-capitalised, extravagantly built, wastefully competitive. The whole point of light railways was to restore independence and provide transport suited to country needs which had been ignored by the monopolistic large railway companies. Indeed, many of the supporters of the narrow gauge emphasised the importance of a difference in gauge to reinforce the distinctiveness and independence of the light railway. However, a physical link with a main line, and thus the use of standard gauge, did permit the possibility of through running, and operation by a main line company permitted hidden subsidies in the form of renewals and repairs to rolling stock in addition to the more obvious benefits of reduced administrative costs. The argument which was felt to be most persuasive, however, was that the existence of a light railway would be a benefit to the main line company because improved transport would increase traffic 'enormously beyond what it could have been had carts and omnibuses remained the only means of communication'.[31] That the main line companies were aware of this is clearly evident in the GWR's negotiations with lines it absorbed, such as the Lampeter & Aberaeron Railway. The North Eastern Railway (NER), too, was conscious of the contributory value of the traffic it derived from the North Sunderland Railway and was thus content to ignore the light railway's growing burden of debt (see Chapter 5).

However, even when the neighbouring main line company was friendly a flexible approach was required in operation and construction which would be possible only with a modification of Board of Trade regulations and public opinion: minimal earthworks and fencing; frequent use of level crossings, often without gates; light rail and slow speeds; reduced station accommodation, probably with no platforms; preparedness by staff to work more than an eight-hour day;[33] and willingness by traders and passengers to accept higher rates and fares.[34] A change in attitude by Parliament and the public was considered necessary if finance was to be forthcoming for light railways. There was a recognition on the part of the more informed commentators that even for the better schemes there must be a preparedness to accept that direct losses would have to be offset against indirect gains.[35] Landlords must not expect direct compensation for the land they lost to the railway.[36] It was argued that Parliament should offer railway promoters the same compulsory purchase powers that existed for new street building and improved sanitation.[37] The crippling effect of passenger duty[38] and local rates and taxes was often referred to,[39] with the suggestion that light railways should be granted some relief.

The question of who was ultimately to benefit from the construction of light railways significantly affected the mode of financing: was a railway built in the interests of the state, the shareholders, the community it served or some neighbouring mainline railway?[40] If the railway was considered to be in the interest of the state, then the state should either provide financial support, as was the case in Ireland, or empower local authorities to do so.[41] If shareholders were to bear the brunt of the costs, it was generally agreed that such lines with dubious prospects of profit would not be built. If the local community was considered to be the major beneficiary of the line, then many light railway proponents were prepared to argue that local ratepayers should be obliged to participate even to the extent of a guarantee of a 4 per cent return to shareholders by means of a rate.[42] Needless to say, this view excited opposition. Discussing the proposed Witney Burford & Andoversford Light Railway at a meeting of Gloucestershire County Council, Colonel Sir Nigel Kingscote opposed a council grant. He believed that the county council should not speculate with ratepayers' money and that funds should be found in the locality.[43] Thirty years earlier A. C. Pain had argued that finance should ideally come from the locality, which would benefit to such an extent that any outside shareholders should be offered preferential dividends. Pain addressed the issue of landowners accepting shares for land: the larger landowners should give their land; the less substantial should take shares; while the smallest should be paid by the railway company.[44]

Finally, the role of main line companies excited both hope and suspicion. On the one hand, the value of the contributory benefit derived from feeder lines was considered high enough to justify building such feeders.[45] On the other, the case was argued that association with main line companies was not in the interests of agricultural railways:

The whole bent and training of the rank and file of the main line is towards solidity and lavish expenditure and with the advent of heavier loads and higher speed this tendency will become more and more pronounced. The *métier* of the light railwayman is to eliminate expenses, superfluity and complexity, in every shape or form, and to evolve a type of line on which efficiency of action is combined in every department with the greatest simplicity of equipment.[46]

The debates as to what a light railway should be were ultimately inconclusive. The engineers and those with special knowledge of or enthusiasm for transport were unable to provide clear guidance to railway promoters and operators as to how they should construct and run light railways or how best to finance them. The specialists even expressed dissatisfaction with the new legislation for which they had campaigned, and indulged in quibbles over lesser problems of defining a light railway. Lacking a clear body of principles, it is perhaps small wonder that the light railways that were built came in all shapes and sizes, and that the much-admired networks to be found in some European countries never had their equivalent in Britain.

Notes

1 See p. 162.
2 W. M. Acworth, *Journal of the Royal Agricultural Society of England* (*JRASE*), V (1894), p. 647.
3 W. M. Acworth, *Journal of the Royal Society of Arts*, 15 February 1895.
4 W. M. Acworth, Royal Commission on Agriculture, 1896, Q.917.

5   Sir Arthur Heywood, *Minimum Gauge Railways*, p. 47.

6   J. C. Mackay, *Light Railways for India, the United Kingdom and the Colonies*, p. 1.

7   Sir J. Wolfe-Barry, *Proc. I.C.E.*, CXXVII (1897).

8   W. H. Cole, *Light Railways at Home and Abroad*, p. 5.

9   PRO, RAIL, 1023, vi (1900).

10 Harrison Veevers, 'Light railways', *Railway Magazine*, October 1915, p. 279.

11 See pp. 163–7.

12 R. B. Grantham, 'Agricultural railways', *Trans Inst Surveyors*, 24 February 1873.

13 E. R. Calthorp (with E. O. Mawson), *Pioneer Irrigation and Light Railways*, p. 178, claimed the use of narrow gauge could reduce construction costs by 75 per cent.

14 Mackay, *op. cit.*, p. 33.

15 *Ibid.*, p. 73.

16 G. Frank Burns, 'Railways of 2 ft 6 in. Gauge', *Railway Magazine*, December 1927, p. 447.

17 W. M. Acworth, *JRASE, op. cit.*, pp. 657–8.

18 Mackay, *op. cit.*, p. 19.

19 Calthorp (with Mawson), *op. cit.*, p.192.

20 A. C. Pain, 'Light railways and tramways', *The Field* (1873).

21 'Light axle loads and low speed working are the first conditions of cheap construction and economical working, not gauge', Cole, *op. cit.*, p. 7.

22 RC 1896, Q 30795.

23 RC 1919, Q 7071.

24 PRO, MT 58–280, 318.

25 Min, *Proc Inst C.E.*, CXLVII (1902), p. 387.

26 Technical Correspondence Agency submission to the Board of Trade on *Light Railways for Agricultural Districts*, December 1894, p. 11. This seventeen-page typescript is one of the most detailed and informed documents in the light railway debate.

27 S. Ballard, *Cheap Railways for Rural Districts*, p. 3.

28 W. H. Delano, 'Secondary or narrow gauge railways for agricultural districts', *JRASE* (1881), p. 385.

29 A. C. Pain, 'True and false economy in light railway construction', *Min Proc Inst C. E.*, CXXX, believed that roads were inappropriate for light railways, but his argument was that they were too direct and that true economy was to lengthen rather than shorten lines: the more stations and sidings the better.

30 *Railway Times*, 26 November 1859.

31 Acworth, *JRASE, op. cit.*, p. 649.

32 Ballard, *op. cit.*, p. 5.

33 Mackay, *op. cit.*, p. 14.

34 Acworth, *JRASE, op. cit.*

35 *Ibid.*

36 Ballard, *op. cit.*, p. 5.

37 W. Sturge in discussion of Grantham, *op. cit.*, p. 173.

38 Mackay, *op. cit.*, p. 85.

39 E. R. Calthorp, 'On some aspects of the light railway problem', *The Land Agents' Record,* 16 March 1895.

40 Technical Correspondence Agency, *op. cit.*, p.15.

41 Mackay, *op. cit.*, p. 85.

42 Ballard, *op. cit.*, p. 8.

43 *Transport*, 20 July 1900. For further consideration of this point see pp. 79–80.

44 Pain, 'Light railways and tramways', *op. cit.*, p. 12.

45 Technical Correspondence Agency, *op. cit.*, p. 7.

46 Calthorp, *op. cit.*

4
Light railways in practice

The Light Railways Act was a milestone in the history of administration and the regulation of railways. Parliament delegated to a commission responsible to the Board of Trade the power to confer statutory authority on railway companies, a matter which hitherto had required private Acts of Parliament. Included in the powers administered by the Light Railway Commission was the authorising of compulsory purchase of land and the crossing of highways. The Act had been passed amidst high hopes that it would lead to a major expansion in the numbers and extent of minor railways, especially of railways which would benefit the life and economy of rural districts. It was apparent quite soon, however, that these developments were not taking place. Light railways were not being built in large numbers, and their effects on rural life could at best be described as marginal. The Act was primarily intended to improve transport in rural areas but its terms did not exclude other applications, and in the event most lines operated under Light Railway Orders were not rural. Urban tramway companies particularly took advantage of the new law, for the Tramways Act of 1870 was hedged with restrictions which could be circumvented by use of the Light Railways Act.[1] By 1914 one-third of the applications approved by the Light Railway Commissioners were for tramway purposes, 350 out of 900 miles constructed.

In a review of light railways in Britain and Ireland, J. Tatlow of the Midland Great Western Railway of Ireland drew attention to the tramway element[2] and reflected on the usefulness of analysing the returns to 'ascertain how many of these schemes serve rural and agricultural districts and are really Light Railways such as it was the object of the promoters of the act to encourage and what number are of the nature of urban or sub-urban tramways'. The agricultural lines, he felt, must be useful but the proportion of such applications to the total must be somewhat

disappointing to the promoters of the Act.[3] Even so, Mr Ritchie said in a
Commons debate in February 1900 that the promoters of the Act had not
contemplated all the developments which had occurred but that although
some schemes had a tramways element the Act must be considered a
signal success.

There was a rush of applications in 1896 and the following two years
for Light Railway Orders and it is a reasonable assumption that some
minor railway schemes were delayed so that advantage could be taken of
the provisions of the light railway legislation. Interested parties would
have been aware of the parliamentary debates on the bill of 1895 and
would have been prepared for the Act of 1896. Certainly, twenty-eight
applications had been put to the Light Railway Commissioners by
December 1896 and a further fifty-seven by November 1897, while the
year ending November 1898 saw eighty-eight applications, the largest
annual total. With so many applications it was not unusual for companies
to wait longer for their Light Railway Orders to be confirmed than the
time it took to get a private Act. However, enthusiasm soon began to
wane. By 1904 annual applications had dropped to under twenty, and ten
years later the figure was down to two.

In the early years many projects were rejected because they were
outside the scope of the Act, and of the schemes which were granted
Light Railway Orders a high proportion failed to be built. Promoters of
rural railways were unable to raise capital, a familiar problem, for the
public anticipated a poor return on investment.

It was common to blame the Light Railways Act itself for the fact that
light railways were not being built as expected. W. H. Cole picked on the
well-worn question of defining a light railway and declared that the Act
was too vague and left the Light Railway Commissioners to distinguish,
using no published criteria, between light railways and other sorts of
railway.[4] The 1896 Act was criticised by Sir Arthur Heywood, whose
particular interest was the private agricultural railway, on the ground that
many landlords whose estates would benefit from improved transport
were reluctant to build railways because of the problems which were
created when a road had to be crossed. He remarked that though most
local councils were prepared to permit such crossings there could be no
guarantee that subsequent councils would. With such lack of security a
landowner would become prey to a change of policy and thence the
unfortunate owner of a suddenly truncated railway line. Sir Arthur felt
that the Light Railways Act should have included measures to provide
security in such cases, or at least a formal system of arbitration in the event

of disputes. Of the measure generally the best he could say was that 'fortunately the Act has been taken very quietly' and that although there were 'some cases in which farmers would be the gainers by a light railway, but these [were] an infinitesimal proportion of their whole number'.[5]

Amendments were made to the legislation by means of the Light Railways Amendment Act of 1901, but this was described by the *Light Railway and Tramway journal* as 'disappointing and inadequate'.[6] That was a natural reaction, for the new Act did nothing to meet the criticisms of those who thought the government should be doing more to create light railways. It merely continued the life of the Light Railway Commission for another five years, provided a salary of £1,000 per annum for an additional Commissioner and set the limit for special advances at £750,000.

Table 4·1   Light Railway Orders confirmed

Year	Orders	Mileage	Estimated cost (£)
1901	49	337	2,629,725
1902	33	149	1,192,000
1903	37	179	2,019,800
1904	21	97	801,300

The *Railway Times* drew the conclusion that the 1896 Act had failed, basing its judgement on the 1904 Report from the Light Railway Commissioners which had drawn attention to the decline in the number of orders confirmed, only a few of which would ultimately be built. The decline was blamed on excessively stringent conditions of construction, which increased costs, and inadequate financial support from local funds; this was not the expansion of a transport system which would develop agriculture.[7] By 1910 the annual report of the Light Railway Commissioners was strongly critical of the 1896 Act for failing to generate light railways in country districts: 'in its present form the Act does not adequately secure certain essential conditions — namely cheap capital, cheap construction, and cheap working'.[8]

In terms of a large-scale network of light railways a rather more sanguine commentary came in a report to the Board of Trade in 1912 by Lieutenent-Colonel H. A. Yorke.[9] This report, ostensibly on the Belgian experience, elaborated on the sparseness of facilities: fencing was undertaken by landowners; signals were virtually unknown, as was block working; passengers and goods could be picked up along the length of the line and the few stations that existed were either cafés or village shops; guards issued tickets; average speeds rarely exceeded 12 m.p.h. Yorke then related these practices to the English situation: the British public would be unlikely to accept speeds below 25 m.p.h. and if these were achieved the practicalities of operation would demand the introduction of block working. He then approached the subject of gauge. Given that light railway operation was significantly different from conventional railway operation, narrow gauge served a useful function in that it effectively marked the distinction. The use of narrow gauge lent itself to street and road working, and the main objection to it, the cost and delay inherent in transhipment, had been exaggerated and could be minimised by the use of wagons with detachable bodies. Narrow gauge may not have significantly reduced construction costs but with the current high price of land in England every foot counted. The often rehearsed argument in favour of standard gauge was that it would permit main line wagons to be used on the light railway but Yorke gently reminded the Board of Trade that as main line wagons were rarely full anyway they would be ridiculously uneconomic to operate on the little-used railway. He felt that the few steam-operated light railways in England were in every respect but name conventional branch lines with main line standards of construction and operated according to main line ethos. The solution was narrow gauge: 'The fear of a break of gauge has been exaggerated in England and to its influence must in a large measure be attributed the absence of light railways in our rural districts'.[10] Returning to the Belgian experience, Yorke isolated finance as the crucial difference between the two countries. In Belgium the railway system was state owned and the poorer lines were carried by the more profitable. In England, on the other hand, the railways — privately financed — would object to the development of a large system of competing light railways financed by the state.

The Light Railways Act of 1912 was a further attempt to encourage the development of a light railway network to aid agriculture.[11] Three issues provoked particular interest in the railway press:[12] the problem of light railway schemes which turned out to be too substantial to be promoted under light railway legislation; the problem of finance; and the red herring of electric trackless trolleys.

It was felt that too many light railway projects were being brought before the Light Railway Commissioners only for them to be rejected as being outside the scope of a Light Railway Order with attendant financial loss and waste of time for both parties. Promoters would perhaps be put off making a second attempt in the usual way by means of an Act of Parliament. Clause 1 of the bill proposed that if this were the case the Light Railway Commission would promote a bill in Parliament to which the original promoters would speak. This clause was accepted. Attempts to ease the problem of financing light railways raised a number of doubts: the Board of Trade inserted a clause in the bill by which applications by light railway promoters for advances under the Development and Road Improvement Fund Act had to be referred to the Light Railway Commissioners for a report.[13] These advances were available under the earlier measure for light railway schemes which developed agriculture or the fishing industry. More contentious was a clause by which local authorities would guarantee a return on debentures and ordinary shares. The Board of Trade believed that it was less permissive than the original Act of 1896 and that it was fundamental to the encouragement of light railways in agricultural districts. This clause was dropped. The bill was also shorn of its trackless trolley clause. This had said that the Light Railway Commissioners should be empowered to authorise trackless trolley systems but its critics believed that such a system would infringe the rights of highway authorities and that its benefit to agriculture was negligible.

The real problems with the development of light railways did not derive from the Light Railways Act itself. True, it contained no precise definition of a light railway, leaving it to the commissioners to exercise discretion in accepting applications from operators of tramways in London. Even so, together with the Act of 1868, the new Act quite adequately set out the criteria under which light railways could be designated and the conditions under which they would operate. The main problem with the 1896 Act was not the acceptance of light railway schemes but the funding of them. The intention of the Act had been to create light railways; so far it had brought forth little but Light Railway Orders.[14] In the absence of guarantees of financial support from local or national government, it was proving too difficult to raise capital even for lightly constructed lines in rural areas where the likely amount of traffic held out no promise of a dividend. It was a problem recognised by contempories, as some of the views already cited indicate.

When proposals for the amendment of the Light Railways Act were being discussed in 1901 the *Light Railway and Tramway Journal* carried out an investigation into the working of the Act by circulating questionnaires to various experienced, informed and interested parties, although most of them were city and borough engineers whose experience was of urban tramways rather than of railways. Most respondents expressed general satisfaction with the principles of the Act, while suggesting administrative changes, such as the idea proposed by Colonel Stephens that there should be a model Light Railway Order which would save 75 per cent of the Commission's time. However, there were some, such as H. L. Godden, an engineer associated with several light railway schemes, who did argue that while the Light Railways Act had eased promotion it had done little to assist with the raising of capital (see Appendix B). The question of financial support from government, and especially the use of local rates to finance light railways, was a contentious one. It was easier to concentrate on amending administrative clauses.

Light railway applications, 1896–1914

Applications for Light Railway Orders were divided into two classes, A and B. The former related to light railways schemes on acquired land and relying mainly on steam traction; the latter were those that ran along the roads and generally used electric power. Class A applications were mainly for lines that may be called true light railways, while class B were the urban electric tramways. Class A lines were generally longer, and required less capital, since most of them were built on cheaper land in country districts. Of all the applications up to November 1914, 249, or 47 per cent were Class A; this represented 58 per cent of the total mileage and 48 per cent of the total estimated cost (see Table 4·2). Commissioners seem to have preferred less-ambitious projects in so far as, on average, lines submitted to the Board of Trade for confirmation of a provisional order were shorter than the average for initial applications. The Commissioners may have been justified for light railways with extensive mileages planned were prominent amongst those that failed either to be built of completed. The Mid Suffolk managed half its planned 42 miles; the Ackworth & Lindsey Light Railway was a particularly ambitious project for a line of 53 miles carrying coal to Immingham docks, but none was built, not even the revised 5 mile long version.

The table in Appendix A lists the Light Railway Orders granted during the first ten years of the Light Railways Act's existence. It can clearly be seen that urban tramways, from Southend and District and London United to West Manchester and Leicester and District, came to predominate over the rural railways for which the Act had been intended.

Table 4·2 Light railway applications, 1896–1914

	Applications		Submitted to Board of Trade		Submitted as % of applications	
	Class A	*Class B*	*Class A*	*Class B*	*A*	*B*
Number	249 (47%)	279	165 (48%)	157	66	56
Mileage	2,752 (58%)	2,010	1,488 (69%)	655	54	32
Estimated cost	£18,301,160 (48%)	£19,274,742	£9,504,402 (60%)	£6,308,397	49	133
Average length	11·0	7·2	9·0	4·2		
Cost per mile	£6,647	£9,589	£6,387	£9,631		

Table 4·3 Light railway applications, 1896–1914, total figures

	Applications			Approved			Rejected			Withdrawn		
	No.	*Miles*	*Est. Cost (£)*	*No.*	*Miles*	*Est. Cost (£)*	*No.*	*Miles*	*Est. Cost (£)*	*No.*	*Miles*	*Est. Cost (£)*
Class A[a]	249	2,752½	18,301,166	171	1,554¾	10,030,656	46	738½	5,133,912	29	290½	1,929,240
Class B[b]	279	2,011	13,274,742	158	671	6,417,790	65	631¾	5,882,739	55	452	3,705,875

[a] In addition two schemes, total 8½ miles, were deferred, and one of 4¼ miles was not dealt with.
[b] One scheme, 14½ miles, was deferred.

Even the 'proper' light railways were not all opening up the neglected country districts. There were lines built to serve mineral workings, such as the Brackenhill Light Railway, and the Tickhill Railway in the South Yorkshire coalfield. The Harrington & Lowca Light Railway was built to serve part of the Cumbrian coalfield. The Snailbeach District Railway in Shropshire was a narrow gauge mineral railway. There were plans for this to become an extensive concern renamed the Shropshire Minerals Light Railway, but they foundered and the company ended up in the Colonel Stephens group. Other light railways were built to serve industry. The Corringham Light Railway, opened in 1901, crossed 2¼ miles of the Essex marshes to a new explosives factory at Kynochtown. The place was renamed Coryton when Cory Brothers Ltd took over the factory in 1921 to convert it into an oil refinery. This company operated the railway until it closed in 1952, running regular passenger services as well as the oil trains. The Great Central Railway used the Light Railways Act to build short railways into the new docks the company was building at Immingham. Three of these lines were authorised as the Grimsby & District Light Railway in 1906, the Grimsby & Immingham Electric Railway, and the Barton & Immingham Light Railway, both in 1907. The Nidd Valley Railway was built in 1907 to serve the reservoirs of Bradford waterworks. Passenger services, mainly for workmen, operated on this railway of 13 miles from Pateley Bridge until 1929. Military needs provided yet another use for the light railway legislation; the London & South Western Railway operated the Amesbury & Military Camp Railway, 4½ miles long, for the benefit of army bases on Salisbury Plain.

A few railways authorised or built before 1896 applied for Light Railway Orders in order to take advantage of the less-exacting requirements for way and works. The Lambourn Valley Railway was one of these. Construction of the line had begun in 1873, but was halted, and the same happened at the next attempt in 1883. It was not until 1898 that the line was opened, and in 1904 it obtained a Light Railway Order. The Mawddwy Railway in mid-Wales had been opened in 1867, but was closed to passengers in 1901 and to goods in 1908. In 1911 it was re-opened as a light railway, operated by the Cambrian Railways, in which form it survived until 1951. The Burry Port & Gwendraeth Railway was another Welsh line, built to carry goods only in 1869, but reconstituted as a light railway, with the addition of a passenger service, in 1909. Occasionally railways built after 1896 were similarly transferred to management under a Light Railway Order. The Kingsnorth Light Railway was a short private railway converted into a light railway in 1927.

The Sand Hutton was another private line built in 1912 as a 15-in. gauge miniature railway on the Yorkshire estate of Sir Robert Walker. As Sir Robert pursued his interest in agricultural railways, he rebuilt his line as a public light railway with an extension to a junction with the North Eastern Railway at Warthill. It continued to be of very narrow gauge, 1 ft 6 in.

The organisation and management of light railways followed the pattern already well established in the promotion and operation of local networks and branch lines. Some were built by the major railway companies. As well as the Great Central's lines around Grimsby and Immingham, there was the Maidens & Dunure Light Railway, a line of 19½ miles between Alloway Junction, south of Ayr, and Girvan. It was opened in 1906, the property of the Glasgow & South Western Railway. The London & South Western Railway was responsible for the Basingstoke & Alton Railway in Hampshire, while in Essex, the Great Eastern owned the Kelvedon Tiptree & Tollesbury Railway.

The main line companies operated the lines of a number of independent light railways. Sometimes this was at the Board of Trade's insistence. The Welshpool & Llanfair Railway's Light Railway Order, for example, specified that their line was to be operated by an existing company; it was therefore leased to the neighbouring Cambrian Railways. The Goole & Marshland Light Railway, which served the rich agricultural area of the Isle of Axholme and Hatfield Moor, was worked at first by the North Eastern and later by the Lancashire & Yorkshire Railway. There were several lines worked by the GWR: the Lambourn Valley, for example; the Wrington Vale; and the Lampeter, Aberaeron & New Quay Light Railway, which is discussed in more detail in the next chapter.

Lines owned or operated by main line companies accounted for about two-thirds of the mileage of light railways built up to the end of the First World War. That left a small and rather mixed band of completely independent railways. They included the narrow gauge Vale of Rheidol, although that, too, was to be taken over by the Cambrian Railways after ten years of independence. A few of the independents, among them the Mid Suffolk and the Cleobury Mortimer & Ditton Priors Railway, were included in the grouping of railways in 1923. Others, though, remained independent even beyond nationalisation. They included the North Sunderland and the Derwent Valley, and the railways that were members of Colonel Stephens's Associated Railways. All of these retained the freedom from the remote, city-based management of the main line companies, a desire for which had motivated many rural railway companies down the years. The price they paid, however, was a poverty often worse in its effect than that which neglectful management at headquarters could inflict on branch lines. To take extremes, while management by the Cambrian, and especially the GWR, gave the Vale of Rheidol the shot in the arm which helped the railway adapt to the growing tourist traffic, the Shropshire & Montgomeryshire Railway struggled along with run-down antique rolling stock including a horse tramcar from London hauled by curious little locomotives bought from industrial concerns.

The gauge of the tracks was another mark of the individuality of light railways. The confused debate as to the merits of standard and narrow gauge resulted in railways being built to gauges ranging from the 15 in. championed by Sir Arthur Heywood and adopted by the Romney Hythe & Dymchurch Light Railway built in 1926 up to the standard gauge. By the beginning of the First World War fourteen different gauges had been used on light railways (Table 4·4). The only semblance of uniformity

Table 4·4   Gauge of light railways[11] in Britain and Ireland

Gauge		Mileage
ft.	in.	
1	3	7·25
1	11½	61·37
2	0	4·50
2	3	24·29
2	4	3·16
2	4½	8·63
2	6	29·81
2	7½	5·00
2	8½	1·625
3	0	637.94[a]
3		34·625
4		20·44
4		13.00
		851·64
4	8½ Class A[b]	463·815
4	8½ Other	197·375

[a] Some 570 miles of 3 ft 0 in. gauge lines were Irish.
[b] Built on acquired land.

similar to the widespread use of metre gauge on the continent was the
gauge of 3 ft to which many light railways in Ireland were built.

Rural light railways

If the urban tramways are excluded from the reckoning, most of the Light
Railway Orders granted were for schemes that fitted in well with the
intentions of those who had pressed for new legislation to bring into
being rural railways. The same could be said of the small number of light
railways built under the earlier legislation of 1868: the Culm Valley, for
example, or the Highworth Light Railway, both purely country branch
lines. The new Light Railways Act seems to have inspired or revived
plans for lines into neglected country districts. A glance at the list of Light
Railway Orders in Appendix A shows that most of the light railway
schemes, especially the more ambitious projects, were in the sparsely
populated, agricultural regions. The Wrington Vale Railway, one of the
first to be authorised, in 1898, was promoted by local farmers to improve
transport for their milk. The West Country was well represented among
light railway schemes, as attempts were made to penetrate further into
Cornwall, with the Lizard Railway, authorised in 1898, the 21-mile
Penzance Newlyn & West Cornwall, and the Padstow Bedruthan &
Mawgan Railway. In Devon there was the Devon & South Hams Light
Railway, of 13¾ miles, authorised in 1905. East Anglia was another region
where light railway schemes proliferated, including some of the most
ambitious: the Mid Suffolk was to be 42½ miles in all, filling an extensive
area without railways between the two GER main lines to Norwich and
to Lowestoft; the Bury & Diss Railway, 27¼ miles, authorised in
1901, was planned with similar intentions. The Witney Burford and
Andoversford Light Railway, a line of 23¾ miles which obtained its Light
Railway Order in 1904, was intended to traverse parts of the Cotswolds
passed by railways which kept to the main valleys. There were light
railways proposed for some remote parts of Scotland, including the Wick
& Lybster and Cromarty & Dingwall Railways.

The intention to aid the development of rural areas was set out in the
prospectuses of most light railway companies, with the lavishness of
language that was common to such documents. The opening of the
Derwent Valley Railway would mark 'an epoch in the history of
Yorkshire agriculture', while the prospectus for the Rother Valley
Railway expected 'a large traffic will spring up both in passengers and
goods as soon as the line is open'.[16] The Aeron valley, apparently, had

'capabilities possessed by few districts'. The Axminster & Lyme Regis Light Railway pointed to further benefits in that it was to serve two of the 'most attractive watering places' in Lyme Regis and Charmouth.[17]

Problems facing light railways

A further look at the list of Light Railway Orders in Appendix A prompts the thought that many of the railways are unfamiliar names. The reason is that many of those lines that were granted Light Railway Orders were never built; scarcely half the authorised mileage of light railways came into existence. The casualties included most of the examples quoted in the preceding paragraphs. Burford remained a small, isolated Cotswold town until the growth of motor transport. Bury and Diss were not connected by light railway; nor were Leighton Buzzard and Hitchin. Barely half of the Mid Suffolk Railway's planned 42 miles were completed when funds ran out. As a result, some of the company's principal objectives were never reached, among them the junction with the GER line at Halesworth, and the long branch through the town of Debenham which progressed only $1\frac{3}{4}$ miles to the village of Aspall. The Lizard never got its light railway, for the GWR decided to run buses there instead: that in a nutshell was the problem all light railways were up against, but there was more to the failure of light railways to live up to the expectations of dividends to the proprietors or development of the rural economy.

One of the fundamental principles of light railways was that capital and operating costs should be appropriate for the light traffic of country districts. There was some success in achieving this aim, at least before the First World War, for although the major railways were unable to prevent operating ratios becoming less favourable, a number of light railways were improving their performance (see Chapter 5). Even at their best, though, the finances of rural railways were delicately balanced. Capital and overhead charges were high, and after 1920 it became virtually impossible to control operating costs unless maintenance was skimped and renewals abandoned. On the other hand, to put a bus or lorry on the road was cheap and easy: war surplus stock was available; men had acquired new expertise; and there were gratuities to invest.

Any railway, even a lightly built one, needed a considerable amount of capital invested in it. It needed land. It needed permanent way, stations and other engineering and building works. It needed locomotives and rolling stock. The problems facing rural light railways in particular were that, however hard they tried, they were limited in their ability to reduce their initial capital investment. In any case, it can be argued that several of these railways seem not to have tried very hard, and saddled themselves with heavier capital liabilities than they need have done. Examples of this would include the Mid Suffolk Railway's branch to Debenham, which, never completed, remained a burden on the 'main' line, and the scale and cost of the engineering on the Lynton & Barnstaple Railway.

The result was that while most rural light railways were loaded with a capital extremely high in relation to their prospective earnings, some never looked like surviving. That the capital burden was high for all light railways can be simply demonstrated. In the forecasts made before the Lampeter & Aberaeron Railway was built it was said that the capital needed would be £88,000. With net revenue expected to be over £3,300 a return of 4 per cent would be earned. In fact, the line cost £100,000 to build so that it would have needed net revenue of £4,000 to earn 4 per cent, and this never happened. The company rarely broke even on its operations with gross revenue consistent around £3,500. The problem of relatively high capital costs and absolutely low traffic was made worse by a failure of such minor railways to work at the 50 per cent or 60 per cent of total expenditure which the prospectuses had claimed.

Often the major contribution to the heavy burden of capital was that the cost of land was far higher than estimated. Ever since public railways had been built railway companies had come up against this problem, and light railways were no exception. Land on the Aberaeron branch, much of which had been given 'at agricultural prices' was valued at £6,074, nearly 10 per cent of the value of the construction contract. The cost of land on the Easingwold Railway was £2,300, double the estimated figure. Land costs on the Lynton & Barnstaple were four times greater than the original estimate, and the estimated outlay on the Swindon & Highworth Light Railway in 1882 was £28,000, whereas the actual cost reached £45,000.[18] The cost of land on the Culm Valley Railway, despite the optimism of its prospectus, escalated and there were difficulties settling demands for compensation which delayed the opening of the line. The high cost of land went some way towards defeating the object of a line being light railway, while excessive demands for compensation suggest that some landowners at least were not charitably disposed towards railway extension. The Reverend A. Legge objected to the Bentley & Bordon Light Railway because fields would be divided and cattle cut off from supplies of water, which would reduce the value of the land.[19] This railway was built mainly to meet the needs of the War Office, and was operated by the London & South Western Railway; the government used its power to overcome such objections as the Reverend Legge's, while the large railway company had no worries about raising the finance. For independent companies, negotiations with landowners over the value of land could be more difficult and expensive. In September 1898 the shareholders of the Kent & East Sussex Railway were told that progress towards completion had been delayed because of opposition from landowners.[20]

The high cost of land helped to keep up the costs of construction for light railways. One of the principal benefits expected from light railways was that they should be cheaper to build than conventional railways. W. M. Acworth thought that they should cost no more than £5,000 per mile, but this was not often achieved.[21] Only a handful of standard gauge lines came within sight of Acworth's figure, and none at the time at which he was writing. Light railways built after the 1896 Act varied considerably in cost of construction: the Wick & Lybster, operated by the Highland Railway, £3,371 per mile; the Derwent Valley Railway, £5,474; the North Sunderland Railway, £6,205; the Mid Suffolk Railway, £9,626; and the Headcorn extension of the Kent & East Sussex Railway, £13,447. Narrow gauge railways were cheaper to build, despite sometimes having to negotiate difficult terrain, with the Vale of Rheidol Railway costing £4,340 per mile and the Welshpool & Llanfair Railway £5,922.[22] Building a light railway through easy country did not necessarily lessen the cost of construction, as the North Sunderland Railway discovered. Nor did light railway status necessarily make the costs less than minor railways authorised by conventional Act of Parliament. The railway to Minehead in Somerset cost £7,272 per mile, the Ramsey branch in Huntingdon-shire, £7,477 per mile, which compared quite well with some of the light railways just cited; the two narrow gauge light railways did not improve on the £4,571 per mile which the original Ravenglass & Eskdale Railway cost to build in 1873, much less the £2,143 for the Talyllyn Railway in 1866. Again, estimates were often left far behind by the actual costs of construction: construction of the Nidd Valley Railway came to double the estimate.

Despite the virtually unanimous agreement that a railway would be beneficial to the locality, and the bold talk of the tons of coal and the number of sheep that would travel by train, when it came to finding the money to invest in the railway people were less sure. Almost all light railway companies had difficulty raising capital. Several failed completely to do so. Central and local government were little more eager to invest than the landowners, farmers and businessmen of the district served by the railway. When the Light Railways Act was being passed the expectation was that local authorities would be encouraged to support country lines, but they did so on business terms which were unwelcome to the railway promoters but most laudable as far as ratepayers were concerned. The idea that rural transport should be a public service had almost no support; the councils wanted to know how their money would be secured and how their 3 per cent was going to be earned.

The county council and local councils in Cardiganshire hotly debated the advisability of advancing money to light railway projects and there was ultimately investment in the Aberaeron branch. In Yorkshire in 1902 the rural district councils of Escrick and Riccall obtained a Light Railway Order for the Derwent Valley Railway, the first district councils to do so.[23] The two councils guaranteed a minimum dividend of 3 per cent on ordinary shares for ten years with a maximum liability of £1,500, provoking local landowners to promise to meet half to that sum. This was one of the most effective co-operative efforts between landowners and councils in the promotion of light railways.

Little money from central government went into light railway schemes. Provision was made in the Light Railways Act for the Treasury to make grants and loans, but the funds were scarcely tapped. Only £200,000 of the £1 million set aside for loans were taken up. Most of that sum, and all the money laid out in grants-in-aid, was taken up for light railways promoted by the main line companies. They were obviously sound financially, which the new independent companies for the most part were not; the uncertain way in which most light railway companies were founded made them no more likely to gain loans from the Treasury than from the local authorities. Instead, they had to rely on private capital.

Promoters of light railway companies usually at first tried to sell ordinary shares to members of the public. This method rarely met with much success. An alternative was to try to persuade a neighbouring main line company to take on some or all of the investment. By the 1890s, though, the larger companies were less keen on taking on such marginal (in respect both of geography and profit) commitments. The Cambrian Railways, for instance, rejected several pleas from local people for the revival of a project to build a branch from near Llanidloes to the village of Llangurig, although the idea was taken seriously enough for a survey to be conducted as to possible traffic.[24] The population around Llangurig was about 200–300, and the company could expect no more than about twenty-five people to travel to Llanidloes market each week. In an area once rich in lead mines mineral traffic might exist. The survey noted the continued production at the Nantiago Lead Mine, 4 miles beyond Llangurig, from which 92 tons and 142 tons of ore were transported to Llanidloes in 1912 and 1913 respectively at 15s a ton. There would be incoming traffic of lime, perhaps 75 tons out of 150 tons would go by rail, and coal, 200 tons out of 300 tons. The remaining traffic would consist of livestock, for around 7,000 sheep were exported annually from Llanidloes. To set against a projected annual revenue of £217 were working expenses, based on three daily trips, typical of other local branches, of £670 7s 4d. The expenses did not include any allowance for maintenance of rolling stock and permanent way. The report concluded that there was little chance of revenue ever matching working expenses, and the project was dropped. However, in 1917, local initiative revived the scheme, even to the extent of a continuation through the mountains to Yspytty Ystwth, making use of German prisoners of war as cheap labour. Even the prospect of a cut-price extension failed to move the Cambrian. Indeed, that company's officers in drawing up the report in September 1917 not only commented on the absence of traffic but felt that the extension as proposed would provide a shorter route to Aberystwyth and Carmarthen than the Cambrian Railway's present main line and would thus 'pull down rates and fares'. Llangurig did not get its branch line.

When light railway companies ran into difficulties in raising capital unorthodox methods might be resorted to. The problems facing the directors of the North Devon & Cornwall Light Railway were not untypical.[25] This railway, built in the 1920s, was the descendant of the Plymouth & North Devon Direct Railway, which had foundered, failing in 1904 to obtain a London & South Western Railway guarantee of interest on its preference shares and debentures because of the inadequacy of local traffic. Undeterred the promoters of the North Devon & Cornwall Light Railway obtained their Light Railway Order in 1914, an Amendment Order in 1922 and an Extension of Time Order in 1924. The company had a share capital of £250,000, of which £125,000 was to be provided by the Treasury and £66,000 by various interested local authorities. In the event, local investment was reckoned to be less than £20,000. The original contractors, MacAlpine, withdrew and P. W. Anderson took over with a tender of £192,134, much of which was paid in shares at a discounted price. By February 1925 the contractor was bankrupted. The allocation of shares did not go smoothly, with the Ministry of Transport disputing its initial allocation of 6,250 £10 shares believing that the local councils were being let off more lightly. Local people who had agreed to take shares were looking to escape their commitment; in June 1922 the directors heard that a Mrs Ward claimed she had applied for only one share and not two as she had been allocated; Mr Heard was unwilling to take his ten shares as he had only applied on the understanding that a station was to have been built on a particular farm. The following month the directors heard that James Balsdon, W. G. D. Hale, A. C. Pedrick, R. Crocker, E. Curtis and J. Trump had all refused to take up their shares. Furthermore, the local councils, worried about the issue of debenture stock, were unwilling to pay their initial £2 a share. In February 1923 the directors received a breakdown of the share issue and the arrears of payment after the first four payments. Shares allotted totalled 9,847; the money received was £71,810, leaving the company with arrears of £6,966. The owners of 471 shares had paid nothing at all. Local support was not forthcoming and the company was forced to look elsewhere for its finance. Colonel Stephens for the company negotiated a loan with the British Foreign and Colonial (BFC) Corporation on the following terms: a loan of £12,000 for three months at 6 per cent against £15,000 of the company's debentures on condition that the BFC Corporation was given an option to purchase debentures to the value of £22,000 at the end of the three-month period at 97 per cent of par value, free of stamp duty.

Other companies also sought loans to see them through difficult periods. In 1904 the Mid Suffolk Railway's directors heard that the Scottish Imperial Office would take £12,000 debenture stock for £8,000 provided the company's employees were insured with Scottish Imperial. The following year the same company negotiated a loan of £1,250 from the Capital and Counties Bank for a period of seven months; if it were not repaid within the agreed period the company would hand over all its surplus land and a locomotive to the bank.

An attractive method of financing construction had always been to pay for work in shares. The 1860s in particular had been the age of the contractor, when a number of entrepreneurs, such as Thomas Brassey and David Davies, had built lines, accepting shares in the owning company in part payment for their work. The profits they made on these deals enabled contractors to go on to promote other lines, in part, to keep their gangs together. Such powerful contractors largely disappeared after the financial crash of 1867 and the slowing down of the rate of construction. However, rural light railways, finding it hard to raise capital in the normal way, often paid the contractor and other creditors in shares instead of cash. Although this ensured the construction of many lines it also obscured the fact that local demand was not likely to run high. Of the many companies affected in this way, the Mid Suffolk Railway was faced with several financial problems and its contractors took debentures. The contract accepted for the Lambourn Valley Railway in 1888 was for £111,000, of which £18,000 was in cash, £60,000 in shares and the remaining £33,000 in debentures bearing 5 per cent interest and redeemable at par. The Lee on Solent Railway was operated by the contractor until the London & South Western took over in 1909. The directors of the North Devon & Cornwall Light Railway paid themselves expenses in shares. Payments for land also were often made in shares. This was true on both the North Devon & Cornwall Light Railway, and the Southwold Railway where the Earl of Stradbroke accepted shares in exchange for his land. Landowners on the unsuccessful Lampeter to Llandeilo light railway promised their land in return for shares.

The advantages of being a light railway were also undermined by those companies which invested to excess in permanent way, buildings, locomotives and rolling stock. All minor railways were to some extent affected by the problem of excess capacity. In the expansionist 1850s and 1860s it was held that even in rural areas a railway would generate sufficient new traffic for a line to be self-supporting.[26] Later economists, however, emphasised that under-utilised lines — and virtually all light railways were in this category — were likely to be hit by expenditure out of all proportion to the traffic on the line.

Even the lightest of light railways was likely to be too heavy for the traffic it was expected to carry. William Acworth and C. D. Campbell pointed out that in the case of many lines the capital invested was unlikely to be fully utilised; in other words they were built to a standard far in excess of the requirements of the traffic over the line.[27] The Teign Valley Railway amply demonstrated this fact on those occasions when the GWR line from Exeter to Plymouth was closed at Dawlish because of bad weather and trains were diverted over this normally bucolic branch. Speeds may have been slow but the line took the heavy expresses. On a smaller scale but more regular basis, the North Sunderland Railway carried the bulk of its freight on one train a day, the 4.10 p.m. from Seahouses to Chathill. For traffic such as that lightly constructed permanent way was all that was required, and indeed that was precisely what a light railway should have meant. Yet there were several amongst the standard gauge lines that laid their tracks with rails of up to 90 lb per yard, the same as were used for main lines into the early 1890s. True, the rails were often bought second-hand: the Derwent Valley Railway used 80 lb rail that had seen service on the Midland Railway's Settle to Carlisle line.[28] But that did not necessarily represent a capital saving over the cost of lighter rails, which themselves could be acquired second-hand. More suitable for light railways were the 56 lb per yard rails used by the Mid Suffolk Railway, the 45 lb and 56 lb on the Wantage Tramway, while the West Sussex Light Railway was laid with rails of 41 lb per yard.

Capital savings on locomotives and rolling stock were effected mainly by the purchase of second-hand equipment, at least on the standard gauge lines. Some bought new coaches. The Weston Clevedon & Portishead Railway had six bogie coaches built for it in American style with verandah entrances. Most companies bought any coaches that were available second-hand, and these were often antiquated coaches of four or six wheels, light by any reckoning. The Easingwold Railway, for example, bought two four-wheeled coaches from the North Eastern Railway, later replaced by similar vehicles from the North London Railway; the Mid Suffolk's stock of four-wheelers came from the Metropolitan District Railway. The same was true with locomotives. The Lampeter & Aberaeron Railway started operations with an o-6-o side tank originally delivered to the Severn & Wye Railway in 1873. The Golden Valley Railway hired locomotives from the GWR and from the contractor, but it also owned four ex-LNWR locomotives originally built in 1850–53, and rebuilt between 1862 and 1870, some twenty years before their move to Herefordshire. The Nidd Valley line was initially operated by two former Metropolitan Railway locomotives dating from 1866 and 1869. Even when this railway decided to withdraw them, Colonel Stephens expressed an interest in their possible use on his railways. In Warwickshire, the three-mile-long Edge Hill Light Railway bought two of the London Brighton & South Coast Railway's small 'Terrier' class tank locomotives, forty-five years old. These were popular little engines: the Kent & East Sussex and the Weston Clevedon & Portishead were other light railways to own them, and one is still running in preservation. There were light railway companies, such as the Lambourn Valley and the Mid-Suffolk, that bought new, but not always successful, locomotives. Those on the Lambourn Valley were sold shortly after the line was taken over by the GWR. On the railways owned or operated by the large companies investment in locomotives and rolling stock was of lesser concern as the operating company simply supplied equipment usual for its branches, light or otherwise. For all light railways, though, the employment of second-hand rolling stock was easier for those built to standard gauge. Narrow gauge lines, where the capital burden should have been less, were unable to hire or borrow rolling stock from their neighbours.

Locomotives and other equipment were available second-hand: the Ashover Light Railway owned six American Baldwin locomotives bought as war surplus material, and among its coaches were some built for the exhibition railway at Wembley in 1924. However, the availability of stock was limited, and the proliferation of gauges meant that there was likely to be some outlay on conversion. Instead, it was more usual for the narrow gauge lines to buy new locomotives and rolling stock. The Leek & Manifold Valley bought two 2-6-4 tank engines from Kitson's of Leeds, one of which was given the name *E. R. Calthorp*.

Savings on capital invested in such things as signalling and continuous brakes often proved to be less than it was hoped light railway status would offer. The West Sussex Railway had no signals at all along its 8¼ miles, but most had some form of signalling, at least at the stations. Some light railways found that they had to have continuous brakes on at least some of their stock. The North Sunderland was one railway on which the Board of Trade insisted there should be continuous brakes (see Chapter 5). There were others among standard gauge light railways that upgraded their equipment in expectation of through running from main lines. The Southwold and other light railways were similarly hampered, or found that economies on construction and operation were unacceptable, if not to the Board of Trade, then to a prospective purchaser. When the GWR took over the Highworth line in 1882 it spent an additional £18,000 improving a line which had failed the Board's tests on fourteen counts.[29]

On some railways excess capacity was the result of having to meet peaks in traffic. This affected particularly those lines whose traffic was seasonal. Much agricultural traffic was concentrated into periods shortly after the harvests. Tourists travelled on holiday mostly in summer. There was often an imbalance in the traffic. Westbound trains on the Welshpool & Llanfair Railway usually consisted of three loaded trucks or vans; eastbound trains were often nearly empty. The milk, livestock and timber carried down to Welshpool could not match the volume of coal, basic slag, roadstone and cattle feed that was carried up the line. Periods of heavy demand could be localised even to specific days, causing major operating problems and forcing the small railway to depend upon larger, neighbouring railways for rolling stock. This may be illustrated by the annual Dalis Fair at Lampeter when the Manchester & Milford Railway would dispatch between 100 and 120 wagon loads of cattle. Newcastle Races brought such a rush of passengers to the North Sunderland Railway that the trains had to be double-headed. The railway had to press all of its passenger stock into service and borrow more from the NER.

Light railways which were dependent upon seasonal holiday traffic were particularly vulnerable: on the North Sunderland Railway approximately 80 per cent of the passengers were carried during the summer months. Narrow gauge railways were, of course, unable to borrow rolling stock, so in addition to the excess capacity built into the civil engineering there would also have to be an over-provision of rolling stock. On the Vale of Rheidol Railway 60 per cent of passenger train miles (and passenger train miles accounted for 85 per cent of the total) were run in the second half of the year, the period including the holiday months of July and August. The company's dependence upon the summer season is most completely shown in the figures for total revenue, with 70 per cent of income being earned in the six months to December. The railway was able to spread its expenditure more evenly throughout the year. Such items as 'way and works' and 'locomotive repairs' show higher expenditure in the first six months, suggesting that this period was used for maintenance. The Vale of Rheidol Railway's freight services were abandoned in the 1920s and the winter passenger service in 1931, a victim of bus competition. The three locomotives, two of which were provided new in 1923 by the GWR, and fifteen passenger vehicles, were kept only for the summer season. That the railway survived at all was a tribute to the GWR's promotion of tourism.

The tendency for light railways to be overcapitalised had its effect on the profit and loss accounts, for a high proportion of the operating costs of light railways, as indeed of most independent railways, went on overheads which varied little with an increase or decrease in traffic. Overheads were thus a greater burden for the small lines than for main line companies. 'General charges', the item in railway accountancy covering auditors' and accountants' fees and office and general expenses, represented in 1904 an average of 5 per cent of the costs of Britain's railways (see Table 4·6). However, for smaller companies such as the Vale of Rheidol and the Lynton & Barnstaple Railway it was 8·4 per cent and 11·3 per cent respectively. Besides general charges there were the unavoidable expenses of maintaining the line, all of which had to be met whether one train ran or twenty: ballast was washed out rather than worn away; sleepers rotted even without traffic; wagon mileage, and thus depreciation, was largely unaffected by the size of loads. As the tale of the North Sunderland's brakes shows (see Chapter 5) there were ways of keeping some of these costs down. One way to lessen the burden was to share it. For those light railways like the Basingstoke & Alton, entirely owned by a larger neighbour, the costs were absorbed into the main line

Table 4·5 Vale of Rheidol Railway: revenue and expenditure 1907 and 1908, seasonal variation[30]

		Jan.–June 1907	July–Dec. 1907	Jan.–June 1908	July–Dec. 1908
Expenditure		£	£	£	£
Way and works	salaries etc.	477	423	444	439
Loco power	office salaries	30	30	30	30
	wages	167	192	157	186
	coal	384	537	371	422
	water	11	21	9	12
	oil	28	31	13	34
Loco repairs	wages	85	50	73	70
	materials	74	25	137	32
Carriage repairs	wages	14	29	22	19
	materials	15	27	35	111
Traffic	salaries	269	281	234	270
	fuel	42	22	52	29
	printing	17	35	16	27
	clothes	–	–	13	13
	misc.	12	25	45	23
General charges	directors	–	–	–	–
	auditor	5	5	5	5
	accountant and secretary	36	48	48	51
	office/general expenses	40	43	34	50
	advertising	19	56	20	60
	electric telegraph	20	20	19	20
	insurance	28	39	31	37
TOTAL[a]		1,828	1,998	1,874	1,997
Revenue					
Passenger		920	3,014	955	2,787
Parcels		11	17	13	19
Merchandise		253	211	181	204
Minerals		293	253	309	303
TOTAL[a]		1,582	3,563	1,513	3,357
Number of passengers carried		30,459	79,575	32,020	71,045

[a] Totals are not derived from the table, which merely comprises the main headings.

Table 4·6 Percentage distribution of expenditure: various railway companies compared

Year	Maintenance of way 1	2	3	Loco power 1	2	3	Rolling stock repairs 1	2	3	Traffic 1	2	3	General charges 1	2	3
1908	14·2	17·7	18·1	28·3	36·3	27·7	2·2	0·4	14·8	34·1	33·4	27·4	15·9	9·2	3·2
1909	12·9	14·9	18·2	30·8	43·2	25·9	3·2	0·5	14·7	32·0	30·2	28·5	15·5	7·9	3·3
1910	20·7	17·9	17·1	24·7	44·9	26·6	3·1	0·9	15·9	31·5	33·0	28·0	15·2	7·6	3·2
1911	19·7	14·5	17·3	25·6	31·1	25·9	3·7	9·3	15·9	30·9	31·2	28·5	14·9	7·5	3·3
1912	19·3	15·6	16·4	25·8	32·0	25·7	3·0	7·0	15·8	31·6	32·1	29·1	15·7	9·8	3·4

1 Southwold Railway
2 North Sunderland Railway
3 North Eastern Railway

Table 4·7 Comparison of railway costs in 1913[32]

Expenditure	Standard railway £	%	Light railway £	%
Maintenance and renewal of way and works	11,888,958	15·2	25,529	18·7
Maintenance and renewal of stock	13,322,329	17·1	15,320	11·2
Locomotive power	17,447,018	22·3	38,976	28·6
Traffic expenses	23,458,964	30·0	30,632	22·5
General charges	2,634,646	3·4	13,239	9·7
Miscellaneous	9,402,301	12·0	12,768	9·3

company's business. Centralised administration was one of the benefits offered by Colonel Stephens to the various light railways he controlled and such amalgamations were encouraged.[31]

The running costs of light railways generally were high. Table 4·7 shows how light railways compared with ordinary railways in 1913. The light railway's principal advantage seems to have been in traffic expenses. It could save on staff; on the costs of running a station; and on the issue of tickets, by assigning this to the guard, as on the West Sussex Railway. On the other hand, the costs of maintenance and replacement bore more heavily on light railways (Table 4·7). The large main line companies were able to finance a steady programme of repairs and renewals, and to spread such work throughout the year and over a period of years, whereas lines with small numbers of locomotives, carriages and wagons were likely to find themselves with heavy repair bills at inconvenient times, and, with stock out of traffic, the reduction or withdrawal of service. That was the strait to which the North Sunderland Railway was forced when its locomotives failed; the company was obliged to employ the services of a taxi. To a large extent these problems were the result of the light railways' failure to buy the best equipment: their locomotives were second-hand, underpowered or inefficient, and often all three, with the result that they cost more in coal and maintenance than the equivalent locomotives on main line railways. The same could be said of rolling stock. Light railways paid a smaller proportion of their expenses on the maintenance of carriages and wagons (Table 4·7), but to a large extent they got by without carrying out the maintenance. Hence the fabled decrepitude of many a light railway.

Thus the light railways were falling between two stools. On the one hand, they were laden with greater capital than was bargained for, because the costs of land and construction were higher than expected; in consequence fixed charges and overheads took up a large part of the profit and loss account. On the other, they had insufficient capital to buy the best locomotives and rolling stock, and then insufficient working capital to maintain the equipment. This was a vicious spiral which got worse as time went by. Light traffic and low revenues on the rural light railways made it difficult, if not impossible, to raise new capital for the replacement of locomotives, rolling stock and permanent way. Replacements, therefore, were deferred, and from that deteriorating services and declining traffic would follow; in turn, falling revenue would make the raising of new capital even more difficult. Light railways built in the first decade or so after the Act of 1896 were reaching the point where replacement of equipment was becoming necessary in the 1920s, just when road competition was making itself felt. And so their services went into decline.

People were fully aware of these problems. A Light Railways Investigation Committee was appointed in 1921 to consider the question of light railways in relation to the Railways Bill then before Parliament. The disappointing results of light railways, reported the committee, were less the result of inefficiency or lack of economy than of insufficient revenue and capital. But the committee had come too late. Their sanguine views on the future of light railways and their recommendations for greater support from the government and local authorities were quickly overtaken by events. Already the finances of almost all light railways were heading for complete collapse. Not all light railways actually made a loss on operations, but very few made sufficient profit to meet interest charges and provide for effective maintenance and renewal of equipment. The operating ratio has been referred to already as a guide to performance: it is illuminating to compare the ratio of a number of light railways with that of some other minor railways (Table 4·8).

The Great Western Railway carried out an analysis of the economies of branch line operation in 1926 and concluded that there was little benefit to be gained from converting further branch lines to light railways.[33] All the major railway companies were cautious in their approach to light railways, and their attitude was often decisive for the survival of light railway

Table 4·8 Various railways: percentage operating ratio, 1890–1925

	Operating ratio					
Type of railway	*1890*	*1895*	*1900*	*1905*	*1910*	*1925*
	%	%	%	%	%	%
Light railways						
Southwold	83	85	66	67	63	96
Easingwold		62	72	55	60	98
North Sunderland			69	58	46	103
Golden Valley	196	146				
Minor railways						
Ffestiniog	58	60	67	74	70	90
North Wales Narrow Gauge	88	90	85	87	101	114
Manchester & Milford	99	88	97	97		
All British railways	54	56	62	62	62	83

schemes. The main line railways did not wish to encourage light railways which they thought would be a drain on expenses and yield little revenue. So it was that the GWR abandoned support for the Lizard, and other light railway projects in Cornwall as soon as it had concluded that it was cheaper to run a bus in such an area. The major companies were prepared to work together to defeat light railway projects as the GWR and LNWR did in 1899 to the proposed Wolverhampton & Bridgnorth Light Railway. A memo passing between the two large companies made their position clear: 'I am sure you will agree with the view of this Company [GWR] as to the necessity for the large railway companies to protect themselves and each other against the exploiters who are now rising in every direction under the disguise of light railway promoters.'[34]

Unwilling though they were to see a proliferation of unprofitable rural branch lines, the main line companies were willing to make use of the light railway legislation when it suited them. The GWR dropped the light railways in Cornwall, but it actively promoted a line from Pewsey to Salisbury, a route of 20¾ miles, for which it obtained a Light Railway Order in 1898 and an Extension of Time in 1901. This railway was lost because the War Office took exception to a railway passing close by the camps and firing ranges on Salisbury Plain, and its crossing land owned by the War Department. The GWR tried to persuade it of the benefits the army would derive from the line: easing the transport of materials for building Tidworth barracks, facilitating manoeuvres, reducing costs of moving men and provender, better communication between the camps and Aldershot and via the Severn Tunnel and Fishguard to Ireland. This did not sway the War Office. Nor did the company's suggestion that it would construct the light railway so that artillery could easily pass over it; nor the proposal that speed limits could be imposed or services suspended entirely if military affairs required. Even the suggestion that the GWR would permit the army to build the line, under the direction of the company's chief mechanical engineer, as a practical military exercise, did not sway the War Office.[35]

The Pewsey railway had its origins in an earlier scheme, the Pewsey Salisbury & Southampton Railway, for which an Act of Parliament had been obtained in 1883.[36] It was a straightforward attempt by the GWR to thwart its rival London & South Western Railway (LSWR). The major railways used the light railway legislation as another means of protecting their interests against those of a rival. The Basingstoke & Alton Railway was promoted by the LSWR, it seems with the intention of preventing expansion by the GWR into Hampshire. The GWR saw a take-over of the

Lambourn Valley line as a means of siphoning traffic away from the
Midland & South Western Junction Railway;[37] running the Lambourn
Valley as a light railway helped to reduce the expense of the investment.
In Cardiganshire there was a delicate relationship between the GWR and
the London & North Western (LNWR), and the nominally independent
Lampeter & Aberaeron Light Railway was little more than a pawn in the
larger railway rivalries (see Chapter 5).

The main line companies, often unwilling to commit themselves to the
expensive tasks of promotion and construction, were nevertheless alive to
the benefits of the contributory value of traffic from even the most
moribund of minor railways. In the next chapter it will be shown that
their larger neighbours derived reasonable benefits from the Lampeter &
Aberaeron Railway, the Southwold and the North Sunderland. It was
equally true of other lines. Few people from Wantage would have
Wantage Road station as their ultimate destination and the majority of the
passengers on the Easingwold Railway would not have come from, or
expect merely to go to, Alne. The same could be said of many branch line
passengers, especially where the junction with the main line was a place of
no importance; goods traffic, on the other hand, would almost invariably
travel a greater distance over the neighbouring lines. The people of
Llanfair Caereinion would probably travel only as far as Welshpool, but
their incoming coal and the cattle they dispatched would be carried by the
Cambrian and later the GWR. The Wisbech & Upwell Tramway may
have produced net receipts of only £420 in 1896, or little more than 1 per
cent return on its capital of £41,926

but we must remember that these figures correspond with haulage on the light
section [of the GER] only and that there is a much greater, if unrecorded, profit to
the company due to the additional traffic, more especially in apples, potatoes, and
other agricultural produce created and fostered by the tramway, and carried over
the main line to London at an additional working expenditure which is scarcely
appreciable.[38]

The contributory value of traffic was rarely mentioned openly or
officially but a consciousness of its existence was evident in the support
occasionally given to struggling independent railways. The NER loaned
locomotives to the North Sunderland and wrote off some of the light
railway's debts. The main line companies, however, could not afford to be
too profligate with their shareholders' money, and long and acrimonious
were the discussions when a light railway was eventually absorbed. The
LNER 'bought' the Mid Suffolk Railway in 1921 for £30,231, but nearly

£206,000 had been spent in building the line, whose creditors were lucky to get anything: W. H. Smith & Sons accepted £2,000 in settlement of their claim for £10,902, while the Earl of Stradbroke accepted £460 for his claim for £5,316.[39] The GWR paid £10,000 for the Golden Valley Railway, and, earlier, in 1879, £27,000 for the Culm Valley Railway. In the latter case, when outstanding liabilities of nearly £18,000 had been paid, the shareholders were left with only 5 per cent of their original investment. That was in a railway for which the prospectus in 1872 had confidently predicted dividends of 6 per cent.[40]

Light railways in the community

The issue of railways and their place in the economic and social life of the country has been recently and effectively considered.[41] It may still be asked whether light railways, representing a small fraction of the total mileage yet faced with proportionately a far larger share of problems, influenced the communities they traversed.

The essential question is, of course, whether or not light railways met the transport needs of the communities they served. Undoubtedly they did, although it is in the nature of things that their customers continued to complain. Eventually improvements in road transport provided a challenge to which railways could not respond. Certainly in terms of speed and comfort, and to a large extent in respect of cost, railways revolutionised rural transport. Light railways were no exception. The criticism that they did not pass by every farm gate is unfounded for passengers; had they done so the service would have been so slow and indirect that it would have been quicker to walk to the village station. Freight movement was also enormously eased by the extension of the railway network as costs fell and wider markets were opened up to farmers. The frequency of service affected passengers more than freight, for which a single train each day would have been sufficient. Passenger services on light railways were attuned to the basic rhythm of country life. There were usually no more than three or four trains in each direction daily: an early morning train, one late morning or early afternoon, and one late afternoon. The Easingwold Railway was an exception, being so short that nine trains each was daily could easily be operated, while the Wantage Tramway connected with every GWR train stopping at Wantage Road station. Timetables were always adjusted to suit market days. The Tanat Valley Railway way typical in that on Wednesdays the first train for Oswestry left Llangynog at 7.00 a.m. instead of 7.35 the rest of the week; the last return train left Oswestry slightly later, at 4.50 p.m., and taking nearly an hour and a half reached the end of the line at 6.13 p.m. Country railways rarely catered for those staying out in the evening, mainly because most people stayed at home. The Mid Suffolk, though, in its 1922 timetable did have a late train on Saturdays leaving Haughley at 8.55 p.m.

To say that light railways carried farm produce and agricultural inputs is, of course, to state the obvious. To what extent the appearance on the rural scene of a new railway influenced the nature or form of agriculture is more debatable. The Mid Suffolk Railway abandoned its attempt to improve its schedules to aid cattle marketing because it found that corn-growing was returning to its area. The Kelvedon & Tollesbury Railway, however, played its part in the development of the Tiptree jam and fruit industry. Gilbert Thomas described the railway between the wars thus: 'the line exists primarily for the jam factory that nestles amid acres of its own orchards at Tiptree, and human freight is given every possible reminder that it is of secondary importance'. The 'several passengers' he saw picked up at Tiptree were more than matched by the 'ten wagon loads of jam'.[42] There was a marked increase in local production of milk in the years following the opening of the Culm Valley Railway. The Duke of Buckingham's Wotton Tramway enabled the farms on his estate to supply milk to London. Other goods carried included hay, straw, grain, timber and bark outwards and coal, roadstone and manure from London inwards.[43] The Wisbech & Upwell Tramway carried apples, potatoes and carrots, and the provision of transport facilities for summer fruit encouraged local farmers to turn to such crops.[44] At the opposite side of the country, the development of horticulture and fruit farming was assisted by the Bere Alston & Calstock Light Railway, a line only 4 miles long but which brought its locality into the national transport network, via the East Cornwall and Plymouth Devonport & South Western Junction Railways, when it opened in 1908. The Derwent Valley Railway may not have altered the course of Yorkshire's agriculture but was of benefit to the farmers who used its nine stations and two halts. In 1913 it carried 18,174 tons of merchandise, of which potatoes were a major part. The total rose to a peak of 37,244 tons in 1925. The movement of livestock was also important: the railway carried 1,054 animals in 1913 and 5,679 in 1925. The company helped the development of the National Benzole, Russian Oil and Shell Mex petrol storage depots, and these provided useful traffic. The benefit to local people was less pronounced in respect of passenger traffic, for the line was hard hit by road competition.

The number of passenger journeys fell from a peak of 49,983 in 1915 to 18,430 in 1925 and passenger services were withdrawn the following year. The Axholme Joint Railway (the Goole & Marshland) was heavily committed to agricultural traffic and in 1915 had six stations and fifteen sidings for the benefit of farmers,[45] while the Kent & East Sussex was one of a number of these country lines to gain the epithet 'The Farmers' Railway'. Even a light railway so committed to passenger traffic as the Kinver Light Railway in the Black Country provided a service to agriculture: substantial quantities of milk were carried, enough on occasions to have passenger stock commandeered for the goods traffic.

Coal was a vital element in the rural economy, and had always been a major part of most railways' traffic. Light railways were no exception, coal often being the most profitable part of the goods traffic. It was particularly profitable on the North Sunderland, where the company and the station master at Seahouses jointly entered the coal merchanting business. The same was generally true of other railways of this generation not operated as light railways. The Lynton & Barnstaple Railway was promoted in the 1890s to fulfil similar transport needs to most of its light railway contemporaries, but it had its own Act of Parliament. On this line, too, incoming coal traffic overshadowed the volume of wool, potatoes, hides, sheepskins, rabbits and other agricultural goods carried. Around 1,000 tons of coal were delivered to Lynton station each year, 500 tons to Blackmore Gate, while Woody Bay and Bratton Fleming stations dealt with 150 tons and 30 tons respectively.[46]

The close ties between light railways and their local rural, farming communities were often all but destroyed during the 1920s and 1930s as competing services from buses and motor lorries captured many of the local journeys of passengers and farm stock and produce to market towns. Passenger journeys on the Tanat Valley Railway in mid-Wales shrank from the 67,762 of 1913 to 11,670 in 1938. Most of those travelling on the line in 1938 were making long journeys, not going for a day's shopping in Oswestry, now more likely to be undertaken by bus. Agricultural and goods traffic diminished too: 445 wagons of livestock in 1938 compared with 752 in 1923. That left mineral traffic as the most important part of the Tanat Valley's business in place of the service to farming for which it had been promoted. There were some other light railways built under the Act of 1896 which had always predominantly served mineral or industrial interests.[47] The Tilmanstone branch of the East Kent Light Railway at its peak carried 250,000 tons of coal annually and as late as 1935 the East Kent Railway itself moved over 249,00 tons of freight.[48] The Edge Hill

Light Railway was designed specifically for mineral traffic. A Light
Railway Order was granted in 1919 for a line 5¾ miles long employing
locomotives in conjunction with cable haulage up a gradient of one in six.
In its busiest period the railway moved 200 wagon loads of ironstone a
day and kept 200 men employed in local workings.[49] The Ashover Light
Railway was built primarily as a mineral railway, passenger services being
added as an afterthought.[50]

Many light railways were designed with the tourist trade in mind and in
this respect contributed to the local economy. One such was the Leek &
Manifold Railway, one of only four railways built on the 2 ft 6 in. gauge.
Some light railways largely owed their existence to tourism: the Vale of
Rheidol[51] and the Romney Hythe & Dymchurch for example. Other light
railways which had a strong tourist input into their passenger traffic
included the Lampeter & Aberaeron, the North Sunderland and the
Southwold. Tourism has become the saviour of most light railways that
survive today and still, therefore, the railway contributes to the local
economy; now the railway is as much an attraction for visitors as the
scenery.

Light railways were promoted and built to serve a wide variety of
functions. Most of what could be called the true light railways were
intended to do what the light railways enthusiasts had hoped: improve
transport in neglected country areas. Those that were built performed
valuable services for their localities over many years, carrying jam from
Tiptree, fruit and vegetables to Wisbech, milk along the Wrington Vale,
passengers to local markets. But the irony was that the strongest offspring
of the Light Railways Act of 1896 were the urban tramways, usually
electric, while the country lines for the most part struggled. Many of
those projected failed even to materialise. The Light Railways Act itself
was often criticised for these failures, for not relaxing regulation
sufficiently for light railways to become established. Yet it was less the
regulation of the light railways than their financing that was the problem.
Almost all light railways had difficulty raising sufficient funds, as the major
railways, local investors and local authorities, each for differing reasons,
held back. The major railway companies were cautious of supporting
further branch lines, when their own finances were beginning to show
signs of weakness. The farming community had little spare cash to invest:
landlords whose income from rents had been reduced may have been
prepared to give their land but were unwilling to buy shares on a large
scale. Additionally, the financial stresses created by the depression
brought to the surface tensions between landlord and tenant, and this

found a forum in the deliberations of local and county councils which were given a role to play in the creation of light railways by the Light Railways Act of 1896. In all respects by 1896 the spirit of constructive co-operation among the parties most deeply involved was singularly lacking. The real problem was that the Light Railways Act had come at least ten years too late, for by the time the resultant railways were being planned and constructed they were already facing healthy competition from road transport. Just how healthy this was will be seen in the next two chapters.

Notes

1 W. H. Cole, *Light Railways at Home and Abroad*, 1899, pp. 155–6.
2 IRC 1900, 6, section 38 p.33.
3 *Ibid.*
4 Cole, *op. cit.*, pp. 156, 167.
5 Sir Arthur Heywood, *Minimum Gauge Railways*, pp.49–50.
6 *Light Railway and Tramway Journal*, May 1901, pp.
7 *Railway Times*, 10 June 1905.
8 PRO, RAIL 1054–2, Light Railway Commissioners' Report for 1910.
9 PRO, RAIL 1053–228.
10 *Ibid.*
11 The Light Railway Commissioners' Report for 1911 had described the amendment of the 1896 Act as 'a pressing need'. Interestingly, this report remarked rather complacently that improved road transport 'had tended to stimulate the desire, and to emphasise the need, for better railway facilities, rather than to supersede them'.
12 *Railway Times*, 4 May 1912, 13 April 1912 and 28 November 1912.
13 The Development and Road Improvement Funds Bill had been under discussion in the autumn of 1909. Some fears were expressed that it might trespass on the authority of the Light Railways Commission and if government grants were generally available for rural transport then private companies might be encouraged to make profits at government expense. Further, it was believed that Lloyd George was pushing the bill through with the object of weakening the railways by building improved roads so that the railway system could be taken over by the state, *Railway Times*, 25 September and 9 October 1909.
14 *Light Railway and Tramway Journal*, May 1901, pp.
15 PRO, RAIL 1045–5; Light Railway Investigation Committee Report Appendix C.
16 PRO, RAIL 1057/2711.
17 PRO, RAIL 1110/236; 1075/91.
18 PRO, ZLIB 4–277. T. M. Smith and G. S. Heathcliffe, *The Highworth Branch*, p.7. As with the Culm Valley Railway the Highworth Light Railway was a product of the 1868 Regulation of Railways Act. A. C. Pain was engineer.

19   'The Alton Mail', 8 February 1902.

20   PRO, RAIL 332/3.

21   RC 1896, Q 30896.

22   PRO, RAIL 1023/7. pp. 68–70.

23   *Railway Magazine*, XXIII (1913), pp. 336.

24   Bosley, 'The Manchester & Milford Railway 1860–1906', *op. cit.* for details of the railway to Llangurig.

25   PRO, RAIL 523/1.

26   R. D. Baxter, 'Railway extension and its results', *Journal of the Statistical Society*, XXIX (1866), pp. 549–95; reprinted in Carus Wilson (ed.), *Economic History*, III, p. 65.

27   W. Acworth, *Railway Economics*, p. 16. C. D. Campbell, *British Railways in Boom and Depression*, p.40.

28   *Locomotive*, 5 February 1929.

29   Smith and Heathcliffe, *op. cit.*, pp. 7–9.

30   PRO, RAIL 1110–56.

31   PRO, RAIL 1054–5. Report of the Light Railway Investigation Committee. Appendix on Organisation and Management of Light Railways in the United Kingdom.

32   PRO, RAIL 1054/5, Appendix H.

33   PRO, RAIL 250–336. GWR report on branch lines.

34   PRO, RAIL 258–309, 9 October 1899. The companies had co-operated two years earlier, obstructing a projected light railway between Bridgnorth and Newport. LNWR to GWR 8 March 1897: 'Do you not think it desirable that the answer to Mr Phillips [who had had the temerity to propose the light railway] should be somewhat on the lines of the letters we have recently dispatched to Mr Morris and Mr Price. If you concur and will send us a rough draft of the terms in which you propose to communicate with Mr Phillips I will form a letter to that gentleman similar in language.'

35   PRO, RAIL 258–309.

36   E. T. MacDermot, *History of the Great Western Railway 1863–1921*, II (1964 ed.), p. 182.

37   PRO, RAIL, 1057–2916. On the day of their visit the GWR investigators noted that nineteen racehorses had been walked to Chiseldon station on the Midland & South Western Junction Railway. They were led to believe that receipts at Chiseldon station were £4,000 per annum.

38   Cole, *op. cit.* Survey of the Wisbech & Upwell Tramway, pp. 255–63.

39   PRO, RAIL, 390–386.

40   PRO, RAIL, 1110–93.

41   J. Simmons, *The Railway in Town and Country 1830–1914*, 1986.

42   G. Thomas, *Calm Weather*, pp. 68–74.

43   Contemporary descriptions of the Wotton Light Railway as it was called occur in R. B. Grantham, 'Private agricultural railways', *Trans Inst Surveyors*, 24 February 1873 and W. Lawford and S. W. Haughton, 'On the Wotton Light

Railway', *Trans Inst C E of Ireland*, X (1875), pp.41–4.

44 Cole, *op. cit.*

45 PRO, RAIL, 13–2.

46 G. A. Brown, *The Lynton and Barnstaple Railway*, p. 24. PRO, 2LIB 4/277.

47 W. J. Wren, *The Tanat Valley Railway*, pp. 52, 96.

48 *Railway Magazine*, March 1937.

49 PRO, SPC, 11 328. E. S. Tonks, *The Edge Hill Railway*.

50 J. S. Morgan, *The Colonel Stephens Railways*, p.51.

51 Despite the importance of passenger traffic from the outset, the moving force behind the line was a Mr Green who owned the Rheidol mines which were linked to the narrow gauge railway by an aerial ropeway. J. I. C. Boyd, *Narrow Gauge Railways in Mid Wales*, pp. 196–7.

5

The railways in operation I

The next two chapters examine in some detail a number of light railways. The choice of examples was partly determined by the existence of a reasonable body of documentary evidence, although for few of these lines can the evidence be said to be exhaustive. Just as important, however, the examples are intended to show light railways in different parts of England and Wales, and they also represent some of the main categories of rural light railway discussed in the previous chapter, and authorised under the various Acts from 1864 to 1896. The Southwold Railway was a line built to narrow gauge and operated under Board of Trade certificate. The Wantage Tramway was a roadside line, a form of light railway rarely found in England. The other examples are of railways that were typical of those that the Light Railways Act was intended to encourage, lines built to improve transport into more or less remote country areas. The Lampeter & Aberaeron was authorised by Light Railway Order, and was operated, and then absorbed at the grouping, by a main line company. The Easingwold and the North Sunderland Railways each sought Light Railway Orders after they had been incorporated and the lines constructed. Both remained independent companies, but their relationship with their larger main line neighbour is also instructive.

The Lampeter and Aberaeron Railway can be distinguished from the other railways under scrutiny in that it was completed and operated from the outset by one of the main line companies, the GWR. Later fully absorbed into the GWR it benefited from the economies of scale that this represented: management costs were negligible and repairs and replacement of locomotives and rolling stock were not only easier but cheaper than independent or semi-independent companies were to find. That the line remained in use, at least in part, until 1973 may be seen as a consequence of its having become an integral part of the GWR system;

indeed, rather ironically it was because of the milk factory served by the Aberaeron branch that the erstwhile Manchester & Milford Railway/GWR route north of Carmarthen was kept open. In fact, the GWR and its successor the Western Region of British Railways did well by its Cardiganshire light railways for the Devil's Bridge Railway was grouped in 1922 with the GWR, which then provided it with new locomotives. This was entirely in keeping with the GWR's interest in publicity and tourist traffic. The Aberaeron branch did not receive such dramatic largesse but there is little doubt that it benefited from operation and later ownership by a larger company, which in turn welcomed, though not publicly, the contributory value of the branch's traffic.

The Lampeter & Aberaeron Railway

The Lampeter Aberaeron & Newquay Light Railway, opened in April 1911, was the culmination of more than seventy years of effort to bring railways to this part of west Wales. Numerous lines had been promoted down the years; all had failed, and the line that was built was a shortened version of what might have become a substantial light railway network. Only the section from Lampeter to Aberaeron was built, and hence the 'Newquay' was commonly omitted from the title.

That the line was built at all was a tribute to the strong body of local opinion committed to the idea of improving the standard of living in Cardiganshire by means of railways, which would galvanise fishing, farming and tourism, and revive the fortunes of the lead mining industry. The sincerity and altruism of the many promoters of these schemes cannot be doubted but equally worthy of note was their blindness to the abundant evidence available in the locality of 'failed' rural railways. Companies such as the Mid Wales Railway, the Manchester & Milford Railway and the Carmarthen & Cardigan Railway had all been in receivership, with a heavy burden of debt, an inability to raise new capital and an absence of profitable traffic. These weaknesses were generally applicable in rural areas in all parts of Britain and Ireland; peculiar to Wales was an innate suspicion of landlords' motives on the part of tenants and an even greater reluctance on the part of farmers to co-operate with their neighbours than was evident in England.

Several of the plans for railways in this area were somewhat grandiose, based on hopes for developing Aberaeron or Newquay as ports with railway links to the mining and industrial areas of south Wales. The England & Ireland Union Railway of 1836 was one of the earliest proposals for a railway to reach the coast of Cardigan Bay. The Manchester & Milford Railway was a classic among puffed up trunk routes, reaching neither Manchester nor Milford Haven.[1] The Llandilo & Teifi Valley Railway of 1860, a project which foreshadowed the schemes of the eventual successful promoters, aimed to link Llandilo and Pont Llanio with a branch to Lampeter[2] and thence to Aberaeron.[3] This project took on a slightly more concrete form as the Swansea & Aberystwyth Junction Railway of 1864, which intended to run from the Vale of Towy Railway at Llandilo to the Manchester & Milford Railway at Llanfair Clydogau with a branch to Lampeter. In 1865 this company was authorised to change the route of its branch to Pencarreg and thence to Lampeter, running adjacent to the Manchester & Milford. The scheme was solid enough for plant to be brought to the area but the contractors, Overend and Watson, were bankrupted in the wake of the failure of Overend Gurney and the project fell into abeyance.

Smaller-scale, more locally based schemes to link Aberaeron with the railway network were as numerous, especially in later years. In 1860 David Davies, the contractor who later built the Manchester & Milford Railway, proposed a line between Pencader and Aberaeron by way of Lampeter. Later, between 1876 and 1880, Davies projected a line to Aberaeron from Llanifan[4] and this coastal route was that chosen for the proposed Vale of Rheidol Railway's 2 ft 0 in. gauge Aberaeron Extension Railway in 1898, and the Cambrian Railways standard gauge line to Aberaeron and Newquay in 1904. This last was no new departure for the Cambrian Railways as it had been contemplated that one of this company's constituents, the Aberystwyth & Welsh Coast Railway, should be extended southwards to Aberaeron, Newquay and Cardigan, a scheme not adopted because of the difficult terrain and lack of money.[5]

There were other abortive schemes in the south of Cardiganshire. One such was a plan in 1885 to link Newquay with Llandyssil. A committee formed in Newquay in 1885 commissioned James Szlumper[6] to undertake a preliminary survey of the route. Szlumper estimated that the 15 − mile railway could be constructed for £30,000 including the cost of stations but excluding land, the cost of which, however, was expected to be nominal. At £2,000 per mile this reinforces the suggestion that the line would be narrow gauge.[7] The earning capacity of the line was estimated in relation to the Carmarthen–Llandyssil line, gross earnings on which in 1884 were £12,000. The proposed line was 3 miles shorter and it was believed that traffic, even at 30 per cent of the Llandyssil line's, would provide a gross revenue of £3,640 per annum. After deducting working expenses at 55 per cent there would be left a net income of £1,638 for dividends.[8] The Newquay committee proposed to issue 3,600 £10 shares to cover construction costs with £6,000 for land, plant and legal expenses. With high hopes the promoters embarked upon a series of parish meetings, but too few shares were taken up even to meet parliamentary expenses. By 1870 North Pembrokeshire and the South Cardiganshire coast was the part of Wales most remote from railways, with the people of outlying districts unable to reach local fairs and thus still dependent on travelling dealers.

The final — and successful — phase in the campaign to establish a railhead on the Cardiganshire coast in the area of Aberaeron and Newquay came with the light railway movement at the end of the nineteenth century.[9] One of the first to see the potential of a light railway was F. J. Jayne, Bishop of Chester, and Principal of St David's College, Lampeter, from 1879 to 1886. He was greatly concerned with the economic decline of the area, which was due partly to the collapse of the lead mining industry and partly to the problems of agriculture which were intensified by high transport costs. He felt that a line should be built from the recently opened GWR Newcastle Emlyn branch to Newquay, Aberaeron and on to Lampeter. Finally, anticipating the legislation of 1896, the bishop proposed that as the line would be beyond the resources of the local community so 'the state might be justified in lending Cardiganshire a financial hand'.[10]

During the 1890s the possibilities of light railways were widely canvassed in Cardiganshire. By 1903 two firm schemes were proposed, centred on Lampeter. One was for a line running south through the Pencarreg Mountains to Llandilo. The other was to go north-westward from Lampeter to the coast at Aberaeron with a branch to Newquay. For some people these two light railways were part of a single network, reviving hopes of earlier years for a direct railway link between the Cardiganshire coast, the Teifi valley and South Wales. Such were the complexities of the society and politics, especially railway politics, in this area that the lines had to be promoted separately and only one, the line to Aberaeron from Lampeter, was built.

This was an area of deep divisions and equally strong allegiances: church and chapel; Tory and Liberal; Anglicised landlords and Welsh tenants. There was also a traditional rivalry in this area, as strong as in other parts of the country, between the GWR and the LNWR, which may well have been a complicating factor in local railway promotion.

Although the GWR considered south and west Wales as its own
territory the LNWR had made successful incursions into the area fifty
years before. With the central Wales route to Swansea and via the
Pembroke & Tenby Railway it reached even to the shores of Milford
Haven. It is not too fanciful to assume that the GWR recalled this threat
when, in 1906, it leased the Manchester & Milford Railway and provided
tougher opposition to the link between Llandilo, which was in LNWR
hands, and Aberaeron. The Light Railway Commissioners' report on the
Lampeter Aberaeron & Newquay Railway refers to their rejection of a
clause proposed by the LNWR enabling that company to have through
facilities of every description and through rates and fares between the
light railway and any railway owned, leased or worked by the LNWR.
The Light Railway Commissioners were also to comment, curiously, on
the unusual provision in the Draft Order for the Lampeter & Llandilo
Railway by which its directors would be able to lease or sell the line to
another company. Was the LNWR contemplating an advance to the coast
of Cardigan Bay? Were the rumours of dramatic railway expansion in the
area attendant upon the GWR leasing of the Manchester & Milford
Railway merely a propaganda exercise aimed at swaying public opinion
against the Llandilo line?

The report of the Light Railway Commissioners on the Lampeter &
Llandilo Railway makes it clear that they detected hostility between the
various companies and believed it to be responsible for the proposed
layout of lines in Lampeter. It was apparently intended that there should
be two junctions with the Manchester & Milford Railway in close
proximity to each other: the Aberaeron line branching off to the north of
Lampeter station and the Llandilo line to the south, with a link between
the two light railways running parallel to the established line, than which
'a worse and more ridiculous arrangement [could] hardly be conceived'.[11]

The Lampeter to Llandilo Railway

The major portion of the route between Aberaeron and Llandilo was
promoted as the light railway between Lampeter and Llandilo. This, it
was hoped, would provide a more direct link with the industrial areas of
south Wales. The Light Railway Commissioners heard evidence relating
to the scheme on 14 July 1905. The Commissioners were told that the line
was supported by all the major landowners of the district and that the only
opposition had come from the Manchester & Milford Railway, the
manager of which, T. B. Grierson, unsuccessfully opposed the scheme on

the ground that the new line would siphon off some of his company's traffic. The solicitor for the Llandilo and Lampeter Light Railway refuted this criticism and felt that 'in common fairness they should have been offered proof that the Manchester & Milford Railway was alive. In that county and throughout Great Britain generally it was considered defunct.'[1] To justify the line the promoters claimed that 13,000 people lived in its neighbourhood and that present railway communication between the two towns was exceptionally poor. The cost of cartage was stressed: coal and lime had to be brought in, and timber and farm produce would be sent out. Dudley Drummond, the company's secretary, said that their intention was to establish a junction with the Lampeter & Aberaeron Railway, that support had been promised by the local authorities, and that the only significant engineering feature was the tunnel between the Cothi Valley and Lampeter.

However, the engineering problems were never put to the test. Although its Light Railway Order was confirmed in August 1908, the line failed to materialise, because of its failure to raise sufficient capital. The county councils were not averse in principle to supporting the railway financially and, indeed, Treasury grants were also available, but close liaison was lacking between these sources of finance. Treasury grants depended upon a proportion of the capital being subscribed locally. Local council support depended upon the county council grant being rated on the county as a whole, and neither the district councils nor the county council wished to grant money before the other had done so. The position deteriorated still further when it became apparent that individuals were not coming forward to take up shares. Landowners were prepared to take shares for land but seemed reluctant to take shares for cash, while popular support although vocal was not translated into share purchases. Indeed stormy county council meetings attested to the acute suspicion that landowners were hoping to finance, through an increase in the county rate, a railway which would improve their ability to let their farms at a higher rent.

A meeting of the Carmarthenshire County Council in January 1906 typifies the doubts and suspicion which eventually strangled the railway. The Reverend J. Towyn-Jones said that he did not want money spent unwisely but he thought a railway was badly needed to open up agricultural districts. At this Mr J. Lloyd wondered whether the previous speaker saw Newquay looming in the distance and speculated as to whether he wished to take his family there on holiday. More seriously, Councillor J. Johns favoured investigating the role of the landowners before the council went further, to ascertain how much the landlords were contributing, for he feared that ratepayers might find themselves subsidising increases in land values. He objected 'to a proposition to use the money of the poorest to enrich the richest' and reminded his fellow councillors that the rates were already high and areas not served by the railway had already protested against any likely increase. Mr Johns believed it would be better to pay the Reverend Towyn-Jones's fare to Newquay. Professor Jones asked if the £40,000 required was beyond their borrowing powers. The chairman replied that it was not but Mr Johns retorted that it was. The only outcome of the meeting was to refer the matter to a committee.[13]

When this committee finally reported it recommended waiting until the district councils concerned had raised £10,000 toward the line. The district councils were unwilling, however, to grant money. At Llandilo in April 'an application by the Llandilo to Lampeter railway for £3,000 caused some amusement'. In May Llandovery Rural District Council deferred a decision on £1,500 for the railway. Ultimately some money was promised, but not the £10,000 required by the county council, while private investment barely covered legal costs. In April 1907 Lampeter Town Council agreed to extend the period for which its offer of support was open but the councillors mocked the proposed railway and in November 1907 Llanybyther Rural District Council had to extend its offer for a further six months. But substantial sums were not forthcoming and the trickle of local council money was entirely inadequate.

The enthusiasm for linking Llandilo and Lampeter waned with the extension of petrol omnibus services in the area and the take-over of the Manchester & Milford Railway in 1906 by the GWR, which was likely to provide sterner opposition to the siphoning off of its traffic. Indeed, the GWR's take-over fuelled some very imaginative speculation about new rail links in other directions, for example Fishguard to Pencader and Strata Florida to Llandiloes, with track doubling between Pencader and Strata Florida. The idea of a railway to Llandilo was not dead, however. It was apparently proposed again in 1913, for in that year the GWR and LNWR made an agreement that they would *not* support it by consenting to work it if the line were built. The main line companies adopted this position not only because they felt revenue would be insufficient to meet their operating costs but also because the development of traffic could be only at the expense of existing routes.

A final effort to get the line built was made in 1925 when a local deputation met representatives of the GWR and the LMS at Paddington

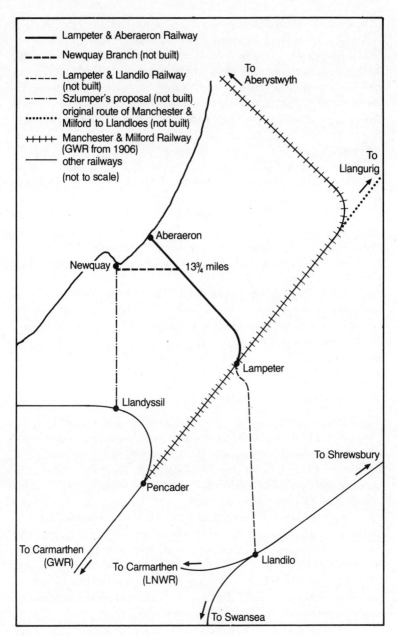

Fig. 5.1 The Lampeter & Aberaeron Railway

to discuss the matter. The estimated cost of the line was £170,000, but state support was said to be forthcoming if one of the main line companies would participate in the project. However, neither the GWR nor the LMS saw much chance of financial success and they doubted both that the construction could be accomplished for £170,000 and that there would be enough traffic from the sparsely populated agricultural districts through which the line would have run. They admitted that traffic in pit props might develop, but believed that the recently reopened lead, copper, silver and gold mines were not flourishing.[14]

The Llandilo & Lampeter was one of the many light railways to be authorised but never built. Its failure was an almost perfect example of the way promises of support, undoubtedly well meant, turned to nothing when it came to putting up the capital for a railway which was likely to earn fairly slight revenues. The peculiar local political rivalries and suspicions of other people's motives added extra spice to what was a common enough story in the promotion of light railways. It is just possible that had this railway been built it would have provided more traffic for the Lampeter & Aberaeron Railway, by virtue of connections with more direct routes to south Wales. As it was, the Lampeter & Aberaeron soldiered on as the solitary outcome of the numerous schemes to develop railway transport in the area between Aberystwyth and Caridgan.

The Lampeter to Aberaeron railway

The foremost promoter of this line was a local landowner and MP, J. C. Harford. In his election address in 1895 he had referred to the importance of state aid in providing a basis for railway extension and he returned to the theme in 1900, urging improvements in the Light Railways Act to benefit poorer agricultural districts. Furthermore, looking to his farming constituents, he joined in the advocation of further reductions in railway rates and increased facilities for farmers to send small amounts direct to customers.[15] Harford was putting some of his ideas into practice by becoming chairman of the Lampeter & Aberaeron Railway Company, which made an application for a Light Railway Order in November 1903. This was for a line from Lampeter to Aberaeron with a branch to Newquay from a point near Ciliau Aeron. The cost of the line as estimated by the engineers, S. W. & A. L. Yockney, was £88,277. To set against this expenditure was the engineers' estimate of revenue of £3,763 per annum.

Table 5.1 Lampeter & Aberaeron Railway: estimated costs for the Lampeter to Aberaeron section

		£
Earthworks		23,016
Permanent way, 13 miles at £2,400 per mile		32,100
Land at £110 per acre		3,750
Rolling stock:		
	£	
3 locomotives	6,000	
6 coaches	2,100	
6 wagons	900	
4 trucks	240	
2 cattle trucks	240	
1 horse box	120	
	9,560	
		9,560
		68,426

Early in 1904 the Light Railway Commissioners met in Lampeter.[16] They heard that passengers travelling between Aberaeron and Lampeter by van were charged 2s 0d single and 3s 0d for a return journey, producing, it was calculated, an aggregate revenue of £6,154 per annum. Councillor Lima Jones claimed that the cost of coal shipped from Swansea to Aberaeron was 50 per cent more than that taken by rail to Lampeter. Other witnesses spoke of a reduction in the number of horses farmers would have to keep, a general revival of agriculture and the encouragement of fishing off Aberaeron once boats did not have to land their catches at Milford Haven. The Light Railway Commissioners reported favourably on the proposed railway and the Light Railway Order was eventually obtained in 1906. Difficulties over the exact route the railway would follow, and more acute problems over the raising of sufficient capital, caused delays in the line's construction, however, and the latter in particular was an ill omen for the future of the company.

The promotion of the railway coincided with expansion in bus services and the take-over of the Manchester & Milford Railway by the GWR, two not unrelated facts for the GWR immediately instituted a bus service between Lampeter and Aberaeron. To some the improvements in road transport reduced the need for a railway, but for others in Cardiganshire problems caused by buses made the railway more attractive. Early buses, with their narrow wheels, wreaked havoc on poorly surfaced roads, causing not only increases in road maintenance costs but also unreliable time-keeping. In January 1907 bus services to Lampeter were suspended for several weeks because of weather conditions, while October of the same year saw the Llandyssil to Newquay bus stuck in mud near Capel Cynon for over twenty-four hours. The GWR came in for particular criticism at a meeting of Cardiganshire County Council in 1908. The county surveyor complained that the railway company's buses, which weighed 4–8 tons each were too heavy even for those roads which had been metalled, and the railway was running a service of six or eight buses daily. A Mr Lloyd operated buses from Newcastle Emlyn of only 30 cwt which was much preferable. The surveyor suggested that the GWR should contribute to road maintenance, a suggestion promptly rejected by the company. Perhaps in retaliation an application by the GWR to put bus stops on the Aberystwyth–Aberaeron road was rejected by the council on the grounds that it was cheap advertising. In May 1908 J. C. Harford argued that an incidental virtue of the proposed railway would be that some bus services might disappear for the road was entirely unsuited to buses and maintenance of the Lampeter to Aberaeron road already cost £600 per annum.[17] The GWR refuted these criticisms of damage to the roads on the grounds that it used rubber tyres. This did not stop the mayor of Cardigan objecting to buses on the grounds that they deposited oil and grease on the roads. The complexity of the relationship between bus services, the railways and the local authorities is well illustrated by the attempt by Lampeter Town Council in April 1908 to persuade the GWR to run a bus service between Lampeter and Brecon which would remove the necessity of a railway to Llandilo, thus saving the council £1,500 promised to the light railway company.[18]

By 1908, as bus services improved and the likelihood of raising money locally receded, the light railway project had been reduced in scope. No longer was the line to run parallel to the Manchester & Milford Railway into Lampeter for money would be saved by effecting a junction a short distance from the town. Additionally, and much more contentiously, the line to Newquay was dropped, although J. C. Harford was adamant that the village would be reached eventually. The company was now looking for less financial assistance from local authorities: £15,000 rather than £20,000 from Cardiganshire County Council and £1,000 rather than £1,500 from Lampeter Rural District Council.[19] The Treasury, having been asked originally for £30,000, now agreed to provide £20,000. The county council was persuaded that its £15,000 investment was a wise move for it would thus avoid annual charges of at least £3,000 in road maintenance. Despite criticisms of the scheme because of its abandonment of the Newquay line, in November 1908 the county council was reported to have borrowed from the Yorkshire Penny Bank on a mortgage of the county rate at 3¾ per cent over forty years.[20] In August the company had accepted Nuttall's tender of £72,864 for construction and in late October Miss Molly Harford cut the first sod.

Negotiations had been in progress for some months with the GWR on the subject of working the line.[21] The GWR had offered to operate the line at 2*s* 0*d* per train mile providing that this was not less than 60 per cent of receipts. When this was queried by the Lampeter & Aberaeron directors the GWR responded in May 1908 as follows:

The point on which we differ is, of course, the estimated traffic on the line. We have no wish to disparage in any way the possibilities of traffic but we are not without experience of lines such as the Lampeter & Aberaeron will be when constructed. [Any arrangement below 2*s* 0*d* per train mile] would be a much more substantial loss to the working company than the GWR directors could, with every desire to assist the countryside, properly be recommended to incur.

Despite this warning in October the directors were calculating revenue differently, on the basis of £12 per mile per week with a charge of 1*s* 9*d* per train mile by the working company (see Table 5.2). The speculation — the castles in the air — continued: 'If 1*s* 6*d* per train mile is arranged it would leave available £3,380 . . .'.[22] Not surprisingly, when agreement was reached in December 1908, it was on the more rational basis of 2*s* 0*d* per train mile with four trains in each direction, six days a week for fifty-two weeks of the year, which would cost £2,995 4*s* 0*d* annually, or £3,000 in round figures.[23] This sum would be retained by the working company for expenses provided the £3,000 was 60 per cent of receipts; if 60 per cent of the receipts produced a smaller figure than £3,000 then the owning company would pay the GWR the difference, but if 60 per cent of the receipts produced more than £3,000 the GWR would remit the excess to the owning company.

In an internal memorandum the GWR rather cold-bloodedly estimated probable receipts of the line as £3,750 per annum and costs as £3,260, but acknowledged that the value of the additional traffic to the Carmarthen to Aberystwyth line might be £3,000.[24] Thus, although not expecting the profits anticipated by the Lampeter & Aberaeron directors, the working company would still make money in the larger context. But, as we have

Table 5.2   Lampeter & Aberaeron Railway:
estimated revenue, 1908

	£
Revenue a £12 per mile per week	7,542
Costs at 1s 9d per train mile	3,325
	4,217
Less fixed charges	1,225
NET REVENUE	2,992

seen, perhaps more importantly by securing its position as the working
company it would prevent the light railway falling into the hands of the
potentially hostile light railway from Lampeter to Llandilo, which, in
turn, appeared to be within the orbit of the LNWR.[25] Although the
LNWR was not thought to be actively supporting the Llandilo line the
junction with the Central Wales line inevitably raised the spectre of
renewed expansion by Crewe into Swindon's territory.

The 'Prospectus of the Lampeter Aberaeron & New Quay Railway',
issued in May 1909, referred to the arrangement by which the GWR
would work the line and drew attention to the total share capital of which
£40,000 would come from central and local government sources.[26] Sir
James Szlumper, 'the eminent engineer', was quoted as saying that the
line would produce £13 per mile per week, which would produce £8,268
annually, leaving £3,307 for dividends once the GWR had taken its 60 per
cent. The prospectus, in common with so many others, claimed that the
Aeron Valley had capabilities possessed by few districts but its
development had been retarded by the lack of a railway. A substantial
passenger traffic, potential investors were assured, was certain for the
GWR was already running motor buses six times a day in spring, eight
times a day in summer and four times in winter between Lampeter and
Aberaeron. The extensive local industry of horse and cattle breeding
would provide traffic, while the fishing industry would be encouraged.
South Wales would provide both tourists and a market for dairy produce,
both of which would use the railway.

However, behind the optimistic tone of the prospectus, usual in such
cases, the directors were facing problems. Doubts were expressed as to
the accuracy of J. W. Szlumper's traffic estimates, to the extent that the
company's solicitor advised J. C. Harford, the chairman, not to pay the

engineer the £50 for his estimate. In fact, Harford was in correspondence with Sir Henry Oakley, who was to be paid 25 gns for his trouble. Oakley's estimate was that the traffic would rise from £10 per train mile per week in the first year to £14 or £15, if the line were operated by the GWR, and he pointed out that the best guide to the traffic was the experience of neighbouring lines: the Manchester & Milford Railway had operated at £9 to £10 per train mile per week but this had been increased by the GWR to £12. J. C. Harford was pessimistic for even at £12 per train mile per week the company could not expect to pay dividends on ordinary shares, of if they did, it would amount to only 1½ per cent. Furthermore, other expenses were mounting up: payment of 3 per cent to any member of the public taking up shares during construction; 3¼ per cent interest was payable on loans from the Treasury, although capital payment was deferred for two years; the prospectus cost £300. Even if the line opened for traffic in July 1910, the company would not receive any income from the GWR until March 1911.[27] With this in mind, and in the interests of short-term economy, the number of halts was reduced from five to three, an expedient which must have reduced the immediacy of the services offered.

The directors found difficulties over the siting of the station in Aberaeron.[28] Three locations were considered, but each had expensive shortcomings. One needed a level crossing over its approach road; the second, a former saw mill at Dolaeron, was rather constricted. The site eventually chosen, Morgan Evans's field, was more spacious but did require an additional crossing of the river, at a cost of £1,000. Valuation of the land along the length of the line did not prove as easy as had been hoped and in December 1908 five of the thirteen people whose land had been valued were holding out for a re-valuation, and the land which in 1903 had been estimated to cost £3,750 was reported as being valued at £6,074 in July 1909.[29]

Meanwhile it was proving difficult to sell the shares of the company. In July 1909 the directors heard that 1,423 preference shares and 112 ordinary shares had been applied for. This was considered unsatisfactory and it was agreed to press the contractors, Nuttall's, to take a further part of their contract in shares. In August it was reported that the shares listed in Table 5.3 had been taken. A considerable number of shares were taken up during the next month, as Table 5.4 indicates, but mainly to the principal directors and the contractor. Sales to the general public were non-existent, and the directors' minutes for the following eighteen months continued to record a failure to interest the public in the railway's shares.

During the course of 1910 the contractor accepted nearly 3,000 further shares. Some payments were in cash, but when payment was in shares, their value exceeded the charge. In March 450 shares, and in June another 1,090 were issued to Cardiganshire County Council, but sales to private individuals were unknown.

In February 1911 matters came to a head as the company ran out of money. The GWR agreed to take £5,000 in debentures, increased later to £6,305, to complete the railway and to assist the company with the Board of Trade inspection. In return the Lampeter & Aberaeron directors were to arrange for the withdrawal of the original contractors. Later, in 1915, additional debentures to the value of £6,500 were issued to J. C. Harford as part security for the overdraft of £8,189 as the company struggled to

Table 5.3 Lampeter & Aberaeron Railway: shares taken up by August 1909

Shareholder	No. of shares
J. C. Harford (director)	200
Colonel Davies Evans (director)	200
Captain Vaughan (director)	200
Lieutenant A. L. Gwynne (director)	200
R. Loxdale	200
F. D. Harford	200
S. W. Yockney (engineer)	1,500
Cardiganshire County Council	300
Nuttall's (contractor)	754

Table 5.4 Lampeter & Aberaeron Railway: shares taken up by September 1909

Shareholder	No. of shares
Lampeter Town Council	250
Lampeter Rural District Council	250
Nuttall's	1,787
Nuttall's	5,000
Isaac Cooke (company solicitor)	1,000
S. W. Yockney	750
J. C. Harford	5,000
Captain Vaughan	5,000

relieve its financial problems. The line itself was used throughout to Aberaeron — unofficially — in January 1911, by which time capital expenditure had reached £92,586. Unofficially the new railway was first used for goods on 12 April 1911, the line being officially opened by Mrs Gwynne, wife of one of the directors, on 12 May 1911.[30]

The operation of the Lampeter & Aberaeron Railway

From the start the relationship between the owning company and the operating company was not particularly happy. The directors of the Lampeter & Aberaeron Railway acknowledged that goods traffic would take time to build up but nonetheless felt obliged to exhort the GWR to greater efforts. In their report for 1912 the directors made it clear that they considered a maintenance charge of £1,459 to be excessive, especially in the light of a wet summer which took its toll of the tourist traffic, and a miners' strike which reduced the GWR's coal traffic by 50 per cent. The effect such problems had on revenue persuaded the directors to look for a reduction in the operating charge of £3,000. Their protest had some effect for the following year the maintenance charge was withdrawn and compensation of nearly £70 was paid in respect of the reduced coal traffic but the operating charge was not reduced. What particularly alienated the Lampeter & Aberaeron directors was that the GWR had reduced its own operating costs by introducing auto-trains on to the line and the more economic operation which obtained from this had not been allowed for in the original negotiations. Another bone of contention was that Newquay traffic was routed via bus services through Llandyssil station on the old Manchester & Milford line (now GWR), a distance of 16 miles, rather than through Aberaeron, which was only 7 miles from Newquay. Not only did the journey to Llandyssil take two hours but the greater damage to roads had to be met by the ratepayers. Finally, the directors were aggrieved to find that the not inconsiderable traffic generated by their railway provided more profit for the GWR than for their own railway because of the relative insignificance of their mileage in the total journey either of passengers or freight.[31]

Despite these signs of dissension, and indeed despite the failure of the promoters to gain a satisfactory return on their investment (by 1920 the directors' report included remarks such as 'the company's liabilities . . . materially increased' and 'impossible to forecast the prospects of the company'), the line did provide considerable benefits to the community it served. The railway brought tourists, gave access to more distant markets

Table 5·5   Vessels unloading at Aberaeron in 1926 and 1927[33]

Year	Total Ships	Flour (tons)	Stone/chippings (tons)	Coal (tons)
1926	24	671	3,103	–
1927	18	701	1,206	490

and reduced the price of some goods; coal, for example, fell from 10s 0d to 2s 4d per ton.[32] On the other hand, the railway did not eliminate older methods of transport in Aberaeron: ships regularly used Aberaeron harbour with cargoes of flour, chippings and coal until 1934 (Table 5.5). In addition to shipping Aberaeron continued to be served by road transport with daily buses to Aberystwyth and a carrier from Newquay meeting every train. A sign of the times was that by 1921 the town boasted two motor engineers. While the population of rural Cardiganshire generally was declining, the population of Aberaeron rose from 1,263 in 1891 to 1,338 in 1911. The population of Newquay remained stable.

In 1913, the railway's third year of operation, total revenue rose above the GWR's charge of £3,000 for the first time. Two-thirds of revenue came from passengers, and holiday traffic represented an important part of this business, as can be seen from the higher receipts in the second half of the year. Goods traffic was fairly constant, consisting mainly of coal and agricultural produce and incoming supplies (see Table 5.6).

Table 5.6   Lampeter & Aberaeron Railway: receipts, 1912 and 1913

	Jan–June 1912			July–Dec 1912			Jan–June 1913			July–Dec 1913		
	£	s	d	£	s	d	£	s	d	£	s	d
Passengers	752	19	3	1,286	7	0	893	12	11	1,522	12	0
Mail	21	10	0	21	10	0	21	10	0	21	10	0
Parcels	35	7	4	57	16	7	37	19	7	55	14	1
Goods	333	18	4	476	7	4	431	10	6	416	18	8
Miscellaneous	2	19	1	11	1	3	8	15	2	11	16	4
Rents	8	11	0	17	11	6	20	18	6	18	12	6
Grass sold	–	–	–	2	19	6	–	–	–	2	9	6
Gross revenue	1,155	4	0	1,843	13	2	1,414	6	8	2,049	13	1
Yearly total	£2,998 17s 2d						£3,463 19s 9d					

During the following years, partly as a result of government control during the First World War, revenue was also fairly constant (Table 5.7), earning the Lampeter & Aberaeron Railway Company about £500 a year after the GWR had been paid. However, the railway's residual income fell far short of meeting the heavy capital charges incurred by the owning company. In 1913 interest charges amounted to £558 12s 3d, well above the £463 19s 9d net revenue. After all receipts and payments had been accounted for the company was left with a loss of £122.[34] This state of affairs was repeated every year, the loss being less than £100 only once, and reached as much as £453 in 1915.

Table 5.7 Lampeter & Aberaeron
railway: gross revenue, 1914–21

Year	Revenue £
1914	3,518
1915	3,468
1916	3,473
1917	3,480
1918	3,496
1919	3,498
1920	3,495
1921	3,504

The Lampeter & Aberaeron Railway after the First World War

Any small railway company that before 1914 had found it so difficult to earn anything above its working expenses, and impossible to cover its capital charges, was going to find the going hard in the 1920s. This was quickly apparent on the Lampeter & Aberaeron. Initially the return to peacetime conditions was something to be looked forward to, and the directors of the company in their report for 1919 had high hopes for the resumption of heavy excursion traffic, even though the line would remain under government control for another two years. Reviewing the war years, the directors felt that the GWR should have suspended the charge of £3,000 because the guaranteed service had not been maintained. Although they did not find the GWR in a benevolent mood, their

Table 5·8 Lampeter Aberaeron & New Quay Light Railway: balance sheet, 31 December 1914

CAPITAL AND LIABILITIES

		£ s d	£ s d
CAPITAL			
Authorised			120,000 0 0
Issued			
22,497 Ordinary Shares of £1 each fully paid			22,497 0 0
21,953 5% Preference Shares of £1 each			
Amount received in respect thereof			20,203 0 0
MORTGAGE DEBENTURES		£ s d	
Great Western Railway	4%	5,128 0 0	
Edmund Nuttall	4%	400 0 0	
James Nuttall	4%	100 0 0	
G. G. Lynde	4%		1,500 0 0
Cardigan County Council	3½%	12,450 0 0	
Aberaeron Rural D. Council	4%	1,650 0 0	
Aberaeron Urban D. Council	4%		850 0 0
Lampeter Town Council	4%	875 0 0	
Lampeter Rural D. Council	4%	875 0 0	23,828 0 0
H. M. TREASURY LOAN			
Debentures of £22,000 @ 3½% have been issued in respect of this loan			22,000 0 0
SUNDRY CREDITORS			18 15 0
UNION OF LONDON & SMITH'S BANK			
Loan Account		689 6 11	
Overdraft Current Account		11,172 17 8	11,862 4 7

CAPITAL EXPENDITURE AND OTHER ASSETS

	£ s d	£ s d
CAPITAL OUTLAY ON WORKS		
Duty on Capital	312 10 0	
Capital Formation & Preliminary Expenses	1,838 15 2	
Land	8,084 2 5	
Construction of Way	81,672 9 4	
Salaries, Wages, Office, Printing, Income Tax Stamps & Law Costs &c	2,832 14 7	
Interest, Bank Charges &c	3,966 5 10	98,706 17 4
DUE FROM GREAT WESTERN RAILWAY in respect of		
Traffic receipts		518 7 1
PETTY CASH in hand		2 5 6
PROFIT & LOSS ACCOUNT		
Balance 1st January 1914	1,085 9 6	
Add Net loss for year per Revenue Account	96 0 2	1,181 9 8

Table 5.8 cont.

£7,675 Debentures have been issued and
deposited to secure the Guarantors
of the above Bank overdraft

	£ s d
	100,408 19 7

(total: 100,408 19 7)

We have examined the above Balance Sheet and accompanying Revenue Account with the books and vouchers relating thereto, and hereby certify the same to be correctly drawn in accordance therewith, and exhibiting a true and correct view of the state of the Company's affairs as shown by the books of the Company. The liability for accrued interest on Loans and Debentures is not included in the above Accounts, and the amount of traffic receipts has been taken from returns furnished by the Great Western Railway Company.

February 10th 1915   H. GRAHAM KING, Chartered Accountant, 17,   Ironmonger Lane, London, E.C. ⎱
⎰ *Auditors*
H. M. BRITTAIN, Chartered Accountant, 34,   John Street, London, W.C.

REVENUE ACCOUNT – FOR THE YEAR ENDED 31 DECEMBER 1914

	£ s d		£ s d
Bank Interest and Charges	569 10 9	TRAFFIC RECEIPTS per Great Western Railway, agreed amount thereof for year ended 31st December 1914	3,518 7 0
Office Salaries and Accountancy	32 12 0		
Rent and Office Expenses	8 12 11	Deduct amount retained by Great Western Railway, being their minimum charge under the Working Agreement	3,000 0 0
Stamps on Debentures	1 10 0		518 7 0
Lamp Standards	2 4 0	Transfer Fees	0 2 6
		Balance Net Loss for year carried to Balance Sheet	96 0 2
	614 9 8		614 9 8

Table 5·9   Lampeter & Aberaeron Railway
Company: annual losses, 1913–19

Year	Loss (£)
1913	122
1914	96
1915	453
1916	194
1917	201
1918	178
1919	204

optimism concerning improved traffic was well founded, although the report for 1919 laments their inability to increase their share of the profits. A year later, however, the directors were pessimistic about their company's future. Their main complaint was that high interest rates were making it almost impossible to service the company's debt, but there was cause for concern in the traffic figures. Goods traffic had substantially increased in volume over what it had been immediately before the war, but the resurgence in excursion traffic was not coming up to expectations and passenger traffic was soon beginning to decline (Table 5.10). By 1921 the company's expenses had risen to £895 and its loss for the year to £395.[35]

The grouping of 1923 took the Lampeter & Aberaeron Railway completely into Great Western ownership. Shortly afterwards, in 1926, this line was included in a detailed investigation which the GWR made into 53 of its branch lines, with the intention of discovering where economies could be made. The report of this investigation gives a detailed account of the receipts and expenditure on the Aberaeron branch for 1925, and these are summarised in Table 5.11.[36]

The principal economy proposed was the reduction in the number of staff by five from its total of fourteen. Two porters at Talsarn, whose primary employment had been controlling level crossing gates, would be withdrawn; the gates would be replaced by cattle grids. Also to go would be the station masters at Felin Fach, Ciliau Aeron and Aberaeron. Whether this was precisely what took place is nowhere revealed, but numbers employed on the line did fall by five. A further economy proposed was the abandonment of the electric train staff system, but this

Table 5.10 Traffic on the Aberaeron Branch: 1913, 1923, 1933 and 1938

Year	Staff	Wages (£)	Total receipts (£)	Tickets issued (No.)	Parcels and miscellaneous (No.)	Parcels and misc. receipts (£)	Total passenger receipts (£)	Gen. merchandise forwarded (Tons)	Gen. merchandise received (Tons)	Coal and coke charged received (Tons)	Other Minerals received (Tons)	Coal and coke not charged forwarded and received (Tons)	Total goods (Tons)	Total receipts for goods excluding coal and coke not charged (£)	Livestock forwarded and received (Wagons)
1913	9	561	9,612	60,108	na	675	4,087	1,550	2,145	2,022	1,697	1,868	9,286	5,525	268
1923	14	1,930	21,686	51,628	15,177	1,146	5,679	2,161	5,381	1,553	4,601	3,739	17,520	16,007	432
1933	9	1,274	14,795	20,654	16,590	1,027	2,689	4,216[a]	4,338	2,840	2,582	1,681	15,732	12,106	330
1938	10	1,528	13,749	12,178	14,099	402	1,604	617	7,222	2,737	3,047	1,861	15,531	12,145	289

[a] 1933 was an exceptional year for this category. No other year between 1923 and 1938 saw this traffic exceed 1,000 tons.
na Not available
Source: Great Western Railway Station Statistics

Table 5·11 Lampeter–Aberaeron Branch: receipts and expenses, 1925

RECEIPTS	Passenger £	Parcels £	Goods £	Total £	1924 £		± £
Lampeter (Aberaeron Branch only)	577	13		590	677	−	87
Silian Halt			103	103	17	+	86
Talsarn Halt	428	35		463	542	−	79
Felin Fach	327	169	2,930	3,426	4,207	−	781
Ciliau Aeron	577	319	1,805	2,701	2,724	+	23
Aberaeron	2,416	500	7,827	10,743	13,258	−	2,515
TOTAL				18,026	21,425	−	3,399

Passenger Traffic   Worked by autotrain   4 trips each way

Goods   1 train each way

1925 1,031 Cans of milk

376 trucks of livestock

Goods tonnage – forwarded and received: mainly coal, roadstone, bricks and grain

Coal and minerals   8,696 tons

General goods   5,975 tons

Daily average of wagons dealt with

Coal and minerals   forwarded 0   received 6

General goods   forwarded 5   received 8

Table 5·11 cont.

Expenditure	Traffic Dept staff paybill figures	1924	1925
% of Traffic Receipts	Station	£	£
	Felin Fach	640	610
	Ciliau Aeron	308	317
	Aberaeron	1,127	1,126
	Junction Staff	278	287
13.04		£2,353	£2,350 – £2,350
	Loco Dept engine and tram running expenditure		
	Coaching – coal consumption	31.1 lbs per mile	
	Freight – coal consumption	39.0 lbs per mile	
	Maintenance, renewal and working cost – coaching	18.9d per mile = £3,389	
26.90			4,850
	Maintenance, renewal and working cost – freight	21.97d per mile = £1,461	
16.61	Engineering Dept maintenance and renewal		2,995
1.30	Signal Department maintenance and renewal		235
0.27	Clothing		48
0.26	Fuel, lighting, water, general supplies		46
1.46	Rates		264
59.84	TOTAL		10,788

does not appear to have proceeded. The predicted annual saving was put at £522.

One benefit of operation by the GWR is that the Lampeter & Aberaeron Railway was included in that company's station statistics, some of which are summarised in Table 5.10. All the receipts for 1923 show a healthy increase over those for 1913, but wartime inflation accounted for much of that. A closer look at the different categories of traffic reveals the trends affecting the railway. Passenger traffic never returned to its pre-war volume, a clear reflection of the growing use of motor transport. The number of tickets issued fell by 60 per cent between 1923 and 1933, and revenue by a corresponding amount. Parcel numbers and revenue stayed constant, perhaps reflecting an increase in small goods consignments dispatched by passenger train. The volume of goods carried had almost doubled between 1913 and 1923, but began to fall away during the 1920s. Two categories, coal and coke and general merchandise received, maintained their volume and receipts, while others generally declined quite substantially. These two categories included most of the goods being brought in over long distances, on which the growth of road transport had as yet limited impact. Motor competition was more strongly felt over short distances, as the decline of nearly a quarter in livestock traffic between 1923 and 1933 indicates.

The decline in traffic on the line continued between 1933 and 1938, but at a slower rate. 'Tickets issued' fell by a further 40 per cent but passenger revenue by only 30 per cent; 'general merchandise forwarded', however, remained constant, while 'general merchandise received' rose steadily and reached its greatest volume in 1938, at 7,222 tons. Total goods traffic fell by no more than 200 tons between 1933 and 1938; receipts actually rose, albeit by only £39. Total revenue in this period declined by just over £1,000, a fall of 7 per cent.

The only item of expenditure included in the station statistics was the cost of staffing the railway.[37] As Table 5.12 shows, the increased number of staff in 1923 compared with 1913 could be justified on the grounds that each man was earning the railway nearly half as much again. However, the fact that weighed more heavily with the GWR management was that the total labour bill had risen far more quickly than receipts. Total receipts in 1923 were 126 per cent higher than those for 1913; the wages bill had risen by 244 per cent. It was this that caused the GWR to seek a reduction in the number of staff in 1926, and pressure to contain the labour bill continued throughout the 1920s and 1930s. Railwaymen's wages rose steeply during the period of government control during and after the First World War:

Table 5·12   Lampeter & Aberaeron Railway: staff, 1913–38

Year	Number of staff	Wages (£)	Receipts per man (£)
1913	9	561	1,068
1923	14	1,930	1,549
1933	9	1,274	1,643
1938	10	1,528	1,374

these wages and working hours were protected by the Railways Act of 1921. Not only did this impose a particular burden upon the smaller railways but the freedom of road passenger transport from such controls meant that the railway companies found it increasingly difficult to compete. In 1932 the lowest basic wage on the railways was 40s, whereas bus drivers' and conductors' wages were sometimes as low as 25s and 15s respectively.[38]

The Aberaeron branch lost its passenger service in February 1951. The opening of the milk factory at Felin Fach in the same year, however, provided a considerable boost to goods traffic. The line from Felin Fach to Aberaeron was lifted in 1965 and the remaining sections between Carmarthen and Felin Fach were closed in 1973.

Notes

1   For a full treatment of railway development in Cardiganshire see P. Bosley, 'The Manchester & Milford Railway 1860–1906', M.A. thesis, University of Wales, 1978.

2   *Herapath's Journal*, 28 November and 5 December 1860.

3   *Haverfordwest and Milford Haven Telegraph*, 13 July and 3 August 1864.

4   Lewis Cozens, *Aberaeron Transport*, p. 4.

5   *Haverfordwest and Milford Haven Telegraph*, 3 October 1860 and 13 July 1864. *Herapath's Journal*, 13 December 1860 refers to a 'Welsh Coast Railway' which would run along the coast of Cardigan Bay.

6   J. Szlumper had been engineer of the Manchester & Milford Railway.

7   In a letter to *The Times*, 7 September 1895, from the Bishop of Chester entitled 'A Light Railway for Cardiganshire', the 1885 scheme was said to have been of 2ft 0 in. gauge.

8   This proposal, with the neighbouring Manchester & Milford Railway operating at 85 per cent, was a trifle unrealistic.

9   Royal Commission on Land Use in Wales and Monmouth, 1896, XXXVI. Appendix presented by A. C. Humphreys-Owen MP in answer to Q 47981.

10   *The Times*, 7 September 1895.

11   PRO, MT 58–318.

12   *Carmarthen Weekly Reporter*, 21 July 1905.

13   *Ibid.*, 26 January 1906.

14   PRO, RAIL 258–309/3, GWR Secretarial Papers.

15   See pp. 13–14.

16   PRO, MT 58–280

17   *Cambrian News*, 22 May 1908.

18   *Ibid.*, 10 April 1908.

19   *Ibid.*, 1 May 1908.

20   *Ibid.*, 20 November 1908.

21   PRO, RAIL 1057–477.

22   PRO, RAIL 339–1, 6 October.

23   PRO, RAIL 339–1, 29 December 1908, and PRO, RAIL 1057–477, 9 December.

24   PRO, RAIL 1057–477.

25   PRO, RAIL 1057–477, 18 December. The same attitude of mind was evident in the negotiations for the purchase of the Golden Valley Railway by the GWR. The GWR paid under £10,000 for the hopelessly insolvent railway whose revenue in 1896 was £1,569 against expenditure of £1,930. A GWR memo, however, noted that the railway created for its larger neighbour traffic to the value of £3,740 in 1896. C. L. Mowatt, *The Golden Valley Railway*, p. 81.

26   PRO, RAIL 1075–140.

27   PRO, RAIL 1057–476, 22 March 1909. PRO, RAIL 236–719/19. Sir Henry Oakley had earlier advocated the development of light railways. In 1877 he wrote of Market Deeping's proposed railway that there should be 'some light line . . . which would serve as a feeder and be worked by horse or steam car in a very inexpensive manner'. I am indebted to Professor Jack Simmons for this reference.

28   *Cambrian News*, 4 December 1908.

29   PRO, RAIL 339–1, 14 July 1909.

30   PRO, RAIL 339–1, 16 May 1911.

31   PRO, RAIL 1110–236, Report for 1913.

32   *The Railway Magazine*, XXXIV, (1914) pp. 333–5.

33   Lewis Cozens, *op. cit.*, pp. 83, 84.

34   PRO, RAIL 1110–236.

35 PRO, RAIL 339–1, Directors' Report.
36 PRO, RAIL 250–736.
37 PRO, RAIL 266–45.
38 P. Bagwell, *The Transport Revolution from 1770*, p. 254.

6

The railways in operation II

The railways considered in this section differ in respect of date of construction, authorising legislation and gauge, and while three were railways in the accepted sense, one was a roadside tramway. However, they have in common the fact that they were proposed, built and operated by independent companies. The degree of independence varied considerably. The Wantage Tramway and the Southwold Railway, opened in the 1870s, were both inspired by the Tramways Act of 1870 although one was a standard gauge tramway and the other a narrow gauge railway. Neither of these companies received support from their larger neighbour, respectively the GWR and the GER; indeed, the GWR operated a bus service in competition with the Wantage Tramway while the Southwold's requests for support were not heeded by the GER.

The benefits to the Easingwold Railway from the NER were variable. At the time of the inception of the railway the Easingwold's directors were critical of the hostile attitude of the larger company of the joint station at Alne although the relationship improved with the North Eastern Railway (NER) carrying out locomotive repairs and hiring out replacement locomotives. An entirely different situation can be found in Northumberland. There a benevolent local NER administrator based in Newcastle was motivated partly by sentiment, referring to the North Sunderland as 'the little railway', but equally by a hard-headed realisation of the profits involved in the contributory value of traffic fed on to the NER system at Chathill. The impression gained is that although the North Eastern Region was as aware of the value of the North Sunderland Railway's traffic as the NER had been, it was less able to provide the general support which was needed. Moreover, with the locomotive situation reaching crisis point support from British Railways would have had to have been both specific and large scale.

The Southwold Railway

Southwold, on the Suffolk coast, with a population of 2,109 in 1881, was primarily a small fishing town with herrings, sprats, sole and cod landed. Other industries included the production of salt, an iron foundry and a brewery. The tourist trade was undeveloped. As Wantage had been bypassed by the GWR so Southwold was bypassed by the East Suffolk Railway, and the town depended upon a horse omnibus and the carrier's cart for its public transport. Dissatisfaction was strong enough to produce demand for improvements. The Blyth Valley Railway of 1865 was a standard gauge project to link Southwold and Halesworth.[1] The Tramways Act of 1870 inspired the Southwold & Halesworth Tramway of 1872, which collapsed through lack of money. This scheme, promoted by the Lowestoft Yarmouth & Southwold Tramways Company Ltd, would have been a roadside line and its cars would have been horse-drawn.[2] The Southwold Railway itself dates from October 1875, when a series of public meetings dominated by A. C. Pain and R. C. Rapier (of the local engineering firm of Ransome & Rapier) occurred. Both of these men had experience of, and commitment to, the employment of the narrow gauge. The company's prospectus described the project as being a line of 8 miles 63 chains with a capital of £40,000 in shares and £13,000 debentures. The gauge was not to be less than 2 ft 6 in. and speed and weight limitations would be expected. The journey time would be thirty minutes.

The Southwold Railway Company was incorporated by Act of Parliament on 24 July 1876. The line, 8¾ miles long from Southwold to the junction with the GER at Halesworth, was built to a gauge of 3 ft and opened to traffic on 24 September 1879. Six months later the company obtained a certificate from the Board of Trade granting power to operate the line as a light railway. Some restrictions were imposed by this certificate, principally that the railway must be operated according to the one engine in steam principle, and that speeds should not exceed 16 m.p.h. The early months of the company were not without incident; the contractor was reluctant to start work until all the land had been bought and this, together with local party political rivalry, led to a change of directorate which weakened the local flavour of the line.[3] However, local support for the railway remained strong.[4] Too isolated, Southwold was 'consecrated to the use of a few exclusives more or less remotely connected with the aristocracy'. The railway would make the town better known to the money-spending classes to the benefit of the tradespeople and lodging house keepers: 'If the few wealthy drones will not advance a copper it behoves the intelligent and aspiring to do all they can to support that universal benefactor, the railway.'

By July 1876 £3,000 had been raised but with Southwold Corporation accepting a rent charge for land and the Earl of Stradbroke feeling obliged to take the value of his land in shares some signs of financial pressure were evident. Indeed, the cost, originally estimated at £30,000, eventually rose to £90,000, partly because of the necessity of building a swing bridge over the River Blyth. This bridge was to prove a major headache for the railway. Not only was its initial cost high but when an extension to Kessingland in the direction of Lowestoft and the GER was proposed it was felt necessary to convert the entire line to standard gauge. This would have involved major, and costly, work reconstructing the swing bridge. The extension and conversion to standard gauge were taken as far as the company's obtaining a Light Railway Order in 1902. But raising the finance proved impossible: all that the available money could achieve was the moving of some fences and the widening of a number of bridges, including the swing bridge, in 1906. Ironically, it was not used as a swing bridge after 1914.'

Despite this the company was not especially over-burdened with the sort of financial problems which crushed many minor railways, and while it enjoyed a near monopoly of transport to Southwold it operated profitably enough. When motorised road transport appeared the line was severely hit. It declined especially rapidly after 1926, when Southwold Corporation authorised buses to pick up passengers in the town itself. Although the rail journey was still quicker than that by road, the bus was cheaper and its route was more convenient for people's homes. Moreover, a direct service to Lowestoft made the railway practically irrelevant. The Southwold Railway responded by cutting wages, and fares from 2s 3d to 1s 6d for return journeys, but its measures were inadequate and the line was closed in 1929. One of the first light railways to succumb, it showed a remarkably rapid transition from profit to defeat.

Despite its early demise it would be difficult to believe that the railway had not contributed to the prosperity of the town. Its population, which fluctuated around 2,100 between 1841 and 1881, rose after the railway was opened and reached 2,311 in 1891 and 2,800 in 1901. The growing holiday trade must have owed something to improved transport. The number of apartments listed in *Kelly's Directory* rose from three in 1865 to forty-nine in 1886 and 120 in 1912. Day-trippers used the line in great numbers and it was reported for August Bank Holiday 1899 there had been 'brilliant sunshine and a cloudless day, and as a consequence, Halesworth was almost deserted. The Southwold trains were crowded throughout the day, there being 415 return and 33 single tickets issued.' Some of these passengers enjoyed an eventful return journey for with six full carriages the weight was too much for the engine, which failed to climb the incline into Halesworth station. Intending to split the train and pull it into the station in two sections, the locomotive crew must have given the rear section a parting push for the three rear carriages set off down the line unattended and did not stop before they reached Blyford.[6]

Interestingly, the railway did not bring about the collapse of the local carrier network. In 1865 Southwold was linked to the outside world by a coach to Lowestoft three times a week and a daily horse omnibus to Darsham railway station on the GER, while carriers operated to Beccles three times a week, Halesworth and Yarmouth daily, and Lowestoft daily but with two services on Wednesdays and three on Mondays and Fridays. By 1896 the horse omnibus to Darsham, and carriers' wagons to Halesworth and Yarmouth, had all disappeared, their routes easily covered by the railway. There remained carrier services weekly to Beccles, daily to Lowestoft and, locally, a daily service to Blythborough and Wangford. These were still operating in 1912, by which time there was a motor bus service between Southwold and Lowestoft, its timetable depending on seasonal trade. The carriers survived if their routes were not competing directly with the railway. Once, however, a regular motor bus service speeded up the journey to Lowestoft the Southwold Railway's weakness in not serving the main town of the district was laid bare. What is also evident here is the flexibility of the road vehicle as a means of transport which was entirely unmatched by the railway.

Traffic and receipts
An analysis of the Railway Returns shows clearly that passenger traffic dominated. Revenue from passengers was consistently greater than that from goods traffic, as Table 6.1 shows.

Table 6·1   Southwold Railway: traffic and receipts, selected years

Year	Passenger numbers	Passenger revenue (£)	Goods revenue (£)	Total revenue (£)
1884	73,138	1,924	862	3,143
1904	110,486	2,798	1,711	5,888
1924	84,126	4,236	2,323	6,944

Until the end of the nineteenth century first-class passengers consistently contributed 10 per cent of the passenger revenue, an unusually high proportion for a minor railway. For the last few years of the railway's life it is possible to determine the number of passengers originating on the line. At that time the majority of first-class passengers originated off the line while most of the third-class journeys started on the line, suggesting an incoming first-class tourist traffic, local third-class day-trippers and third-class journeys to market.

The total number of passengers rose steadily in the 1880s and 1890s, reaching 105,000 in 1899 and then levelling out to remain above 100,000 in all years but one to 1912. Post-war passenger figures were significantly down, never exceeding 88,000, and this was before the advent of a truly competitive omnibus service in 1926. The Southwold Railway appears to have been run efficiently judging by train miles which remained constant, while absorbing a 50 per cent increase in the number of passengers.

Goods traffic also reached a peak at the turn of the century. The picture with regard to mineral traffic was one of growth from 1880 to 1901, levelling off to 1907, and then a fall to 1913. The immediate post-war

Table 6·2   Southwold Railway: origin of passengers, 1922 and 1925

| | Number of passengers | |
	First class	Third class
1922 total	1,273	86,905
Originating on line	376	63,053
1925 total	1,161	82,162
Originating on line	401	60,995

Table 6·3   Southwold Railway: passenger numbers and train miles, ten-year averages

Years	Train miles	Number of passengers
1880–89	30,668	70,479
1885–94	30,198	76,167
1890–99	29,299	87,252
1895–1904	29,956	100,225
1900–09	30,352	104,658

period showed a considerable revival in such traffic, particularly in respect of mineral traffic originating on the line.

General merchandise exhibited the same steady rise in the 1880s, and 1890s but without the corresponding fall immediately before the First World War: the year 1912 saw the largest amount of merchandise carried. The post-war period saw a dramatic fall in such traffic, from 6,686 tons in 1912 to 3,515 tons in 1925.

The Southwold Railway was successful in keeping expenditure in check and avoiding dramatic swings. Expenditure exceeded £3,000 per annum for the first time in 1893 and £3,360 only once up to 1912. These figures are most notable for the burden imposed by general charges; the smaller the railway, the greater the burden of general charges.[7]

Table 6·4   Southwold Railway: mineral traffic, in tons, 1881–1925

Year	Coal	Other minerals	Total	Other minerals originating on line
1881			3,335	
1891			6,722	
1901			10,776	
1911			5,950	
1922	8,995	1,562	10,557	257
1923	8,488	3,321	11,809	653
1924	9,096	2,547	11,643	659
1925	8,470	1,828	10,298	1,096

In the absence of an alternative, the measure of profitability most generally applied to railway companies is the operating ratio; expenditure expressed as a percentage of revenue. Through the later years of the nineteenth century the figure for Britain's railways rose; that for the Southwold Railway fell (Table 6.6). This suggests an efficiently operated line with at least one lucrative source of traffic: passengers.

The situation after the First World War was dramatically different. The operating ratio over the period 1922–25 averaged 96.75 per cent as revenue fell back to pre-war levels and expenditure increased.

The Southwold Railway Company appealed to Southwold Corporation and to the LNER for assistance. Despite the benefits the company had brought to both,[8] assistance was not forthcoming and the railway

Table 6·5 Southwold Railway: expenditure 1882, 1892, 1902, 1912 and 1922

Year	Total (£)	Maintenance of way (£)	(%)	Locomotives (£)	(%)	Stock repair (£)	(%)	Traffic expenses (£)	(%)	General charges (£)	(%)
1882	2,275	455	20	661	29	14	0·6	785	34	323	14
1892	2,839	707	25	793	28	98	3·0	870	30	336	12
1902	3,854	528	14	1,027	27	119	3·0	1,044	27	431	11
1912	3,485	675	19	902	26	105	3·0	1,102	32	549	16
1922	8,026	1,426	18	1,984	25	374	5·0	2,768	34	1,084	14

Table 6·6 Southwold Railway: average operating ratio, 1880–1912, compared with national average

Years	Southwold Railway	National average
1880–89	86·0	52·2
1885–94	84·8	53·9
1890–99	80·1	56·4
1895–1904	70·5	59·7
1900–09	62·4	62·4
1905–12	62·3	62·5

which in 1927 carried 81,704 passengers and earned net receipts of £751 was closed in Apr·¹ 1929.

The Easingwold Railway

The Easingwold Railway linked the town of Easingwold with the main line of the NER at Alne, a distance of 2 miles 37 chains. Easingwold, which, before the railway depended upon one carrier to York and another to Alne station, was a town of 1,932 people in 1891 with 190 'commercial premises',[9] although it was dismissively referred to by W. M. Acworth in 1896 as 'entirely rural'.[10] At the outset the line was not technically a light railway for the Board of Trade had insisted upon interlocking signals and other attributes of main line railways: a Light Railway Order was obtained in 1928, but that only confirmed the reality that the line had been operated as a light railway from its opening. So much was this so that the Easingwold Railway was held up as an example of what a light railway should be, especially by W. H. Cole and W. M. Acworth. 'The Easingwold Railway was a model frequently quoted', it was noted in *The Locomotive* for March 1912.

Various schemes emerged in the second half of the nineteenth century to bring the railway to Easingwold, but nothing transpired until plans were drawn up by a Mr Copperthwaite and a company came into being on 23 August 1887. At the launch of the company in October 1887 the people of Easingwold were encouraged to take shares in a scheme, the capital for which was to be allocated as shown in Table 6.7. The prospectus claimed that the railway served an area of some 21,000 acres, with a population of 2,044 in Easingwold and another 2,000 locally. The industry of the area was entirely agricultural. The main crops were wheat, barley, oats, rye, beans, peas, potatoes, turnips, mangolds, carrots and hay, which would produce 8,000 tons of traffic annually, to which would be added 1,000 tons of general merchandise and 10,000 tons of coal. Wool, cattle, machinery and road metal would, it was hoped, push up the annual total to some 25,000 tons. The directors of the company were local: Sir George Wombwell, J. H. Love, George Hudson-Smith and the Hon. F. H. Dawney, and they had high hopes that the line would be completed within three months.[11] But in July 1890, with little or nothing having been achieved, the directors commissioned a new report on likely costs of construction: they had by this time risen to the figures shown in Table 6·8.[12]

In December 1890 the Board of Directors reviewed the situation. A major target for criticism was the NER, which, it was thought, was

Table 6·7 Easingwold Railway: estimated capital costs, October 1887

		£
Contract for engineering work		5,136
NER charge for Alne station		312
Locomotive etc.		1,035
Four cottages		600
12 acres of land		1,200
Tools, furniture, etc.		500
	TOTAL	8,783

Table 6·8 Easingwold Railway: estimated capital costs, July 1890

		£
Parliamentary and law charges		1,000
Land		1,200
NER connection		1,000
Permanent way and works		8,010
Equipment		2,100
Contingencies		1,000
Engineers' costs at 4 per cent		572
	TOTAL	14,882

charging too highly for the works at Alne station and it was remarked: 'They [the NER] understand the art of taking care of themselves.' Secondly, the directors were critical of the cost of land, especially that part of the land owned by Messrs Whytehead 'who though largely benefitted by the line, threw every obstacle in the way . . . obtaining prices for their land largely in excess of its value'. Thirdly, the directors were worried at the failure of the company to sell shares. Finally, they anticipated difficulty in operating the line when it was completed. Should they approach the NER to work the line for them? Should they obtain plant (locomotives etc.) on hire? Should they approach a third party to provide the plant and work the line for them?: 'In the light of past experience the [directors'] Committee is averse to approaching the NER.' The committee thought the line would pay and become valuable and did 'not attach any weight on this question to the opinions of any NER officials'. [Ultimately the directors convinced themselves that the Easingwold Railway Company could operate the line more cheaply than the NER. Economy of operation was to be the watchword and the appointment of a secretary was rejected, for the duties could be done as easily by the station master at Easingwold: 'The necessity of doing away with all expenditure not indispensable [*sic*] to complete construction and equipment on a very moderate scale is so obvious that the committee feels it is hardly necessary to do more than allude to it.'[13]

Operation[14]

The Easingwold Railway was opened for traffic in July 1891. In the event it must be considered one of the most successful of light railways, surviving as it did into the post-nationalisation period as an independent company. But even this company's experience demonstrates a gulf between expectation and reality in its formation. The projected cost of engineering was £5,136 but the reality was £11,973; locomotive and carriage costs were expected to be £1,035 but were, in fact, £1,420; and land which was estimated to be £1,200 cost £2,300. The local committee had anticipated that the total of building and equipment would be £8,783; the line when opened had cost £16,961, nearly double the estimate.

Goods traffic took a number of years even to approach the estimated figure of 25,000 tons, reaching 24,401 tons in 1909. However, this figure was never achieved again. On the other hand, passenger traffic, representing 40 per cent of the total revenue, must have been more encouraging and in 1892 the number of tickets sold was 42,708. The figure rose to 43,104 in 1893, but 1894 did see a falling off from this, to

39,717, coinciding with the introduction of second-class travel. It appears likely that the shift from third class to second class was encouraged by the parliamentary trains being the first and last each way. W. H. Cole concluded that on such short journeys travellers were prepared to pay a little more and make use of second-class facilities. From this he argued that light railways might be justified in charging higher rates for, although on such short journeys the increased charge would be a matter of indifference to the passenger, the increased revenue would help the company to survive. In 1896 fares were 3*d*, 4*d* and 6*d*, for third, second and first class respectively. Return fares were double.

Table 6·9   Easingwold Railway: passenger receipts, 1893 and 1896

Number of passengers		Description	Half-year ended 31 December					
1893	*1896*		*1893*			*1896*		
			£	*s*	*d*	£	*s*	*d*
494	432	First class	12	4	9	10	14	0
	17,439	Second class	–	–	–	284	8	6
23,238	2,315	Third class	275	5	6	26	3	0
		Season tickets	3	14	0	3	16	0
23,732	20,186		291	4	3	325	1	6

After the disturbance caused by the introduction of second-class travel in 1894 passenger traffic remained constant at around 40,000 until there came a sharp fall in 1910 to 33,888 and a further drop in 1911 to 27,392. By 1922 the number of people using the railway had fallen to under 11,000 but picked up to 34,360 in 1924 from which time a steady decline in numbers set in. During the period 1892–1912 passenger revenue was remarkably constant, remaining between £600 and £660 per annum in all years but three. In the immediate post-war period passenger revenue was substantially higher, £1,437 in 1922. Before 1914 passenger revenue represented around 40 per cent of the total revenue but after the First World War it slipped to 33 per cent. Passengers were offered a very generous train service by the standard of rural railways, with nine trains daily in each direction. Although this was attractive it clearly did not prove sufficiently so. For passengers, rather more than with goods, the essential requirement was a rapid service to York. In this respect the

Easingwold Railway was an easy target for road competition; not only was the railway journey indirect but there were delays in changing trains at Alne.

Train mileage remained constant in the years before 1914 at an annual average figure of 13,893 miles, varying from this by more than 1 per cent on only three occasions: 1910, 1911 and 1912, when the annual train mile figures were 14,165, 14,105 and 13,445 respectively. The more hostile financial climate after 1918 brought a reduction in train mileage and in 1924 the figure was down to 9,908 train miles. Thus, in the period up to 1914 the Easingwold Railway coped with a substantial passenger traffic and an increasing freight business but held its train mileage steady. In the 1920s reduced traffic forced a curtailment of services to reduce costs but this in turn made the railway a less-attractive proposition. If performance is measured by the operating ratio, the Easingwold Railway was not inefficiently run. During the twenty-year period from 1893 the company's operating ratio averaged 66·8 per cent, with high and low points of 88 per cent in 1893 and 55 per cent in 1905. For the purpose of comparison, the national figure for the same period was 60·5 per cent while figures for some typical rural railways were: Southwold Railway 68·5 per cent; Mid Suffolk Railway (1904–12) 97.7 per cent; Manchester & Milford Railway (1893–1905) 89·6 per cent. After the First World war, however, the picture changed dramatically: the operating ratio for the period 1922–25 averaged 100·5 per cent as competition increased and the company struggled with the unfavourable legacy of wartime control. The direct effect of wartime control had been a reduction in working hours coupled with an increase in wage and raw material costs. The two areas of expenditure in which labour costs would be most significant ('locomotive power' and 'traffic expenses') show the most dramatic increases.

Table 6·10   Easingwold Railway: expenditure, five-year averages, 1893–1912

Years	Total (£)	Locomotive power (£)	Maintenance of way (£)	Traffic (£)	General charges (£)
1893–97	1,054	361	146	363	68
1898–1902	1,255	418	253	372	92
1903–07	1,312	464	198	401	89
1908–12	1,584	501	213	531	160
1922–25	3,394	1,293	317	1,180	212

In 1896 train staff consisted of two men who doubled as drivers and guards and one fireman who at times was relieved by one of the driver/ guards. The station staff comprised an agent, two clerks and two porters, one of whom was guard for the last two trains. Permanent way was maintained by two platelayers. Commenting favourably on the virtues of such interchangeability of duties, W. H. Cole remarked 'Such versatility is the very essence of economical light railway working.'[15] Another contemporary writer, W. M. Acworth, was less impressed.[16] Describing the line's first full year of operation, 1892, he directed criticism at the railway's high level of expenditure which was disproportionate to its length and traffic. 'General charges', which covers office and Board costs was singled out at £129 as absurdly high for a railway only 2 mile long (total expenditure £1,256). Acworth claimed it to be double what it would be were the line operated by the NER and although the traffic warranted only one locomotive he pointed to the extra costs involved when the engine required repairs.[17] On those occasions the Easingwold Railway was dependent on the NER to carry out the repairs, and as a source of the replacement locomotive, which would have to be hired.

The Easingwold Railway officially became a light railway in 1928 in order to take advantage of any chance of reducing costs. In fact, there was no reduction in staffing, which was to remain virtually constant: two drivers who doubled as guards, one fireman, one station master, two clerks, four porters and two platelayers. The number was reduced after the Second World War to four, by which time the service had been reduced to two trains daily in each direction.[18]

Final years

Revenue, which averaged over £3,400 per annum in the early 1920s, fell to £1,161 in 1938 with a loss for the year of £117. Dividends fell from the 4 per cent paid in 1910 to 1 per cent in 1931. The Second World War saw a revival in the fortunes of the railway and the best year, 1943, saw revenue reach £7,048 with a profit on the year's operation of £2,240 and a dividend paid of 3 per cent.

The revival did not survive the war and substantial losses were sustained in 1947 and 1948. Passenger traffic was hit the hardest; in 1947 passenger receipts totalled £18 0s 8d, with one first-class passenger, accounting for the 8d, and 635 second-class passengers.[20] After the ending of passenger services in 1948 revenue fell from £2,385 in 1949 to £1,723 in 1956 with a steady decline in traffic; coal traffic fell from 2,450 tons to 1,375 tons between 1949 and 1954. Conversely, expenditure rose,

Table 6·11   Easingwold Railway: revenue and expenditure, 1938–48[19]

Year	Total receipts (£)	Total expenditure (£)	Net result (£)	Debt to other companies (£)	
1938	1,161	1,664	− 117		22
1939	1,246	1,696	− 128		145
1940	1,775	1,656	378		
1941	2,174	2,225	180		555
1942	3,860	2,435	1,662	CR	1,429
1943	7,048	5,025	2,240	CR	1,247
1944	5,912	9,370	− 3,326		637
1945	3,737	3,345	461		492
1946	4,124	3,320	906		
1947	2,802	4,830	− 1,838		1,934
1948	3,640	5,307	− 1,582		3,405

particularly in respect of wages. But it was the problem of the replacement of its locomotive which probably contributed most to the eventual closure of the railway. Acquired in 1903, the locomotive was declared beyond repair in 1948–9; replacment costs were estimated between £3,500 and £4,000 and the Easingwold Railway was left with no choice but to hire an engine from British Railways at £40 per week.

Postscript: the Brandsby Road Motor Services
In his book on the Easingwold Railway K. E. Hartley[21] remarks that it joined with the NER in offering a road delivery service to Brandsby and neighbouring villages. This service, and the Brandsby Dairy Association which established a co-operative purchasing system for member farmers, was lauded by E. A. Pratt in his book *The Transition in Agriculture*: 'The road motor service has . . . had most encouraging results and it has . . . shown that such services may serve an extremely useful purpose in villages off the beaten track of rail communications and not having sufficient traffic to warrant the building of a branch line of railway.'[22]

The North Sunderland Railway

The North Sunderland Railway was authorised in 1892 to build 4 miles of railway between North Sunderland and its harbour development at

Seahouses, on the coast of Northumberland, and Chathill on the NER's main line to Berwick. The share capital was established at £28,000, of which £7,000 was in the form of debentures. Engineering works included the following: two bridges under roads, two level crossing gatehouses, one terminal station, one intermediate station, three culverts, light cuttings and banks and rails at 70 lb per yard, single track.[23]

The purpose of the railway was to serve the local fishing industry, recently boosted by the construction of the harbour at Seahouses by Lord Crewe's Trustees. In 1891 Seahouses had six large fish-curing establishments, often working day and night despite the fact that their produce had to be carried 5 miles by road to Chathill; of the 1,700 tons of fish landed at Seahouses that year 748 tons were carted to Chathill for transhipment to the NER. The following year these figures had risen to 3,000 tons and 1,108 tons respectively, with a further 477 tons of fish manure and refuse leaving Chathill. Seahouses was thought to be capable of development into an important tourist resort and the railway was expected to produce a building boom, for not only was there no worthwhile accommodation other than public houses but also there were 'splendid sites for villa residences'.[24] Finally, the North Sunderland Railway was surrounded by good agricultural land, while both roadstone and coal could be extracted locally. With such potential for passenger and goods traffic it is not surprising that local landowners proposed to build a railway, and money was rapidly forthcoming to finance the necessary Act of Parliament, since the North Sunderland Railway pre-dates the Light Railways Act of 1896. However, delays in raising capital meant that the first sod was not cut until May 1896. Disputes with the contractor over the advance payment of a surety of £1,000 to the company led to the appointment of a new contractor. The line was eventually opened for goods traffic on 6 August 1898.

In an attempt to reduce costs the company turned to the Light Railways Act of 1896. Ostensibly the Light Railway Order was sought for an extension of the North Sunderland Railway to Monkhouses near Bamborough. Although the branch was not built, the Order, dated 13 August 1898, remained in force, covering the original line. The Commissioners in their report to the Board of Trade were suspicious of the company's motives; they criticised the estimated cost of the extension, which, at £11,227, or nearly £8,000 per mile, was significantly more than the original line's £5,000 per mile: 'It certainly looks as if the original capital was insufficient and that it was proposed to make up the deficiency by a heavy estimate for this line.'[25] The North Sunderland Railway clearly hoped that the Order would enable it to dispense with the use of the continuous brake, which would be inoperable because of the company's policy of running all trains mixed. If this was the objective the company's directors were to be disappointed for from the correspondence between the North Sunderland Railway and the Board of Trade it became clear that the Board was not prepared to permit any relaxation of regulations. The Inspector's report had noted that the company had purchased passenger vehicles from the Highland Railway but that these were not fitted with the continuous brake. Attention was then drawn to the fact that although the Light Railway Order had stipulated a speed limit of 25 m.p.h. there had been no limitation on length or weight of train and thus the Board of Trade could not sanction operation of the line without the use of the continuous brake. Continuous brake had thus to be used and the company reported on 3 December that all its passenger vehicles were so fitted. Five days later the Board of Trade offered the concession that each train could contain one unbraked wagon. The North Sunderland Railway was, however, to be plagued with problems with regard to its continuous brakes; in the period of government control during the First World War the company was issued with a waiver, the brake mechanisms were subsequently never maintained and ultimately this was to starve the railway of passenger rolling stock.

At the public inquiry for the Light Railway Order the reasons for building a railway from the NER at Chathill to Seahouses on the Northumberland coast were set out once again. Fundamentally the line was to carry fish and tourists. The area's principal landowner, Lord Crewe's Trustees, having already expended £30,000 on improving harbour facilities at Seahouses, felt 'the scheme would hardly be remunerative without adequate railway facilities to provide a quick delivery for the fish'.[26] Authority was looked for, and obtained, to extend the line to Monkhouses and through to Bamburgh: 'Monkhouses would form a very desirable place for bathing',[27] and Lord Armstrong was expected to build a siding on from there to Bamburgh. The line, opened in August 1898, was expected to provide an impetus to fishing (Seahouses was already the principal kippering centre of the North-east) and assist agriculture for the carting of produce was otherwise considered prohibitive: 'henceforward the district through which the railway runs will be smiled on by fortune and the efforts of the company amply repaid'.[28]

Traffic: Estimates and Reality

A number of traffic estimates exist for the railway. In 1891 expected traffic for three communities served by the railway was as set out in Table 6.12. In addition to this the locality was exected to produce 130 head of cattle and 1,200 sheep for carriage on the line.[29]

An estimate produced in 1893 by Mr J. Baker, who was associated with the Easingwold Railway, concentrated on the value of the likely traffic and thus the company's receipts. In a preliminary statement Baker estimated that the fish landed at Seahouses would average 2,000 tons, although the previous year had seen 3,000 tons landed and with the benefit of an improved harbour and rail communication they might expect to draw in boats from other harbours and a total of 5,000 tons might be expected. Such a note of optimism, typical of traffic estimates, was continued with the statement that the imminent withdrawal of the Bird Protection Society from the Farne Islands would mean that the tourist trade would be boosted by the prospect of boat trips. Finally, Baker had heard that coal was about to be mined at Beadnell, and that would further boost trade. His estimate, based on such speculations, is given in Table 6.13.

Table 6·12   North Sunderland Railway: expected goods traffic, 1891

	Coal (tons)	Fish (tons)	Manure and chemicals (tons)	General goods (tons)	Potatoes (tons)	Total (tons)
North Sunderland and Seahouses	1,500	1,800	290	150	300	4,040
Bamburgh	600		100	50	100	850
Beadnell	100	100	50	20	100	370

The net revenue of £1,320 per annum was considered sufficient to pay both a 5 per cent dividend on the £21,000 cost of construction (£1,050 per annum) and interest at the rate of 4 per cent on £7,000 debentures (£280 per annum).

Perhaps a more useful estimate of traffic was that in an article in the *Alnwick and County Gazette* published in May 1896. In a report on the progress of the company the newspaper identified traffic dispatched from Chathill station on the NER which might be expected to be carried on the line then under construction. These are given in Table 6.14.

Table 6·13   North Sunderland Railway: estimate of traffic, 1893

	£
Passengers (including tourists): 50,000 at 4d	833
Fish, 2,000 tons	
Fish manure, 500 tons ⎫	600
Timber ⎬	
Salt ⎭	
General merchandise	400
Minerals (including coal from the NER)	150
Mails	40
Limetone, brick earth	200
Coal from local mines	200
Whinstone for road repairs	50
Agricultural produce	150
Advertisements	20
TOTAL	2,643
Assume working expenses at 50 per cent	1,323
NET REVENUE	1,320

Table 6·14   North Sunderland Railway: estimated traffic at Chathill, 1895

From North Sunderland area	*Tons*
Kippered and pickled herrings	949
Fish manure	277
Fish refuse	255
For despatch to North Sunderland area	
General goods	1,546[a]
Coal	2,541
Livestock	11,859

[a] Average 1,500 tons for three years.
Source: Alnwick and County Gazette.

Two conclusions stand out from these estimates. First, the new railway was expected to double the fish traffic; and secondly, experience had apparently still failed to convince promoters that the assumption that any small, independent line could be worked for 50 per cent of receipts was entirely untenable.

The estimated traffic was always in excess of what was actually carried. The supposed 50,000 passengers never materialised: the greatest number actually carried was 28,904, in 1902, but in the period before the First World War the figure hovered around 23,000. The figure projected for total revenue, £2,643, was approached on one occasion: £2,262, in 1910. On average, from 1898 to 1912, the figure was less than two-thirds of the projected amount. Not surprisingly the operating ratio only once fell to 50 per cent; however, the average, 1898–1912, was 62 per cent, a very good figure for any railway, and the three years 1910–12 saw the average fall to 51 per cent. It follows from this that profitability never achieved the estimated sums. The greatest net revenue figure was £1,216 in 1910, but the average from 1898 to 1912 was under £650.

After the First World War

In the inter-war years the North Sunderland Railway sank abruptly into unprofitability, an operating profit of £735 in 1922 gave place to a loss of £615 in 1931.[30] An operating profit was achieved on four occasions between 1923 and 1939, and the average result for that period was a loss of £221 per annum. The Second World War did not bring a return to profitability, and losses from 1940 to 1945 averaged £489. Precise details of traffic are difficult to glean, but for 1923 a picture of passenger traffic flow is available and is given in Table 6.15.[31]

The previous year's total number of passengers was only 10,100 but the total for 1923 of 26,331 was well in excess of the immediate pre-war figure, suggesting the revival of the local tourist traffic. This is perhaps borne out by the imbalance between total passengers and passengers

Table 6·15 North Sunderland Railway: passenger traffic, 1923

	First	Class Second	Third	Total
	No.	*No.*	*No.*	*No.*
Total (*a*)	235	23,782	2,314	26,331
Number originating on North Sunderland Railway (*b*)	77	7,756	1,938	9,771
	%	%	%	%
(*b*) as percentage of (*a*)	32·7	32·6	83·7	37·1

originating on the system. With nearly 67 per cent of first- and second-class passengers originating off the system, but only 16 per cent of third-class passengers, the dependence of the line on 'external' traffic is clear. Such traffic would be most susceptible to road competition.

Fish was obviously an important element in the company's traffic but it was not separately recorded in the Railway Returns. For the year 1928 a record of fish traffic exists, however, providing a monthly analysis of fish dispatched in wagons and in parcels. A total of 510 tons of fish and 3,700 parcels of fish in packages of under 2 cwt were carried on the railway.[32] In 1946 the railway dispatched 1,290 tons of fish and received 112 tons. In the course of the year 724 wagons were dispatched from Seahouses, the largest monthly total being 152, in July. This traffic had achieved such a status on the line that passenger services were cancelled so that the fish specials could be operated by the one locomotive in steam. The unfortunate passengers were taken to Chathill by bus.

Passenger bookings off the line were still essentially local: for example, in March 1928 eighty-six passengers were booked on to the LNER, of whom forty-eight were bound for Newcastle and twenty for Alnwick, while in August 1928 of the 143 passengers travelling off the line ninety-seven were booked for Newcastle, twelve for Alnmouth and nine for Edinburgh. Passenger traffic was both seasonal and declining; by 1947 it was claimed that of the total number of passengers 4,000 were carried during the summer and 1,200 during the winter months.

The problems facing the North Sunderland Railway and its importance to the LNER were such that the larger company undertook a thorough investigation in 1931. The relationship from the beginning had been close: the LNER, for example, took a generous attitude over the division of receipts on through rates,[33] permitted the growth of a substantial debt, despite the requirement of an agreement of 1899 that accounts would be paid monthly, and reduced the charge for the use of Chathill station.[34] The LNER agreed with the North Sunderland Railway's view that its revenue 'has decreased because of industrial depression and road competition',[35] noting in July 1931 that 'the small railway is being severely hit by road competition and trade depression'.[36] The LNER position throughout the 1930s and 1940s was consistent and was indicated clearly by the District Passenger Manager in July 1929: 'We would be the losers if the line were closed.'[37]

The inspection in 1931 was carried out by the District Passenger Manager's Office.[38] The LNER had three plans in mind: to continue the North Sunderland Railway's operations unchanged; to cut out the passenger service; or to reduce the passenger service. The LNER officials were unwilling to support the second or third options as they would drive traffic on to the road but still leave the North Sunderland Railway with the expenses of staff and maintaining equipment. They argued that the only satisfactory option to continuing the current service was the complete closure of the line. This could be done by establishing a railhead at Chathill but the proviso was stated that at certain times the demands of the fish traffic were such that two road vehicles would be needed. A second vehicle, underemployed for much of the year, would be a positive drain on the LNER.

The question of the profitable employment of two vehicles was raised in a second report, on 18 November 1931. One possible solution was that a local haulage contractor could be hired on busy days; the point was made, however, that only short notice could be given and this might prove unsatisfactory for both the haulier and the fish. A new problem was then raised. Most fish then reached Seahouses station between 3.30 p.m. and 4.00 p.m., but some consignments arrived right up to departure time of 4.10 p.m. If road transport supplemented or replaced the train service, loading could not be done later than 3.40 p.m. at Seahouses if the consignment had to reach Chathill to be checked, booked and

Table 6·16   North Sunderland Railway: traffic at Seahouses, 1930

Passengers booked	2,046	Tickets collected	3,405	
Horses out	3			
Horses in	5			
Cattle out	15	Wagons out	41	
Cattle in	2	Wagons in	27	
Dogs out	25			
Dogs in	41			
			Tons	*Cwt*
Parcels out	4,135	Miscellaneous fish	534	13
Parcels in	4,511	Parcels fish	155	17

	Goods forwarded	*Goods received*
	(Tons)	*(Tons)*
Carted	73	260
Not carted	193	967
Minerals	56	2,547[a]

[a] This was an exceptionally inflated figure because of a one-off demand for roadstone.

transhipped in time for the 4.35 p.m. fish train. The report also included a detailed analysis of traffic on the line in 1930, which is set out in Table 6.16.

The LNER inspector's report did not produce any change in the service provided by the North Sunderland Railway. For the inhabitants of Seahouses and North Sunderland who depended upon the line, whether as passengers, tradesmen or customers, this must have been a relief. It was not only the fish trade that would have posed problems for road transport; goods traffic including mineral traffic was substantial, some 2,900 tons in 1928, 4,096 tons in 1930 and 2,444 tons in 1931. In addition to this there was considerable parcels traffic, valued in 1929 at £4,157, numbering 8,768 units in the year ending 31 October 1931. Not only would the LNER have suffered through the loss of contributory traffic but the people the line served would have had to discover an alternative, and probably less satisfactory, method of transport.

Table 6·17 North Sunderland Railway: passenger and parcel traffic at Seahouses, year ended October 1931

Month	Passenger bookings	Tickets collected	Packages of fish under 2 cwt	Other parcels	Total out	Total in
November	40	98	91	29	120	239
December	119	94	93	69	162	333
January	124	99	186	33	219	248
February	56	60	196	25	221	230
March	89	86	339	34	373	334
April	117	168	683	51	734	386
May	124	263	630	47	677	349
June	158	534	525	53	578	375
July	227	520	402	125	527	607
August	355	1,185	273	170	443	534
September	239	230	199	88	287	374
October	116	73	68	54	122	296
TOTAL	1,764	3,410[a]	3,685	778	4,463	4,305

[a] Tickets issued at stations other than Seahouses.

The end of the line

The steady operating losses that the company had made during the 1930s had meant that essential maintenance and repairs had been kept to a minimum while the friendly assistance of the LNER acted only as a

Table 6·18   North Sunderland Railway: fish traffic ex-Seahouses, year ended October 1931

Month	Miscellaneous fish					No.	Parcels fish				
	Tons	Cwt	£	s	d		Tons	Cwt	£	s	d
November	36	18	156	2	10	91	4	11	24	14	2
December	69	13	286	4	7	93	5	3	23	16	2
January	86	18	363	4	5	186	8	14	44	7	4
February	47	5	201	0	10	196	9	19	50	10	10
March	17	17	88	1	5	339	16	5	87	3	11
April	51	14	253	11	7	683	33	8	176	15	9
May	81	14	352	15	3	630	29	18	157	9	3
June	59	6	259	3	0	525	24	8	1,281	18	11
July	48	3	219	2	9	402	18	4	99	11	5
August	39	2	158	14	5	273	12	13	64	15	7
September	26	0	118	10	7	199	8	17	46	0	11
October	38	9	165	4	5	68	3	7	19	11	4
TOTAL	602	19	2,621	16	1	3,685	175	7	2,075	15	7

palliative; it was not intended to be, and never was, the drastic remedy that the railway required. The line, in fact, was simply wasting away. One problem reported by the LNER engineers was that of brakes. North Sunderland Railway trains ran loose coupled contrary to the Regulation of Railways Act of 1889 and the company's own Light Railway Order, which stipulated that passenger vehicles should be controlled by continuous brakes.[39] With gradients falling towards Seahouses it was the company's policy to run with a guard's van at the rear of all trains but the LNER engineers doubted whether this would be sufficient to stop a train if the locomotive's brakes failed. Both locomotives, *Bamburgh* and *Lady Armstrong*, steam and diesel respectively, were equipped with Westinghouse brakes but that on *Bamburgh* was out of order. No continuous braking was thus possible because the various systems on the passenger stock were defective. The North Sunderland Railway which had run unbraked mixed trains from the time of government control during the First World War thus found itself in a dilemma. It must equip all its passenger vehicles with vacuum brakes, but this was too expensive; or it might repair the Westinghouse brakes on the steam locomotive but then it would have to run separate goods trains and this would place an intolerable burden on the company. An LNER report on the rolling stock drew attention to the effects of a failure to maintain and renew equipment on an adequate basis (Table 6·19).[40]

Table 6·19 North Sunderland Railway: rolling stock, August 1939

Second class	Holds 30 people but no luggage
Saloon	Hand brake works on two wheels
Third class	Six compartments
(No. 60883)	Westinghouse brake untried
Third class	Six compartments, dual braking
(No. 60916)	Westinghouse brake defunct, no lights
	Left unused in siding at North Sunderland because of derailments

In winter months passenger traffic was carried in the second-class saloon. In summer trains consisted of the second-class saloon, 60916, 60883, and a third-class brake hired from the LNER. In the absence of the LNER brake, luggage on the North Sunderland Railway was carried in a fish van. The demand created by race days was met by using all the company's own stock, hiring two or three carriages from the LNER and running both locomotives in tandem.

Not only was the coaching stock in a parlous condition, on 16 November 1939 the poor state of the permanent way caused a reduction in maximum speed to 15 m.p.h. The LNER was able to report, however, that 500 sleepers had been bought, that track was being relaid and even that brakes were being overhauled.

The financial position of the North Sunderland Railway deteriorated sharply after the war, as indicated in Table 6.20. Between 1936 and 1948, while income doubled, expenditure rose over threefold and the consequent operating loss increased nearly tenfold. One important ingredient in rising costs was increased wages. In 1931 the line's station master, J. Cuthbertson, received 65s 6d a week; the driver, R. Simpson, 58s 6d; T. Willis, a porter, 19s. In 1948 R. E. J. Pawson, the station master, received 117s 6d a week; T. Willis, promoted from porter to driver after twenty-one years; service, 97s 6d; and a porter, 84s 6d. Overall the company continued to employ the same number of staff, although in 1948 only two, T. and R. Willis, had been with the company since before the war.[41]

The North Sunderland Railway, in common with all other railways, was hit by an increase in locomotive fuel costs; in the case of the North Sunderland, however, the problem was exacerbated by mechanical problems with its diesel locomotive which forced greater reliance on the steam locomotive and the more expensive fuel, coal. The LNER was

Table 6·20   North Sunderland Railway: income and expenditure, 1936–48

	1936	*1946*	*1947*	*1948*
Gross receipts	£	£	£	£
Passenger train traffic	845	2,220	1,743	1,861
Goods train traffic				
General merchandise	242	787	553	670
Minerals	43	37	52	21
Coal	228	233	227	251
Livestock	7	12	7	8
Miscellaneous	7	4	4	3
TOTAL INCOME	1,372	3,293	2,586	2,814
Expenditure				
Maintenance: way and works	394	870	621	641
Maintenance: rolling stock	114	1,638	1,057	1,273
Locomotive expenses	317	1,255	1,503	1,746
Traffic expenses	608	1,241	1,217	1,505
Miscellaneous expenses	198	261	184	143
TOTAL EXPENDITURE	1,631	5,265	4,582	5,308
LOSS	259	1,972	1,996	2,494

concerned about this state of affairs. A memorandum from the Mineral Section to the Rates and Development Section in March 1946 recorded the increased fuel costs set out in Table 6.22. In March 1947 the LNER reported to the North Sunderland Railway's directors that annual running costs for the steam locomotive *Bamburgh* had risen from £227 17s 4d in 1945 to £503 3s 9d in 1946, while the comparable figures for the *Lady Armstrong* were £101 13s 8d in 1945 and £52 9s 0d in 1946, representing an overall increase of 69 per cent.

On the evidence of the company's own trading, rising annual losses and an accumulated indebtedness to the Railway Executive (£17,071 in 1948), closure was inevitable before or after nationalisation. However, the North Sunderland Railway together with the Derwent Valley and Easingwold Railways, was not nationalised. Considering the position of the railway in the light of the nationalisation proposals, the LNER District General manager wrote to the General Manager at York[43] that if the North Sunderland was not acquired then it would have to put up its charges which would destroy its traffic, or cut wages which would leave it with no one to work its services. There was also the problem of

Table 6·21 North Sunderland Railway: engine mileage, 1944–46[42]

Year	Steam locomotive	Diesel locomotive	Total
1944	5,040	–	5,040
1945	5,676	10,644	16,320
1946	13,660	5,013	18,673
1947	–	–	18,176
1948	–	–	19,712
1949	–	–	18,226

Table 6·22 North Sunderland Railway: coal consumed and price per ton, 1944–45

Year	Tons	Cwt	Price per ton				Total annual costs		
			s	d			£	s	d
1944	86	13	37	7			162	18	7
					Cost				
					£	s	d		
	63	18	41	7	132	17	0		
1945	38	13	45	1	87	2	5	219	19	5

locomotive power. Not only was the annual cost of hiring expensive, £1,140 in 1947, but the North Sunderland Railway had already written to the Ministry of Transport pointing out that it was dependent upon the smallest LNER locomotives, a type then obsolete.

The District General Manager indicated the inevitable subsequent cost of nationalisation. If the line were to be provided with a new locomotive, even one of an obsolete type, the cost would be £3,000; if, however, the permanent way were to be strengthened to take larger locomotives, the cost would be £14,500. Nationalisation, therefore, appeared to be an expensive option but in the view of the Newcastle District manager, whose office ran the North Sunderland Railway, the closure of the line could not be done without great inconvenience to the people of Seahouses in respect of fish, coal and holiday traffic. He argued that the Transport Commission should support the railway for the same reasons that other small branches' losses had been swallowed up by larger railway companies for years: contributary value. Thus, a body of opinion existed among the management of the old LNER that the North Sunderland Railway was worth subsiding. The North Eastern Region analysed the North Sunderland's results in 1947–48, making out the case for maintaining the small line (Tables 6.23, 6.24 and 6.25).[44] The results of closure, it was stated, were likely to be as follows.

Parcels and small consignments would be routed through Belford as a result of which the Belford motor van mileage would rise from 2,959 to about 9,000. This would necessitate the acquisition of a new 2 ton lorry.

Fish traffic would probably be lost to rail except for small consignments, which were expensive to handle. The loss of the fish traffic would represent a loss to British Railways of £4,200 per annum.

Passengers would almost certainly forsake the railway for the road for their entire journey rather than drive first to either Chathill or Belford. This would cost British Railways a large proportion of the £5,126 derived from the North Sunderland Railway passengers in 1946.

Coal was expected to be road hauled. It is interesting to note that trading in coal was the only profitable business venture conducted by the North Sunderland Railway. The sale of coal was one of the duties of the station master at Seahouses, who took for himself 20 per cent of the profit, the other 80 per cent being allocated to the railway company. In 1947 the amount sold was 2,000 tons, which produced a profit of £330 on a turnover of £5,700.

The NER accountant's office produced a summary of the region's revenue which derived from the North Sunderland Railway showing a reduction of £7,946 per annum, as detailed in Table 6.23.

The value of the North Sunderland Railway to British Railways in 1948 was once again analysed, the conclusion reached being, as before, that the line was worth saving (Table 6.24). Despite this evidence of the direct financial benefit to British Railways of the continued existence of the North Sunderland Railway, no decision was taken to provide support on a regular basis and the matter emerged again in 1949 as the company's losses mounted. On 29th December 1949 the North Eastern Region dispatched a memorandum to the Railway Executive reviewing the North Sunderland Railway's plight. Losses approached £3,000 per annum; cash had been raised by disposing of two derelict locomotives for scrap prices but funds did not stretch to acquiring a new engine and the company was now dependent on British Railways for its motive power; passenger vehicles were in urgent need of repair and unless £430 was spent on maintenance the company would be unable to operate its summer services.

Table 6·23 North Sunderland Railway: contributory value of traffic to the London and North Eastern Region, 1946

	Benefit in 1946	Projected residual revenue if NSR closed
	£	£
Goods	3,481	3,000
Coal	548	180
Passengers	5,126	2,500
Parcels	871	600
Fish	4,700	500
TOTAL	14,726	6,780

Table 6·24 North Sunderland Railway: contributory value of traffic to British Railways, 1947 and 1948

	1947	1948
	£	£
Passengers	2,918	3,642
Parcels	765	970
Fish by passenger trains	5,117	4,244
Merchandise, minerals and livestock	2,443	2,142
Coal	564	524
TOTAL	11,807	11,522

It was estimated that in 1947 had the line been closed £7,350 would have been retained and an additional sum of £420 would have been spent to offset against it as shown in Table 6.25.

Assuming the justice of the memorandum's estimates, the benefit to the North Eastern Region comfortably exceeded the North Sunderland Railway's losses. Certainly the region was prepared to invest in minor improvements even at this time of doubt over the railway's future. New works included additional lighting at Seahouses on platform and access paths, and sockets and fittings for hand-held electric lights in the fish dock at a cost of £28. The railwayman's cottage at North Sunderland had an Elsan closet supplied and fitted for a cost of £10.

It appears, however, that in the end the North Sunderland Railway succumbed to a combination of physical exhaustion and the fact that road transport was already providing an adequate alternative service. In respect of locomotive power the North Sunderland quietly faded away. In autumn 1948 the line was closed to passenger traffic for four weeks because its locomotive was undergoing repairs. Taxis were used to carry passengers instead. With the scrapping of the *Bamburgh* and the *Lady Armstrong*, locomotive 68089, hired from British Railways, was used on

Table 6·25 North Sunderland Railway: projected lost BR revenue if line closed, 1947–48

	£	£
Estimated contributory value (1948)		11,807
Revenue remaining if line closed		7,350
Loss of gross receipts	4,457	
less Working expenses at 33 per cent	1,485	
Estimated loss of net receipts	2,972	2,972
Estimated increased cartage costs	1,250	
less estimated extra carriage revenue	830	
Estimated net increased cartage costs	420	420
Estimated lost revenue if line closed		3,392

Table 6·26 North Sunderland Railway: road journeys due to locomotive failure, 1950[41]

Month	No. of journeys
January	–
February	12
March	10
April	6
May	84
June	–
July	5
August	3
September	–
October	262
November	2
December	2

the line and Beechcroft's taxis were required in 1949 only on six occasions, 6 April and 15, 16, 20, 21 and 22 June. However, 68089 was reaching the end of its effective life and was twice removed from service in 1950 for heavy repairs, in addition to numerous minor breakdowns.

The ease and frequency with which recourse to Beechcroft's taxis was made must have contributed to the belief in the British Transport Commission that complete conversion to road transport was inevitable, a fact made more likely because of the Commission's involvement with nationalised passenger and freight road transport.

In March 1950 copies of a report on the North Sunderland Railway were sent to the Chief Regional Officer, Railway Executive, York and to the Tilling Organisation implying that the withdrawal of passenger services was imminent.[46] First, the road and rail passenger services were reviewed. There were six rail services in each direction, the last train from Seahouses being the 6.30 p.m. and that from Chathill the 7.05 p.m. The bus service was much more attractive, with ten buses in each direction during the week and fourteen on Saturdays, with the last bus leaving Seahouses at 10.35 p.m. and 10.20 p.m. on Saturdays. The report analysed passenger traffic at Seahouses very much with the idea of assessing the impact the suspension of railway service would have on the provision of buses by the United Automobile Company (Table 6.27).

Increases in passenger fares of $33\frac{1}{3}$ per cent in August 1946 and 55 per cent in October 1947 possibly helped to discourage traffic and ease the

Table 6·27 North Sunderland Railway: passenger journeys, 1949

	Ordinary	Season	Total	Average passengers per month
To Seahouses				
October – March	1,275	200	1,475	246
April, May, June, Sept.	1,892	125	2,017	504
July, August	2,129	150	2,279	1,139
TOTAL	5,296	475	5,771	480
From Seahouses				
October – March	1,269	200	1,469	245
April, May, June, Sept.	1,956	125	2,081	520
July, August	2,274	150	2,424	1,212
TOTAL	5,499	475	5,974	498

transition to the roads.[47] The British Transport Commission in March
1950 was openly considering shifting freight traffic to the Road Haulage
Executive, perhaps encouraged by the declining value and quantity of
freight on the line at a time when operating costs were at least twice
revenue (Table 6.28). A survey of the passengers booked at Seahouses in
May 1950 (Table 6.29) showed that the line was very lightly used.

In July 1951 the Railway Executive cancelled the 1939 agreement
between the North Sunderland Railway and the old LNER by which the
former railway would be managed by the latter in return for £10 per
annum. Without the help of British Railways the North Sunderland
Railway was unable to continue operation and the decision was taken to
close the line on 27 October 1951. The final trains left Seahouses at 4.20
p.m. drawn by locomotive 68089: the last three train services of the day
were operated by taxis. 'Road transport has finally conquered';[48] the
engine shed was even converted into a bus garage.

Table 6·28 North Sunderland Railway: revenue, 1948–51

	1948 (£)	*1949* (£)	*1950* (£)	*Jan.–Mar. 1950* (£)	*Jan.–Mar. 1951* (£)
Passenger train total	1,881	1,522	1,256	286	204
Parcels (incl. fish) in above total	1,111	889	699		
Goods	950	712	768	179	148
Miscellaneous	29	91	35		
TOTAL	2,860	2,325	2,059	465	352
Expenditure	5,476	7,658	4,496		

Table 6·29 North Sunderland Railway: daily passenger traffic, May 1950

Service	*Passengers ex-Seahouses*	*Service*	*Passengers ex-Chathill*
7·35	3·4	8·10	3·2
9·15	2·2	9·40	0·2
10·10	0·5	10·50	2·5
1·10	2·0	1·50	1·5
4·40	5·0	6·0	3·8
6·30	0·1	7·5	2·0

The Wantage Tramway

The Wantage Tramway was one of the small band of light railways built under the Tramways Act of 1870.[49] It was promoted to put the Berkshire town of Wantage on the railway map, from which it had been omitted by the GWR's routing its main line some $2\frac{1}{2}$ miles to the north to take it through the Vale of the White Horse to Swindon. In 1874 the Wantage Tramway Company Ltd came into being following public meetings in the town. Its line was built from a junction with the GWR at Wantage Road station to a terminus in the town, with sidings to the gas works and to a separate goods station. Estimates of traffic were, as was usually the case, extremely favourable, for the tramway was expected to carry the traffic shown in Table 6.30.

Proposed rates for the new tramway would cut these costs as set out in Table 6.31: the consequent saving to the townspeople would be £1,446 1s 3d.[50]

The cost of the line was estimated to be between £8,500 and £9,000, and most of the shares were taken locally, £3,000 being subscribed at the public meeting to promote the tramway. By 1889 the company's share capital had assumed its final form as shown in Table 6.32.

Table 6·30 Wantage Tramway: estimated traffic

		£	s	d
$\frac{2}{3}$ of existing passengers:	23,338 at $10\frac{1}{2}d$	1,021	0	9
$\frac{2}{3}$ of existing goods:	17,752 tons at 3s/ton	2,662	16	0
$\frac{3}{4}$ of existing parcels:	23,400 at 3d each	292	10	0
Some intermediate passengers		188	2	6
TOTAL		4,164	9	3

Table 6·31 Wantage Tramway: proposed rates

	£	s	d
23,338 passengers at 6d	583	9	0
17,752 tons of goods at 2s a ton	1,775	4	0
23,400 parcels at 2d each	195	0	0
Intermediate passengers	164	15	0
TOTAL	2,718	8	0

Table 6·32   Wantage Tramway: share capital

	£
1,634 fully paid up £5 ordinary shares	8,170
600 fully paid up preference shares	3,000
TOTAL	11,170

For most of its length the tramway, which was standard gauge, ran alongside the road, which varied between 25 ft and 35 ft wide. The rails were laid on one of the two footpaths and never occupied a width greater than 6 ft. Ordinary rail was used and the maximum gradient was one in forty-four. The company originally employed horsepower to operate its services but substituted steam in 1876, thus reducing operating costs from 8*d* to 7*d* per train mile. The first steam engines were Merryweather tram locomotives, including one double-deck steam tram with fifty-four seats. From about 1880 these were replaced by ordinary Hughes-type locomotives, small 0–4–0 tank engines, bought second hand, only one of which was cased in as a tram engine. They hauled a variety of four-wheeled and bogie coaches owned by the company; goods wagons were worked in from the main line. The use of standard locomotives brought a further reduction in operating costs to 5*d* per train mile. In 1882 it was claimed that average costs for tramway operation for horse and steam power were 1s 1*d* and 8*d* respectively, which underlined the economy of operation evident with the Wantage Tramway.[11]

The people of Wantage clearly derived an advantage from the tramway with a significant reduction in the cost of transport. By the end of the 1870s reductions were calculated as shown in Table 6.33.

During 1878 the tramway carried 15,000 parcels and in the single month of February 1879 it moved 600 tons of heavy goods and 133 tons of light goods such as grocery and hardware.[12]

Table 6·33   Wantage Tramway: transport cost reduction, prices per ton

	By road		By tramway	
	s	*d*	*s*	*d*
Coal	2	6	1	0
Stone and timber	3	6	2	6
General merchandise	4	6	3	0

However, as was often the case, the initial estimates of traffic were entirely optimistic. In 1883 revenue from parcels was £101 against an estimate of £195, and goods revenue was £850 against an expected £1,775. Passenger traffic and associated revenue was, however, higher than had been anticipated. In 1883 the tramway carried 32,893 passengers, earning £814, whereas the estimate had assumed 23,338 passengers and a revenue of £583.[53]

Passenger numbers rose slowly during the nineteenth century, reaching 36,692 in 1895 and 39,044 in 1900. Traffic then increased more rapidly and the tramway carried 54,976 people in 1905. Despite this goods traffic was the most lucrative side of the company's business. In 1912 passenger traffic contributed £1,037, parcels £235 and goods £2,548 to total revenue. Twenty years later the corresponding figures were £1,617, £252 and £3,959.[54]

Fares were thought high in comparison with urban tramways.[55] A uniform class was established in 1889 but special rates were available, for example, workmen's returns at 2s 6d for the week for the full distance. Examples of fares are given in Table 6.34.

Table 6·34 Wantage Tramway: fare structure, 1875–1923

	1875				1889[a]		1923[b]	
	First class		*Second class*					
	s	d	s	d	s	d	s	d
Wantage to Grove Bridge		4		3		2		3
Wantage to Oxford Lane		6		4½		4		6
Wantage to Wantage Road		9		6		6		9
Return	1	3		10			1	0

[a] One class only.

Table 6·35 Wantage Tramway: weekly wages

	1903		1920	
	s			s
Manager	50	Managing clerk		80
Engineer	36	Engineer		86
Driver	24	Driver		60

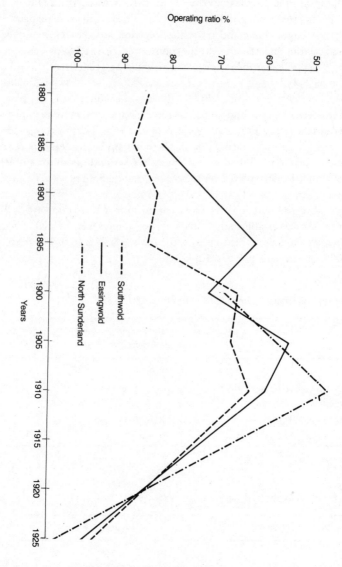

Fig. 6·1 Operating ratios, 1880–1925

In common with all railways the rates of wages rose steeply in the early twentieth century, as Table 6.35 shows. Despite that, the general economy of operation on the Wantage Tramway enabled dividends to be paid on ordinary shares every year until 1914, with the exception of 1899. Between 1903 and 1911 the dividend was consistently high, at 6 per cent, and from 1923 to 1945 payment averaged over 4 per cent.[16]

However, despite this continuing evidence of prosperity, The Wantage Tramway was shorn of its passenger service in 1925. The GWR displayed less sympathy to its small neighbour than the LNER did to the North Sunderland, for it was the GWR that operated the buses which drove out the Wantage Tramway's passenger service. Freight services continued until the closure of the tramway in November 1943 following wartime damage at the hands of the American army. The line was re-opened in February 1944 but it was found that the company's stock of locomotives had deteriorated so seriously that only one engine was available and that was capable of only two trips daily.[17] The need to re-equip the line, together with the closure of Wantage Gas Works by the Oxford Gas Company, depriving the line of some coal traffic, and increased wage bills, persuaded the directors of the tramway to cease operations on 21 December 1945.

Table 6·36   Various railways: percentage operating ratio

Railway	Operating ratio (%)					
	1890	*1895*	*1900*	*1905*	*1910*	*1925*
Southwold	83	85	66	67	63	96
Easingwold		62	72	55	60	98
North Sunderland			69	58	46	103
Golden Valley	196	146				
Ffestiniog	58	60	67	74	70	90
North Wales Narrow						
Gauge	88	90	85	87	101	114
Manchester & Milford	99	88	97	97		
British Railways	54	56	62	62	62	83

Table 6·37 Southwold Railway: expenses and profit, 1880–1925

Year	Mntce of way (£)	Loco (£)	Stock repair (£)	Traffic expenses (£)	General charges (£)	Rates & taxes (£)	Pass. duty (£)	Employee comp. (£)	Legal exp. (£)	Total exp. (£)	Total revenue (£)	Profit (£)	%
1880	431	641	9	700	396	19	10			2,211	2,593	382	85
1881	373	646	48	786	295	19	14			2,192	2,746	554	80
1882	455	661	14	785	323	17	12			2,275	2,856	581	80
1883	529	747	202	769	316	20	47			2,692	3,033	341	89
1884	567	792	202	756	315	22	21			2,735	3,143	408	87
1885	598	813	295	791	318	34	12			2,861	3,262	401	88
1886	536	823	233	741	330	33	12			2,708	2,936	228	92
1887	685	1,083	58	775	330	47	11			2,989	3,098	109	96
1888	608	692	77	835	336	18	12			2,572	2,949	377	87
1889	654	658	13	861	335	30	12			2,563	3,391	828	76
1890	717	712	132	861	335	18	15			2,790	3,353	563	83
1891	776	758	83	816	331	42	14			2,829	3,484	664	81
1892	707	793	98	870	336	41	14			2,859	3,560	701	80
1893	876	773	153	858	329	26	10			3,025	3,659	634	83
1894	713	969	242	919	343	48	9			3,243	3,942	699	82
1895	1,009	1,049	22	960	401	39	9			3,489	4,128	639	85
1896	904	983	131	919	458	86	9			3,484	4,140	656	84
1897	988	760	172	922	445	79	11			3,377	4,169	792	81
1898	850	780	232	965	460	75	11			3,373	4,357	984	77

Table 6.37 cont.

Year	Mntce of way (£)	Loco (£)	Stock repair (£)	Traffic expenses (£)	General charges (£)	Rates & taxes (£)	Pass. duty (£)	Employee comp. (£)	Legal exp. (£)	Total exp. (£)	Total revenue (£)	Profit (£)	%
1899	779	885	109	959	488	85	11	19		3,395	5,223	1,828	65
1900	794	949	98	1,100	433	148	13	22		3,557	5,429	1,872	66
1901	539	1,000	85	1,092	429	159	13	22		3,339	5,893	2,554	57
1902	528	1,027	119	1,044	431	190	13	24	478	3,854	5,626	1,772	69
1903	535	921	96	1,041	445	207	13	17	100	3,375	5,525	2,150	61
1904	512	997	146	1,126	458	152	11	16	100	3,518	5,858	2,340	60
1905	548	909	109	1,094	479	166	12	15	100	3,432	5,116	1,684	67
1906	524	833	106	1,076	491	153	10	16		3,209	5,015	1,806	64
1907	455	784	59	1,117	484	124	10	18		3,051	5,153	2,102	59
1908	431	861	66	1,037	486	128	10	19		3,038	5,149	2,111	59
1909	418	995	105	1,033	503	147	10	20		3,231	5,247	2,106	62
1910	665	816	103	1,042	502	149	10	20		3,307	5,280	1,973	63
1911	675	879	127	1,061	512	147	11	20		3,435	5,546	2,111	62
1912	675	902	105	1,102	549	113	10	20		3,485	5,508	2,023	63
			Mntce Exp.										
1922	1,426	285	1,697 374	2,768	1,084		7			8,026	8,243	217	97
1923	1,099	201	1,598 393	2,559	1,129					7,276	7,395	119	98
1924	1,051	217	1,504 221	2,272	1,114					6,670	6,944	244	96
1925	1,029	141	1,452 192	2,155	1,002					6,220	6,476	250	96

Table 6·38 Southwold Railway: traffic and revenue, 1880–1925

| | No. of passengers | | | | | | | | Revenue (£) | | | | | | | | | |
Year	First class	Third class	Total	Min. (tons)	Merch. (tons)	Coal (tons)	Live-stock	Train miles	Passengers 1	3	S	Total	Dogs pets lgge	Mail	Merch.	Min.	Total goods	Grand total
1880	3,430	62,299	65,749	3,012	1,960			30,818	286	1,459	21	1,766	188	27	468	144	612	2,593
1881	3,044	66,473	70,117	3,335	2,700			30,275	200	1,523	38	1,761	150	30	550	183	733	2,746
1882	3,633	73,692	77,325	4,015	2,567			33,022	214	1,609	49	1,872	176	30	437	251	688	2,856
1883	3,726	63,142	66,868	4,095	3,257			31,170	307	1,507	49	1,863	200	36	593	267	860	3,033
1884	5,009	68,129	73,138	1,730	2,979			29,026	209	1,609	46	1,924	251	30	588	274	862	3,143
1885	4,320	68,543	72,863	4,555	3,199			30,394	229	1,654	47	1,930	223	39	633	343	976	3,262
1886	4,448	64,226	68,674	3,903	2,647			30,286	215	1,505	66	1,786	244	39	533	257	790	2,936
1887	4,621	65,989	70,601	4,341	2,745			30,446	216	1,589	62	1,967	235	30	579	289	868	3,098
1888	4,476	62,586	67,062	5,492	2,700			30,240	222	1,451	46	1,719	211	35	517	374	891	2,429
1889	5,391	67,002	72,393	6,356	3,187			30,400	247	1,633	39	1,919	248	52	619	444	1,063	3,391
1890	5,458	73,197	78,655	5,712	2,907			30,588	257	1,677	52	1,986	235	50	581	366	947	3,353
1891	5,229	72,639	77,868	6,722	3,282			30,536	236	1,679	60	1,975	257	50	588	431	1,019	3,484
1892	5,487	78,513	84,000	6,613	3,268			30,869	235	1,848	33	2,116	240	50	566	433	999	3,560
1893	3,457	83,788	87,245	5,327	3,706			30,150	190	1,966	34	2,190	257	50	617	384	1,001	3,659
1894	2,812	79,498	82,310	7,506	4,579			28,080	151	1,883	33	2,067	322	50	783	548	1,331	3,942
1895	3,088	82,623	85,711	6,817	4,938			27,888	166	1,973		2,167	346	50	864	468	1,350	4,128
1896	3,278	82,025	85,303	6,611	5,343			28,018	184	1,956		2,147	384	50	838	465	1,303	4,140
1897	3,789	88,491	92,280	5,978	4,770			27,846	208	2,048		2,268	376	50	840	427	1,267	4,169
1898	3,466	90,332	93,798	6,664	5,346			28,123	185	2,145		2,334	393	51	873	493	1,366	4,357
1899	4,732	100,621	105,353	8,600	6,320			30,895	207	2,614		2,838	441	50	977	639	1,616	5,223
1900	4,342	99,197	103,539	9,313	6,608			31,258	253	2,468		2,728	452	50	1,082	712	1,794	5,429

Table 6·38 cont

	No. of passengers								Revenue (£)									
									Passengers				Dogs pets lgge	Mail l			Total goods	Grand total
Year	First class	Third class	Total	Min. (tons)	Merch. (tons)	Coal (tons)	Live-stock	Train miles	1	3	S	Total			Merch.	Min.		
1901	4,460	106,336	110,796	10,776	7,363			33,131	267	2,620		2,907	515	50	1,159	796	1,955	5,893
1902	4,415	101,466	105,881	9,576	6,322			33,418	258	2,538		2,822	483	57	1,103	720	1,823	5,626
1903	4,052	105,056	109,108	8,015	5,635			29,265	244	2,577		2,847	514	60	996	570	1,566	5,525
1904	3,614	106,872	110,486	8,460	6,636			29,721	214	2,571		2,798	481	60	1,112	599	1,711	5,858
1905	3,674	99,613	103,287	7,024	5,141			29,498	235	2,430		2,676	529	60	888	552	1,440	5,116
1906	3,098	98,963	102,056	7,429	5,082			29,045	205	2,401		2,615	477	60	911	535	1,445	5,015
1907	3,085	95,036	98,121	8,846	5,236			29,386	208	2,348		2,559	495	60	1,008	633	1,641	5,153
1908	2,836	99,058	101,894	7,041	5,823			29,773	189	2,405		2,605	515	60	1,017	552	1,589	5,149
1909	2,787	98,631	101,418	6,704	6,447			29,031	192	2,404		2,615	515	60	1,136	479	1,615	5,247
1910	2,841	101,356	104,197	6,258	6,566			28,749	192	2,470		2,670	558	60	1,099	433	1,532	5,280
1911	3,185	104,852	108,037	5,950	6,684			30,242	214	2,579		2,806	603	60	1,210	419	1,629	5,546
1912	3,139	100,364	103,503	5,942 Other min.	6,686			31,638	206	2,550		2,765	582	60	1,222	422	1,644	5,508
1922	1,273	86,905		1,562	4,092	8,995	241		157	3,571		5,237			2,506			8,243
1923	1,353	87,136		3,321	3,801	8,488	233		112	3,044		4,555			2,419			7,395
1924	1,188	82,938		2,547	3,814	9,096	100		109	2,931		4,236			2,323			6,944
1925	1,161	82,162		1,828	3,515	8,470	224		104	2,728		4,052			2,045			6,476

Table 6·39 Easingwold Railway: expenses and profit, 1891–1905

Year	Mntce of way (£)	Loco power (£)	Stock repairs (£)	Traffic expenses (£)	General charges (£)	Rates & taxes (£)	Pass. duty (£)	Total exp. (£)	Total revenue (£)	Profit (£)	%
1891	25	182		207	61	9	1	489	635	146	
1892	179	326	5	550	129	23	1	1,236	1,311	55	96
1893	145	371	7	440	88	23	1	1,236	1,404	173	88
1894	133	361	2	333	63	34	29	996	1,559	563	64
1895	173	320	1	330	60	40	28	961	1,552	591	62
1896	125	351	4	355	62	33	29	969	1,636	667	59
1897	156	403	22	358	68	46	29	1,110	1,648	538	67
1898	204	316	10	370	62	45	31	1,051	1,854	794	57
1899	254	483	6	387	103	46	30	1,358	1,794	436	76
1900	261	487	15	376	82	53	30	1,313	1,827	514	72
1901	284	414	23	366	127	61	30	1,336	1,918	582	70
1902	262	393	7	365	87	63	29	1,214	1,982	768	61
1903	230	509	64	364	88	82	30	1,385	1,870	485	74
1904	152	459	66	371	85	76	32	1,252	2,035	781	62
1905	167	374		360	91	69	31	1,105	1,996	891	55

Table 6·39 cont

Year	Mntce of way (£)	Loco power (£)	Stock repairs (£)	Traffic expenses (£)	General charges (£)	Rates & taxes (£)	Pass. duty (£)	Total exp. (£)	Total revenue (£)	Profit (£)	%
1906	221	491	8	457	92	88	30	1,416	2,094	678	68
1907	223	491	2	455	92	87	29	1,403	2,147	744	65
1908	294	482	14	473	95	77	30	1,494	2,122	678	69
1909	280	487	2	482	145	97	29	1,532	2,360	828	65
1910	144	453	15	515	157	94	29	1,422	2,358	936	60
1911	165	666	33	566	213	127	35	1,811	2,489	658	73
1912	183	417	6	622	190	111	32	1,663	2,422	759	69
1922	427	1,111	24	1,228	208			3,340	4,038	698	82
1923	373	1,093	9	1,173	224			3,142	3,449	307	91
1924	408	1,949	46	1,102	205			4,058	3,096	-1,038	131
1925	378	1,019	1	1,160	211			3,036	3,080	44	98

Table 640 Southwold Railway: source of traffic, 1922–25

Year		No. of passengers		Merch. (tons)	Coal (tons)	Other minerals (tons)	Livestock			Total
		1st class	3rd Class				Calves	Sheep	Pigs	
1922	Total	1,273	86,905	4,092	8,995	1,582				
1922	Originating on line	376	63,053	813	13	257		21	220	241
1923	Total	1,353	87,136	3,801	8,488	3,321				
1923	Originating on line	534	64,211	682	44	653		28	205	233
1924	Total	1,188	82,938	3,814	9,096	2,547				
1924	Originating on line	418	61,536	752	50	659		12	88	100
1925	Total	1,101	82,162	3,515	8,470	1,828				
1925	Originating on line	401	60,995	712	14	1,096	4	112	108	224

Table 6·41 Easingwold Railway: traffic and revenue, 1891–1925

Year	No. of passengers 1	2	3	Total	Min. (tons)	Merch. (tons)	Coal (tons)	Live-stock	Train miles	Revenue (£) Passengers 1	2	3	S	Total	Lgge	Mail	Merch.	Live-stock	Min.	Total goods	Grand total
1891	597		20,001	20,598	1,932	4,080			5,826	15		245		261	23	11	223	7	97	327	635
1892	812		41,896	42,708	6,775	5,871			13,324	20		516	28	551	85	25	387	23	217	627	1,311
1893	827		42,277	43,104	5,829	6,688			13,319	21		508	32	544	94	25	499	18	194	711	1,409
1894	805	33,206	5,706	39,717	6,206	7,152			13,987	20	543	69	56	649	77	25	535	27	201	763	1,559
1895	641	33,236	4,628	38,555	5,852	6,780			13,922	17	542	54	43	637	82	25	533	29	202	764	1,552
1896	735	32,503	3,747	36,985	6,211	8,335			13,980	18	531	44		614	87	25	640	24	209	873	1,636
1897	965	33,044	4,340	38,349	5,909	8,487			13,940	24	536	51	52	639	96	25	632	23	206	861	1,648
1898	978	34,547	4,412	39,937	6,437	8,790			13,935	26	561	53		666	127	25	768	20	208	996	1,845
1899	1,037	33,727	4,469	39,233	4,050	12,707			13,797	26	544	56		655	129	25	725	25	203	953	1,794
1900	1,346	33,399	4,500	39,245	4,038	12,817			13,854	34	541	54		656	136	25	749	24	202	980	1,827
1901	1,444	33,917	4,179	39,450	8,111	8,643			13,849	36	530	50	29	645	164	25	667	31	314	1,052	1,918
1902	1,309	33,678	4,630	39,617	8,942	9,621			13,825	32	523	55	29	639	169	25	679	36	373	1,088	1,982
1903	1,435	34,121	4,283	39,839	8,197	8,627			13,817	35	530	49	21	635	159	25	612	35	353	1,000	1,871
1904	1,521	35,884	4,740	42,145	8,210	9,922			13,928	37	559	51	35	682	177	25	711	37	354	1,102	2,033
1905	1,404	35,125	3,780	40,309	9,671	9,482			13,807	34	540	43	32	649	166	25	663	36	408	1,107	1,996
1906	1,093	35,639	3,957	40,689	11,539	10,576			13,920	27	544	44	31	646	184	25	927	35	227	1,189	2,094
1907	898	34,806	3,723	39,427	12,018	10,753			13,869	22	532	41	30	625	170	25	954	44	254	1,252	2,147
1908	811	34,958	4,187	39,960	11,171	10,861			13,957	20	534	50	29	633	174	25	734	44	432	1,235	2,172
1909	607	35,680	2,840	39,127	13,118	11,343			13,872	15	546	31	35	627	173	25	808	51	528	1,387	2,360
1910	487	24,894	8,507	33,888	5,547	11,212			14,165	14	547	21	31	613	182	22	1,063	58	262	1,383	2,358
1911	494	24,686	2,212	27,392	3,121	18,130			14,105	16	546	29	33	624	196	25	1,120	52	271	1,443	2,469
1912	504	24,937	2,782	28,223	6,024	11,450			13,445	16	557	32	39	644	202	25	1,030	45	262	1,337	2,422
1922	69	10,113	676		7,580 *(Other Min.)*	11,889	5,216	8,366		12	972	19		1,437	454	*(Coal)*	1,404	126	492		4,038
1923	177	32,369	1,154		5,147	10,901	5,400	9,020		9	704	10		1,088	349		1,189	132	647		3,449
1924	153	32,957	1,250		5,960	11,833	5,273	18,300		5	680	12		1,028	418		1,131	164	325		3,996
1925	84	27,188	963		5,899	12,203	5,099	16,665		2	541	17		917	384		1,149	167	431		3,080

Table 6.42 Easingwold Railway: source of traffic, 1922–25

| Year | No. of passengers | | | Merch. (tons) | Coal (tons) | Other minerals (tons) | Livestock | | | | Total |
	First class	Second class	Third class				Cattle	Calves	Sheep	Pigs	
1922 Total	69	10,113	676	11,889	5,256	7,580					8,366
Originating on line	69	10,113	676	6,104	–	300	2,046	60	3,586	2,674	8,366
1923 Total	177	32,369	1,154	10,961	5,400	5,417					9,620
Originating on line	43	16,492	519	5,931	–	580	3,208	62	4,501	1,849	9,620
1924 Total	153	32,957	1,250	11,833	5,273	5,960					18,300
Originating on line	46	17,075	727	6,164	–	327	3,062	40	7,338	3,918	13,640
1925 Total	84	27,188	903	12,203	5,099	5,899					16,665
Originating on line	24	14,573	550	5,840	–	238	3,478	48	7,549	3,586	14,661

Table 6·43 North Sunderland Railway: expenses and profit, 1898–1912

Year	Mntce of way (£)	Loco power (£)	Stock repairs (£)	Traffic expenses (£)	General charges (£)	Rates and taxes (£)	Total expenses (£)	Total revenue (£)	Profit (£)	%
1898		175		123	35	6	339	387	48	
1899	118	451	6	258	131	21	1,038	1,436	398	72
1900	170	487	16	272	123	20	1,134	1,640	506	69
1901	147	498	3	288	128	13	1,079	1,652	573	65
1902	295	469	5	307	122	13	1,215	1,783	568	68
1903	202	622	16	322	106	12	1,286	1,885	599	68
1904	177	439		299	125	11	1,051	1,761	710	60
1905	165	372	13	296	114	15	975	1,681	706	58
1906	196	553	8	311	107	16	1,196	1,704	568	68
1907	210	360	77	312	95	22	1,081	1,634	553	66
1908	172	354	4	325	89	17	974	1,557	583	63
1909	162	470	5	329	86	23	1,088	1,851	763	59
1910	186	385	9	345	80	29	1,046	2,262	1,216	46
1911	163	350	105	352	85	59	1,126	2,173	1,047	52
1912	172	354	77	355	108	38	1,106	1,982	876	56

Table 6·44 North Sunderland Railway: traffic and revenue, 1898–1923

Year	No. of passengers				Min. (tons)	Merch. (tons)	Train miles	Revenue (£) Passengers						Mail	Merch.	Live-stock	Min.	Total goods	Grand total
	1	2	3	Total				1	2	3	S	Total	Lge						
1898	25	476	166	667	658	2,126	4,480	2	14	2		18	96		185	4	33	222	387
1899	528	14,109	3,153	17,790	2,558	4,069	16,436	24	423	49	1	497	187	4	510	11	97	618	1,436
1900	665	16,129	2,640	19,434	2,351	6,941	17,236	29	489	41	6	565	234	29	544	18	117	679	1,640
1901	700	17,004	2,947	20,711	4,246	3,707	17,736	34	520	41	4	599	274	20	389	12	218	619	1,652
1902	1,034	24,369	3,501	28,904	5,494	4,336	18,921	36	551	48	10	645	256	20	433	12	282	727	1,783
1903	1,047	19,898	4,932	25,877	4,156	4,180	19,848	52	636	57	5	750	304	20	434	16	212	662	1,885
1904	949	17,555	3,658	22,162	4,066	3,807	18,362	40	580	44	9	673	309	16	388	14	207	609	1,761
1905	1,000	19,478	3,317	23,795	4,970	3,960	17,337	34	476	36	14	560	311	15	372	13	254	639	1,681
1906	846	21,611	3,185	25,642	4,314	4,380	17,185	29	498	34	16	577	337	15	439	14	219	672	1,764
1907	763	21,835	2,639	25,237	3,765	4,162	16,848	25	511	27	12	575	281	15	468	15	131	614	1,634
1908	667	18,302	3,434	22,403	2,829	3,137	16,817	27	548	57	19	651	252	15	335	16	142	493	1,557
1909	758	19,299	3,956	24,103	4,128	3,473	17,114	31	622	41	20	714	328	16	356	15	208	579	1,851
1910	623	19,166	3,059	22,848	10,836	4,065	17,916	26	620	40	32	718	339	20	399	16	567	982	2,262
1911	564	16,984	2,913	20,461	10,529	4,074	18,035	23	543	39	41	646	358	20	447	16	529	992	2,173
1912	464	17,138	3,144	20,746	7,887	3,656	16,801	20	533	44	46	643	362	20	371	15	390	776	1,982
1921	106	8,199	1,795	10,100		1,389	18,382												
1922								9	857	38		1,021		35				1,086	2,917
1923	235	23,872	2,314	26,351	2,414[a] 2,817[b]	3,096													
1923[c]	77	7,756	1,938	9,771	112	1,388													

[a] coal; [b] Other minerals; [c] Originating on line

Table 6·45 North Sunderland Railway: summary of receipts and expenditure, 1922–39

Year	Traffic receipts (£)	Expenditure (£)	Profit/loss on year's operation (£)
1922	2,916	2,181	751
1923	2,675	2,539	114
1924	2,550	2,335	278
1925	2,409	2,501	- 47
1926	2,025	2,522	-444
1927	1,831	2,204	-273
1928	1,423	2,070	-512
1929	1,518	1,981	-356
1930	1,375	1,943	-542
1931	1,249	1,864	-653
1932	1,157	1,409	-407
1933	1,240	1,123	-122
1934	1,274	1,548	-537
1935	1,781	1,681	-196
1936	1,372	1,631	-574
1937	1,609	1,635	-223
1938	1,568	1,628	-288
1939	1,608	1,606	-237

Notes

1 Suffolk Record Office 150/2/5/77-B.
2 Suffolk Record Office 150/10/14-1.
3 *Halesworth Times*, 28 February 1876.
4 It was not unanimous. One correspondent to the *Halesworth Times*, 29 June 1875, applauded Southwold's isolation which ensured that there were 'no cockney tourists who make so many seaside towns objectionable'. The quotation at the end of the paragraph also appeared in the *Halesworth Times*, on 27 June 1876.
5 A. R. Taylor and E. S. Tonks, *The Southwold Railway*, pp. 21, 22.
6 A. Barrett-Jenkins, *Memories of the Southwold Railway*, pp. 20, 21.
7 See p. 60.
8 RC 1896. W. M. Acworth claimed that in 1893 the Southwold Railway's gross receipts were £3,658 but the additional value of the traffic for the GER at Halesworth was £12,123. Q 30922.
9 Kelly's Directory, 1893.
10 RC 1896, Q 30908.

11   K. E. Hartley, *The Easingwold Railway*, pp. 8, 10.
12   PRO, RAIL 167–4.
13   PRO, RAIL 167–5.
14   Cole, *op. cit.* provides a detailed review of the line, pp. 266–72.
15   *Ibid.*, p. 264
16   RC 1896, Q 30990.
17   *Ibid.*, Q 31001.
18   Hartley, *op. cit.*, p. 41.
19   PRO, RAIL 167–70.
20   Hartley, *op. cit.*, p. 30.
21   *Ibid.*, p. 32.
22   E. A. Pratt, *The Transition in Agriculture*, pp. 184–8.
23   PRO, RAIL 533–22.
24   *Ibid.*
25   PRO, MT 58–20.
26   *Alnwick and County Gazette*, 19 March 1898.
27   *Ibid.*
28   *Ibid.*, 6 August 1898.
29   PRO, RAIL 533–20.
30   PRO, RAIL 533–82
31   Railway Returns, 1923.
32   PRO, RAIL 533–83.
33   PRO, RAIL 533–51.
34   PRO, RAIL 533–73.
35   PRO, RAIL 533–23.
36   PRO, RAIL 533–51.
37   PRO, RAIL 533–49.
38   PRO, RAIL 533–25, 12 November 1931.
39   PRO, RAIL 533–53, 26 July 1939.
40   *Ibid.*, 7 August 1939.
41   PRO, RAIL 533–76.
42   PRO, RAIL 533–51, and 533–53.
43   PRO, RAIL 533–68, 24 February 1947.
44   PRO, RAIL 533–83.
45   PRO, RAIL 533–51.
46   PRO, RAIL 533–53.
47   PRO, RAIL 533–73.
48   A. Wright, *The North Sunderland Railway*, p. 44.
49   *The Railway Magazine*, LVI (1925), claimed it was the first passenger steam tramway.
50   S. H. Pearce-Higgins, *The Wantage Tramway*, p. 7.
51   J. K. Rodwell, 'Agricultural tramways', *Proceedings of the West Suffolk Chamber of Agriculture*, 8 March 1882, p. 5.
52   *Ibid.*, p. 7.

53 PRO, RAIL 1053–212, Street and Road Tramway Returns, 1883.

54 Pearce-Higgins, *op. cit.*, p. 52.

55 R. Wilkinson, 'Remembering Wantage's successful tramway', *Berks and Bucks. Countryside*, XVI (1975), pp. 17.

56 Pearce-Higgins, *op. cit.*, p. 138.

57 Wilkinson, *op. cit.*

7

Road competition and the decline of light railways?

In 1896, the year the Light Railways Act became law, Parliament also passed the Locomotives on Highways Act.[1] This repealed the red flag legislation which had required that any locomotive travelling on the common road should be preceded by a man walking 20 yards in front bearing a red flag. Now 'light locomotives' were allowed on to the highways provided they did not exceed 12 miles per hour. The Act was expected to have profound implications for rural areas and country railways. Henry Chaplin,[2] speaking during the second reading debate, suggested that this freedom being offered to road locomotives would push down fares, threaten light railways and provide cheaper transport for agriculturalists.[3] The Select Committee on Traction Engines on Roads (1896) thought road locomotives 'are of great benefit . . . to the agriculturalist . . . They are especially useful in districts where railway communication is not good.'[4]

The British Daimler Motor Company was founded also in 1896, but it was steam traction that the new legistlation was intended to benefit. The idea of motor cars and lorries was still not taken very seriously[5] whereas people 'had no doubt that steam would continue to dominate'.[6] In 1895 there were some 8,000 road traction engines operating[7] and contemporary steam road vehicles were capable of travelling at the rate of a mile in $5\frac{1}{4}$ minutes 'when time was precious'.[8] The cost of working was estimated at 2*d* per ton mile and a 24 h.p. compound Fowler of 10 tons cost £550. Steam-powered road transport took advantage of its new freedom to produce lighter, faster, more powerful and more efficient road locomotives and steam lorries during the next two to three decades, which kept steam very much alive on the roads. Indeed, one of the other debates in the transport world in the early 1920s was whether steam or petrol lorries were the cheaper and more efficient.

In his presidential address to the Institution of Automobile Engineers, which he entitled 'Economy in Road Transportation', Thomas Clarkson stated bluntly: 'it is to the commercial motor vehicle operating upon common roads that we must look for the solution of inland transport problems'. His choice of motive power was steam not petrol and he commented unfavourably on the latter in respect of its efficiency and origins, and he produced figures to establish that a coke lorry cost 3s 10d a day to operate as opposed to the petrol lorry at 10s 0d.[9]

A contemporary advertisement for the Sentinel steam wagon claimed that it was 'the cheapest and best method of transport in the world' and was far superior to the petrol lorry with loads of 3 tons and upwards. A Sentinel could transport 6 tons over 30 miles at a cost of 2d per mile; petrol 5d per mile; horse 18d per mile. On a weekly run to 400 miles the Sentinel would save £15 compared with the internal combustion engine. An apparently less partisan view was expressed in an article in *Modern Transport*[10] on comparative haulage costs over 16,000 miles annually and assuming capital costs of £1,100 for a petrol wagon and £1,000 for steam. The figures are set out in Table 7.1. Wherever lay the truth in the battle between petrol and steam, the latter became increasingly associated only

Table 7·1   Costs of steam and petrol lorries, 1923

	Petrol	*Steam*
Capital cost	£1,100	£1,000
Operating costs	(d) per mile	(d) per mile
Tyres	1·80	1.80
Interest (5 per cent)	0·83	0·75
Depreciation (20 per cent)	3·30	3·00
Lubricants	0·40	0·24
Repairs materials wages	0·51	1·00
Crews' wages	6·00	6·75
Insurance	1·05	1·05
Fuel	3·00	2·50[a]
	16·89	17·09

[a] It is a pity that the type of fuel was not specified for a steam wagon pulling 9 or 10 tons would travel 10 miles per cwt of gas coke but double that with good Welsh steam coal.

Source: Modern Transport, 2 December 1923.

with heavy haulage and remote from the light van and 1-ton lorry sector, where the bulk of commercial vehicles was to be found.

Thus, it was motor transport in all its forms which came to dominate on the roads and provide effective competition for rural railways. Motor lorries were cheaper to buy and easier to operate than steam, decisive points for the farmers and small country traders who needed one or two vehicles at most. Motor lorries were still few up to 1914, but after the war their numbers grew rapidly. The government sold its 60,000 surplus War Department lorries cheaply, and soon the price of new vehicles also came down. The price of the Model T Ford chassis which had been the basis of many War Department vehicles fell from £250 to £85 in 1924. The number of goods vehicles on the roads increased from 62,000 in 1919 to 488,000 in 1939. It was the same story with motor cars. The price of a Morris Cowley, £465 in February 1921, came down to 285 gns in November, and fell further to £225 by the end of the following year.[11] Mass production techniques further reduced the price of all cars and running costs fell to match. By 1939 2 million cars were on the roads.

Expertise in the application of motor vehicles to commercial uses at the expense of the railways developed rapidly. J. L. Clewes, transport manager for Liptons, blamed increased rates and poor service for his company's decision to turn to road transport, and deliveries were made from London to Brighton, a return distance of 123 miles, at an inclusive cost of 32s 6d and 42s 0d respectively. Their fourteen 4-ton lorries distributed 60 tons of food a day with an average run of 70 miles, but the routes had recently extended to Bristol and Sheffield following a recent rail strike. An additional advantage, Liptons felt, had been the reduction in pilfering and damage, for the latter costs totalled £15,000 annually. It was not uncommon for 200–300 eggs to to smashed in a case of 1,200, a loss to Liptons of £5 for the railways carried at owners' risk. In the thousands of cases recently sent by road there had been no breakages.[12]

The rapid development of road transport took a great many by surprise. In 1916 the Selborne Committee, which was a subcommittee of the Committee for Reconstruction and whose task it was to investigate the means of increasing domestic food production, appreciated the growing importance of road transport but still expected to see an expansion of the rural railway and tramway networks. In 1919 F. H. Padwick, President of the National Farmers Union (NFU), argued that light railways had an important part to play and road transport should be regarded as a feeder for the railways.[13] Also in 1919 Professor R. W. Scott reiterated the belief that road transport should be subordinate to the railways and went on to argue that farmers who had invested in light Ford vans were using their capital unwisely for they ran lightly loaded and were so numerous as to damage the roads.[14] The Light Railway Investigation Committee in 1921 concluded that road competition was not a serious problem and that no light railways were in danger of having to close.[15] Light railways were still seriously canvassed into the early 1920s, indeed they were the subject of some revived interest as a means of boosting the rural economy.

Quite considerable numbers of light railways were proposed, especially in the eastern counties of England and in the Highlands of Scotland. Typical was the scheme for the Essex Light Railway & Property Company for a railway of $13\frac{1}{4}$ miles between Chipping Ongar and Dunmow; application was made for a Light Railway Order in 1920. Both national and local government gave serious consideration to the extension of light railways. Holland County Council in 1920–21, for example, promised £423,000 and the neighbouring authorities smaller sums to make up the £550,000 reckoned to be needed to build a network of light railways in the fens.[16] The Ministry of Transport assured the local authorities of its support. Economic recession and cuts in spending caused both national and local government to retract. The fenlands railways, and the others in eastern England, were dropped. One or two new light railways in other parts of the country were actually built, however: the Ashover Light Railway in Derbyshire; and the North Devon & Cornwall Light Railway — both date from 1925. The Totton Hythe & Fawley Light Railway revived a scheme for which the London & South Western had been granted a light Railway Order in 1903, but had allowed to lapse. This, too, was opened in 1925. No doubt they hoped to keep road competition at bay as the Lampeter & Aberaeron Railway had done earlier. In Cardiganshire the rail journey was quicker by twenty minutes than by road and the bus service was suspended. This had been a railway bus service and ironically the railways themselves saw the advantages of road transport for passengers and goods deliveries, and thus their practice was more perceptive than the prophesies of many railway apologists.

Railway motor road services might be said to date from 1903 with the introduction by the GWR of a regular bus service between Helston and the Lizard in Cornwall, where the railway company 'had been in some danger of having to build a costly light railway'.[17] The service was suspended briefly in 1904 because of the poor state of the roads, but survived to be handed over to the Western National Omnibus Company in 1929.

The route to the Lizard was the first bus service operated by the GWR, which came to have considerable enthusiasm for buses in country districts: 'We have been considering the cases in which independent persons run motor services along the roads to our railway stations', the GWR told its shareholders in 1903. 'We do not see why we should not feed our own railways ourselves by means of motor cars. We have therefore given instructions for the purchase of five motors which will each carry twenty-two passengers.' By 1913 the company owned ninety-nine petrol passenger vehicles, four times as many as were in its horse-drawn fleet.[18] The services which complemented (or competed with) rural railways had spread from Helston in Cornwall to Moretonhampstead in Devon, Aberaeron in Cardiganshire and Beaconsfield in Buckinghamshire. There was even a service from Aberystwyth up Plynlimmon using a Morris Commercial coach with chains on its rear wheels. Several other railway companies started their own bus services. The NER and the GER had been among the principal companies running buses before 1914, though none had so extensive a business, or such profitable results, as the GWR. The GER, for one, withdrew most of its bus services in 1913. There were some breakdowns, and much criticism of damage to roads, but the buses provided a generally reliable service. The three GWR buses centred on Aberaeron, 20 h.p. Milnes-Daimlers covered 19,987 miles in the first six months of 1907 with only one breakdown.[19]

The railway companies, bus services were intended to be subordinate to their train services but despite some early losses, probably as a result of mechanical failures and unsuitable roads, the experience gained proved invaluable both to the railways and to their rival operators. By the 1920s the advantages had swung away from train services, and rural bus services were proving more convenient. Buses were more robust, operators more knowledgeable (both perhaps a product of experience gained during the war), and fares were coming down.[20]

The same was true of goods traffic. Whatever the relative merits of steam or petrol lorries, and indeed of electrically powered vehicles which provided an additional choice for delivery work, the operating costs of road vehicles generally (Table 7.1) were less than those of most light railways on which costs per mile ranged between 25*d* and 35*d*. It was the light railways' misfortune that the costs of road transport were falling just when their own costs were rising (Table 7.2).

The greatest disparity was in the bill for labour. For the railways, wages had risen by the 1920s partly as a result of government control of the railways during the war, and a successful strike by railwaymen in 1919

Table 7·2 United Kingdom railways relative operating costs, 1919–21[21]

	1913 = 100			
Year	Wages (drivers)	Wages (porters)	Wages (gangers)	Coal per ton at Pithead
1919	108	150	122	158
1920	143	227	185	240
1921	123	191	156	158

which resulted in a basic 51s a week. All railways were affected by this increase, but the burden was greater for light railways. The eight-hour day and reduction in split-shift working hit particularly those independent companies operating with minimal staff. The only response was payment of overtime or employment of superfluous staff for whom the infrequent train services common on such lines produced enforced idleness. The problem was further exacerbated for light railways by the gradual elimination of mixed duties: station work, for example, was intermittent on rural railways with little responsibility and no great skill involved and any attempt to classify the duties and allocate staff to a 'grade' was inappropriate. In such circumstances it was necessary for light railway practices to be divorced from the main line example (see Chapter 5, p. 114). Meanwhile, there had been no state intervention in the road passenger transport business, and wages for employees of bus companies had not risen to the same extent. But light railways suffered from a number of other disadvantages in dealing with competition from the roads: they were short, slow, indirect and dear.

Light railways on the whole were short. Lorries could compete with rail freight up to a distance of 75 miles and further if a return load was available. Few light railways exceeded 20 miles in length: the Kent & East Sussex Railway, at 23 miles long, and the Shropshire & Montgomeryshire, at nearly 25 miles long, were among the exceptions. Many, including the Vale of Rheidol Railway, the Southwold Railway and the Cleobury Mortimer & Ditton Priors Railway, were around 10 miles in length and some, among them the Wantage Tramway, the Easingwold Railway and the Wisbech & Upwell Tramway, were less than 5 miles. Since much of the general goods traffic of country railways consisted of small loads of agricultural produce, the costs of unloading from farm wagon into light railway train, then transferring after a few miles to a main line train made the alternative of sending a lorry direct from farm to market attractive. For this type of traffic, over distances as small as these, the arguments which had raged about the advantages of standard gauge over narrow gauge in saving the expense of transhipment became quite academic.[22]

Despite the fact that light railways were short they often offered an indirect route through their territory. This was partly because, in order to avoid heavy engineering works, country railways tended to follow the lie of the land, and in so doing frequently meandered round villages rather than went through them. There were numerous examples of stations on light railways, indeed on all rural railways, which were at a considerable distance from the villages they were meant to serve. The three intermediate stations on the Basingstoke & Alton Railway, Cliddesdon, Herriard, and Bentworth & Lasham, were respectively $1\frac{1}{2}$, 1 and 2 miles from the villages they served. Silian station on the Lampeter & Aberaeron was 2 miles from its village. The Tanat Valley Railway advertised two stations to serve Llanrhaiadr Mochnant, each of them $1\frac{1}{4}$ miles from the village. These are distances of villages from their named stations: much greater were the distances between the railway stations and other villages and towns they served. Aspall & Thorndon was the station on the Mid Suffolk advertised as serving the town of Debenham, well over 2 miles away. Newquay, in Cardiganshire, remained some 8 miles from the light railway which it was hoped would serve it (see Chapter 5). Some of the indirectness of light railway routes may be put down to bad planning, although this is a statement made with hindsight.

It is certain, though, that a number of rural railways ran in the wrong direction, a point made all too obvious with the introduction of bus services. Southwold's railway ran inland to connect with the GER at Halesworth: by 1904 Lowestoft further up the coast from Southwold had grown to become the natural centre for the area. The introduction by the GER of one of its first bus services between Southwold and Lowestoft effectively drained the Southwold Railway of much of its local traffic. In the same year the London & South Western Railway (LSWR) linked Chagford and Exeter by bus. How many Chagfordians then travelled to Exeter by way of bus to Moretonhampstead and then via Newton Abbot on the GWR. The East Gloucestershire Railway linked Fairford with Witney some 14 miles distant and thence to Oxford. But Cirencester, 8 miles in the other direction, was the natural centre for the area. Such railways were therefore often failing in one of their main objectives of filling gaps in the rural transport. They were not getting closer to the farms and villages and often they were not going where people wanted to go: therefore people turned to lorries and buses which did. On one light railway, that between Bentley and Bordon in Hampshire, there were no intermediate stations because it was felt that they might interfere with the requirements of the War Office, for whom the line was built. Graciously, the LSWR acknowledged that passengers could get on or off at any level crossing.[23]

Light railways had happily accepted their own speed limitations, secure, so they felt, in their monopoly of passenger traffic. In 1910 the Southwold Railway averaged nearly 15 m.p.h. on its 9-mile journey, the Culm Valley Railway managed around 12 m.p.h., while the Mid Suffolk Railway and the Golden Valley Railway were faster at nearly 20 m.p.h. Such speeds were unexciting but were immensely attractive if the alternatives were to walk or use the cheap, but ambling carrier's wagon. By 1938 the Southwold had closed, the Culm Valley maintained its speed, while the Golden Valley and Mid Suffolk Railways were actually a little slower, in the face of competition from buses travelling no more slowly, often more quickly than the train. Light railways could be criticised for running an infrequent service, although in thinly populated districts it may be said quite fairly that the provision of extra trains would not have brought in any additional net revenue. Indeed, it appeared to be a generally held policy that the most effective means of improving economy of operation was to reduce rather than increase train mileage. A few of the shorter lines such as the Easingwold Railway were able to offer a relatively intensive service with nine trains daily in 1910 and seven in 1938, while the Teign Valley Railway provided eight and seven trains daily respectively. More sparse services were provided in 1938 by the Mid Suffolk Railway with three trains, while the Devon & North Cornwall Railway, and the Golden Valley Railway ran only two trains daily.

A major drawback for light railways was that their fares and rates of carriage were high.[24] Acworth and Cole had argued that this was perfectly reasonable, since the light railways were working in areas where costs were higher, journeys were short and the independent companies could not cross-subsidise little used services as the larger railways could. Acworth argued that light railway companies should have a much freer hand in rate-fixing than the main line companies, balancing what the farmer could pay and what the railway could afford. However, he was certain that the rates would not be low.[25] The situation was no different in the 1920s, for the report of the Light Railway Investigation Committee proposed that a basis for adequate funding of light railways in respect of rates would be to assume that every light railway mile was the equivalent of $1\frac{1}{4}$ main line miles. With hindsight it is reasonable to assume that such a formal increase in charges would have made rural railways even less competitive with road transport. After all, why should passengers pay fares higher than those on the main line to ride in carriages of considerably lower quality and which were hardly more comfortable, if at all, than the bus? Indeed, the rural bus, probably no more indirect than its rail competition, undoubtedly gave a greater sense of speed, and certainly did not cause frustration and delay by pausing to shunt trucks at wayside stations or halts.

The light railways' attempts to counter road competition

The light railway operators cast around for cost-cutting measures. Train mileage was reduced where possible. The train mileage of the Southwold Railway fell from 31,258 in 1910 to 27,915 in 1924, while the Easingwold Railway reduced its mileage from 13,854 to 9,908 over the same period. Reduced mileage did not necessarily require curtailed services but as often as not they were cut. Reduced passenger services resulted in a saving of coal, petrol and oil of £300 per annum according to the reckoning of the Kent & East Sussex Railway. Maintenance was reduced to a miniumum at the expense of reliability; stock was not replaced, let alone updated, lending light railways their rather old-fashioned appearance which, although charming, did not suggest a transport service operating at peak efficiency.

Light railways were not behind-hand at imposing wage reductions as one economy measure. In November 1930 the Kent & East Sussex Railway cut wages to produce, it was claimed, an annual saving of £180 (see Table 7.3).[26] The Southwold Railway, facing sudden demise cut both

Table 7.3 Kent & East Sussex Railway:
wage reductions, 1930

Existing weekly wage	Reduction (%)
Under £2	$2\frac{1}{2}$
£2 – £3	5
£3 – £4	$7\frac{1}{2}$
Over £4	10

wages and fares. Wage and salary cuts had been accepted in 1921, 1923 and 1925, and there were further cuts in December 1928, but to no avail.[17]

The second way to reduce the size of the labour bill was to cut the number of staff. The smaller the railway, the more difficult this was to achieve. Light railways, rarely profligate, had always looked for economies in manning, so that by the 1920s and 1930s there was little room for manoeuvre. The Rye & Camber Tramway could hardly expect to better the 50 per cent reduction in its operating staff, from two men to one man. As early as 1900 the GWR found there was little hope of economising on labour on the Lambourn Valley Railway. The line was already being managed with considerable flexibility. At each of the seven wayside stopping places a lad was employed to do everthing, including cleaning, delivery of parcels and superintending goods traffic. At Lambourn tickets were issued by two girls who also dealt with correspondence. Mr Brain, the station master, assisted in the yard, 'putting his shoulder to horse boxes and trucks as required'. The station master himself travelled by train to Newbury to bank his cash, and was known on occasions to have halted the train on the running line at one of the halts, and with the assistance of a lad to have pushed an empty truck from a siding to attach to the train.[28]

The financial problems of light railways became such that they were reduced to haggling over bills in much the same way as they had done with landowners and contractors when the lines were built. The Kent & East Sussex Railway attempted to defer payments to its auditors, Peat Marwick Mitchell and Co., by offering them 4 per cent debenture stock rather than cash payment: this was rejected by the auditors, who offered to accept payment in instalments instead. In 1933 Peat Marwick reduced their charges for secretarial and audit duties from £75 to £50 and from 50 gns to 40 gns respectively.

One course open to minor railways was some form of co-operation or amalgamation. The advantages offered by co-operative working included a reduction in management costs; interchangeability of rolling stock, gauge permitting; bulk purchasing; centralised workshops; and through running. Light railways built by the main line companies, of course, possessed these advantages from the outset. W.H. Cole in his study of the Wisbech & Upwell Tramway comments that 'no charge was made for direction, management and supervision'.[29] When the GWR assumed ownership of the Vale of Rheidol Railway, it provided new locomotives and, later, entirely refurbished the rolling stock. The shaky finances of the Lampeter & Aberaeron Railway would scarcely have survived the need to supply and maintain locomotives for the line, and the company was therefore fortunate to be able to call upon some elderly Swindon products.

Mergers and working arrangements were, for the most part, not concluded specifically to help meet the threat of competition but rather the financial shortcomings in the early years of the light railways' existence. The farmers and landowners who successfully promoted the Wrington Vale Railway quickly concluded that they had neither the capital nor the expertise to operate the line independently, and they therefore sold up to the GWR in 1901 only two years after the line opened. The same had happened earlier to the Culm Valley Light Railway, opened in 1876 and purchased by the GWR in 1880, the reason being not the competition from road transport but the fact that agricultural traffic was insufficient to support the line's independence. Most light railways not operated by a larger company were omitted from the grouping of railways in 1923, and they generally remained independent, some not even included in nationalisation in 1948. Increasing competition from the roads did, however, tend to force some into closer association with their larger neighbours. As has been seen, the North Sunderland Railway became so dependent on the LNER, and later British Railways' North Eastern Region, as to be effectively a subsidiary company, and the decision on whether the line should be retained or closed was not entirely one for the North Sunderland Board to make.

Another possibility was the amalgamation of two or more small companies, something which was made difficult by the fact that the separate lines had little in common except that they all ran trains. They were far apart from each other and often of different gauge so that there was no prospect of constructing a network of light railways as existed in other countries. The nearest thing to such a network was the association in the 1930s between the Ffestiniog Railway and the joint North Wales Narrow Gauge and Welsh Highland Railway. These were neighbouring lines, connected at Portmadoc. The Ffestiniog was a pioneering railway, authorised in 1836 well before light railways were thought of, whereas the North Wales Narrow Gauge and the Welsh Highland made use of the 1896 Act. However, none of the participants gained much from their closer association.

One light railway group was put together. This was Associated Railways, controlled by Colonel P. S. Stephens, who appeared to devote his entire life to constructing and operating a string of light railways.[30] The Stephens empire comprised a disparate collection of seven minor railways as far flung as the East Kent Railway, the Weston Clevedon & Portishead, and the Shropshire & Montgomeryshire Light Railway. The principle of the group was to offer the railways economies in the costs of management and central services. Much was achieved: management of the whole group was reckoned to cost no more than £800 per annum, and engineering and locomotive superintendence each cost only £350. There were plans for further grouped organisation but they ran up against problems: the question of compensation for the railway officers who would have to be dismissed, varied job specifications rendering co-ordination difficult; and the vast array of incompatible equipment on the different railways in the group, reaching even to such matters as the height of buffers above the rails — all of this making standardisation a long, drawn-out process indeed. There were attempts to standardise, for instance in the introduction of Ford petrol-engined railcars on three of the railways in the 1920s. Not least of the problems was that Colonel Stephens himself was difficult to get on with and unpopular, even though he was pouring a lot of his own money into his railways. The quirks of his management and the perennial shortage of money largely negated the efforts at group management. Far from presenting an efficient defence against road competition, the members of Associated Railways were characterised by a spirit of 'make do and mend'; almost the only thing they had in common was a dilapidated quaintness, appealing to the visitor but not to the local people trying to get to market. Even so, the principle of combined management was a sound one, and it may fairly be said that 'there should have been other Colonel Stephenses running other groups of utility built and cheaply run country railways'.[11] One further example of co-operative effort was the Association of Smaller Railway Companies, which sought to co-ordinate and represent the interests of small 'owning' companies whose lines were worked by main line companies (see Appendix C).

Economising on mileage and services, maintenance and wages, or merging with larger companies had limited impact on the fortunes of light railways. Meanwhile a number of technical innovations were put forward intended to make the operation of rural railways more economical, or to add an entirely new dimension to rural transport, fulfilling the aim of a transport system so flexible as to be able to serve individual farms. Many suffered from appearing as rather eccentric novelties, while capital costs, if less than for an ordinary light railway, were still higher than the purchase price of a lorry or a bus. Those involved in rural transport generally were not convinced by off-beat ideas and those new departures that were tried generally had some rails fixed firmly on the ground. Of the seven described briefly below only the miniature railway really made a mark on transport in this country, and that mainly in respect of private or pleasure lines.

Road cars for light railways

These were developed during the First World War and were essentially ordinary cars adapted to carry rail wheels in addition to their road wheels. Conversion took an hour and these vehicles also carried a form of turntable; two men could turn a car in three minutes. Some 150 were in use in France during the war.[32]

Agrails

The Minstry of Reconstruction published proposals for a series of rural tramways. These very basic tramways were considered preferable to roads because of the cost of improving rural roads and the fact that rail running costs were some 25 per cent cheaper than those for roads. 'Agrail' would require transhipment, but construction costs were two-fifths those of a standard gauge railway. If a proposed line was longer than 1 mile, then 'agrail' was preferable despite transhipment problems.[33]

Aerail ropeways

There were two types of these: monocable, in which a single cable supported and propelled the load; and biocable, with support and transport using separate ropes. Such ropeways could carry 300 tons an hour and were capable of operating over distances of 45 miles. It was argued that a ropeway moving 500 tons on a 2-mile line cost 7 18s 0d, with wages at £6 5s 0d being the largest element. Total repair costs over thirteen years stood at £85 9s 6d. Construction costs for ropeways were around £3,000 per mile.[34]

Road–rail system

Road freight required good roads and the payload of a lorry was fairly small; light railways had not lived up to expectations with standards and costs both too high. However, a road–rail system would combine the advantages of both; adhesion from the road where adhesion was high and the load on rail where resistance was low. Such a system was in service in Nigeria, with 26 miles of track on 2 ft gauge with a ruling gradient of one in twenty-five. Here the cost of contruction was £1,200 per mile. The Stronachie Distillery at Forgandenny in Perthshire operated such a system with a one in twelve gradient.[35] The driving wheels of the tractor would not be on rails but between or outside the track on stone, concrete, wood or earth. The greater adhesion would mean steeper gradients and lighter track. The tractor, as at the distillery, would be convertible to conventional roadwork merely by replacing the rail 'steering' bogie with road wheels. Rail weight could be reduced from 40 lb or 50 lb per yard to 16 lb per yard, while gradients and curves could be one in fifteen and 30 ft radius respectively instead of one in forty and 150 ft radius. Thus road–rail could actually go through producing areas.[36] Construction costs for such a form of transport would be £1,250 per mile compared with £5,000 per mile for a conventional metalled road.

Miniature railways

The keenest supporter of miniature railways was Sir Arthur Heywood. In 1896, in a letter to *The Times*,[37] he argued the case for narrow gauge feeder lines, emphasising the advantages to be derived from a gauge so strikingly different from standard gauge that its operators and users would be prevented from thinking in standard gauge terms: 'Narrow gauges exceeding 30 inches approximate so closely to a full size line as to forfeit, to a considerable extent, the advantages of either system.' He condemned the attitude of so many engineers who treated lines of less than 2 ft gauge as 'mere toys'. At his own home he had operated a 15-in. gauge line for many years, carrying thousands of passengers without accident, as many as 120 on a single train over gradients as steep as one in twenty. The goods traffic was carried in all weathers up a long gradient of one in eleven. In the same year, 1896, Sir Arthur had built for the Duke of Westminster a 15-in. gauge railway to connect Eaton Hall with the GWR 3 miles away at Balderton; branches to the estate workshops and brickyards took the total length of the line to 4½ miles. The cost of constructing this line was £4,928. An additional £965 was spent on equipping the line with a four-coupled locomotive weighing 3 tons in working order (cost £400), a bogie passenger coach and more than thirty goods wagons. Initial investment, therefore, came to a total of £5,893 or £1,309 per mile. The railway was designed to carry 6,000 tons of goods a year, and by 1905 the costs of doing this were put at 1s per ton mile. Working expenses for the first two years are detailed in table 7.4.

Despite the example of successful operation presented by Sir Arthur Heywood the very narrow gauge was not really taken seriously for public railways. A few were built, notably the Romney Hythe & Dymchurch, the Fairbourne, and the reconstructed Ravenglass & Eskdale Railway.

Table 7·4   Eaton Estate Railway: working expenses and performance, 1896–97

	1896			1897		
	£	s	d	£	s	d
Wages, driver and boy	115	3	4	115	12	0
Wages, platelayers	145	8	8	94	15	8
Locomotive coal	19	15	0	19	17	7
Oil, stores, sundries	8	1	10	9	7	1
	288	8	10	239	12	4
Material hauled (*tons*)		6,067			5,896	
Number of days in steam		225			207	

Some were empowered by Light Railway Order, but their importance lay more in the business of tourism than in dealing with the economic or social needs of rural areas.

Portable railways

The Decauville system provided an entirely portable railway network for individual farms.[38] The trackwork was prefabricated in 4 ft, 8 ft or 16ft sections, with a rail of 9 lb per foot. Gauge was normally 16 in. or 20 in. and it was claimed that one man could easily carry a 16 ft section of either gauge. The all-metal construction obviated the need for wooden sleepers, which were susceptible to rot, and the unitary method of construction required minimal ballasting. Fowler's of Leeds who built the system in England were so confident of its usefulness and capabilities that they offered the railway on a month's trial to clients, the only charge being the freight costs to and fro.[39] In 1860 16 in. gauge track cost 3s 6d per yard.

Monorail

The Caillet system of monorail, which was already in use in France, was seen as an attractive alternative to light railways for the movement of farm produce and light goods.[40] In 1910 the *Country Gentlemen's Association Estate Book* published an article on the benefits attendant upon the use of monorail.[41] The article concluded: 'of the advantages of a light railway to an estate there can be no question'. The major stumbling-block was the capital cost, and this was reduced by some 75 per cent if a monorail system was adopted. Such a monorail consisted of a single load-bearing rail of as little as 9 lb per yard weight, the 'truck' being balanced by a man or horse or wheel supporting a pole set at right angles to the truck. The system was so light that it could be laid on a temporary basis across fields, providing transport at one-sixth of the cost of horse transport at one-third of the time. To illustrate the point, an example was taken presupposing 3 miles of 'line' worked by horse, each truck to carry 2 tons and each car twelve passengers, and carrying up to 80 tons and 200 passengers daily (see Table 7.5). Despite the existence of a monorail line in Ireland and extensive provision at the Front during the First War where both the Caillet and the Lartigue systems were in operation, the latter using self-balancing panniers, the system did not appeal to farmers in England and Wales.

There was an evident unwillingness to invest in such radical and obscure solutions to the problems of rural transport, for they did not offer clear advantages over the conventional railway sufficient to meet competition from the roads. The fundamental differences between the forms of transport were rapidly becoming clear. The farmer might be prepared to invest in a Ford van, but then he would not expect to pay for repairs to the road to his farm gate. So it was with all: it was easy and

Table 7.5 Monorail costs

Construction	£
3 miles of Caillet monorail with points and ballast	600
Levelling, ballasting, laying	300
Two passenger cars	120
Four goods trucks	120
Four horses	160
Contingencies (including possible horse track)	700
	2,000
Working expenses per week	£
Interest and depreciation	2
Wages for two men	2
Keep for four horses	2
	6
Traffic needed to produce £1 per day[a]	s
Twenty passengers at 6d	10
Parcels	5
Goods	5

[a] Such a minimum traffic would, however, require only one man and two horses.

getting cheaper to buy a lorry, a bus or private car and leave the cost of the highway to be borne out of rates and taxes. Light railway companies, indeed all railways, were left searching for operating economies which might keep them in some way competitive with motor vehicles.

One widely canvassed economy was the railcar or rail motor. Several types were produced: steam rail motors, consisting of a small steam engine mounted into a bogie coach, were introduced in the years before the First World War; in the 1920s and 1930s came railcars, powered by petrol or diesel engine. Some of the main line railway companies carried out quite extensive experiments with rail motors with a view to introducing them on branch lines, including the light railways they operated. The GWR was early in the field and undertook extended experiments with steam rail motors in the Stroud valley in Gloucestershire, an area the railway considered to be particularly threatened by road transport. The experiment was the subject of a special General Manager's report in 1903[42] and the results seemed sufficiently encouraging for the company by 1910 to have instituted thirty-five separate rail motor services and 140 new 'halts'.[43] Advantages were felt to be greater acceleration, which would reduce journey time, easier handling at terminal stations, with no 'running round' or turning, and the increased possibility of more intermediate stops.

In the event the GWR railcars had a chequered history and the company achieved most of its objectives with auto-trains comprising a small locomotive and carriage so designed that the driver could operate the locomotive from a cab in the coach. Not only did this formation prove more reliable mechanically but it was also flexible in operating terms because it circumvented the railcars' weakness of being unable to pull supplementary coaches and wagons satisfactorily. Railcars continued to have attractions because they were cheap to operate and maintain. When the GWR looked at this question again in 1926 it was concluded that rail motors were cheaper to operate even than the auto-trains (table 7.6).[44] Petrol and diesel railcars offered yet further savings. Still, railcars lacked flexibility and power, however: 'a rail motor cannot work a goods train, is not adapted for shunting, and has difficulty in getting up steep gradients which are common on branches'.[45]

All the disadvantages remarked upon by the GWR were experienced when railcars were introduced on light railways, as they were both by the main line companies and by the independent railways. In consequence, railcars did not supplant the conventional operation of locomotive and coaches as perhaps might have been expected. The Lambourn Valley

Table 7·6   Locomotive running maintenance and renewal, costs per mile

	s	d
Steam engines (GWR as a whole)	I	I I
Steam engines (GWR subsidiary branch lines)	I	6¾
Auto-engines	I	5
Rail motors	I	4

Railway, while still independent, hired steam rail motors from the GWR at a cost of £420 in an attempt at economy. It was not an entirely successful experiment because the rail motors had difficulty coping with heavy trains. A similar experiment in 1936 by the GWR on the same line with a railcar specially designed for branch line work was also less than satisfactory, this time because the railcar could not shunt the mixed trains which were usual on this line.[46]

Even so, a number of light railways did persevere with railcars and were satisfied with the savings that could be achieved. The Derwent Valley Light Railway bought a Sentinel steam rail motor in 1925 which promised well. Locomotive running expenses in 1924 were £2,915 but after the introduction of the Sentinel were only £1,357 in 1925. This engine was capable of hauling three coaches weighing 42 tons and 150 passengers on a line with a ruling gradient of one in 150.[47] The Sentinel cost £1,400, but savings of 7d per train mile compared with the cost of hiring steam locomotives from the NER were expected to pay for it in eighteen months.[48] The Derwent Valley Railway also made use of petrol rail motors, Ford vans fitted with rail bodies to seat thirty-six people.[49] Insubstantial, even curious in appearance, being nothing more than two buses running back to back, these petrol railcars were used on a number of other light railways. Colonel Stephens was especially quick to take up the petrol railcar, buying Fords and some others designed more specifically for railway use, such as the Drewry rail motor built new for the Weston Clevedon & Portishead in 1922.

Light railways in decline

The Derwent Valley Railway's Sentinel and Ford railcars never had a chance to fulfil their promise, for passenger services on this line were withdrawn in 1926 and the Fords sold to the County Donegal railways. This was just one of a succession of closures that left the light railways of

England and Wales in a sorry state by 1939. Several lines had closed completely, among them the Southwold, the Leek & Manifold and the West Sussex Railway. More, like the Derwent Valley, suffered the loss of passenger services; the Goole & Marshland and the Wrington Vale were others in this situation. The Vale of Rheidol was unusual in losing its goods services, a portent, perhaps, of the future for other lines in holiday areas.

Those that remained open, in whole or in part, especially the independent companies, were almost invariably in a run-down condition. The Colonel Stephens railways epitomised this, for they had become curiosities, with their ramshackle collections of rolling stock, apparently held together by string and sticking plaster, while the trains running along such lines as these travelled slowly enough for passengers to pick fruit in season from hedges as they passed.

Rural railways which were too often characterised by short hauls, indirect routes, low speeds, infrequent services, stations distant from villages, possible transhipment, higher rates and small seasonal loads, and debilitated by a shortage of money were falling victim to competition from the roads. Road transport's attractions of speed and cheapness had the most immediate effect on the railways' passenger business. The bus and the private car had delivered the more damaging blow; freight and mineral traffic had a greater immunity because in all probability the journey over the light railway was but a small proportion of the distance to be travelled, and because for most goods traffic speed was less important.

Lines where the passenger traffic had been of most importance, such as the Southwold Railway, were among the first to close. For others passenger services could be dispensed with in an attempt to save money. The Welshpool & Llanfair Railway was typical in this respect. The GWR, which took over operation in 1923, started its bus service in 1925 in direct competition; although the service was reduced in frequency after initial enthusiasm, the railway passenger service was withdrawn in 1931[10] The threat to freight services was apparent from the early 1930s as lorries were becoming more efficient. The GWR opposed applications for extensions of their licences by local carriers, of whom there were nine at Welshpool and one at Llanfair Caereinion; increasingly loads were being carried direct to farmers, bypassing the railway and avoiding transhipment. The threat was temporarily lifted because of the wartime fuel shortage and the simultaneous boost to domestic agricultural production which the war created.[11] What was surprising after the war was not the line's closure but the fact that it survived until 1956.

The fact that the Southwold Railway, most certainly one of the most efficient light railways, closed as early as 1929 while others less well managed carried on demonstrates that there were no hard and fast rules determining the survival of these lines. All were suffering from road competition by the mid-1920s. Most were making losses and all had insufficient reserves to invest in modern railcars or other innovations which might have helped resist competition.

For each company there were special circumstances. The Southwold Railway's early demise was due partly to the fact that the line went in the wrong direction. People wanted to go to Lowestoft but the railway could take them only to Halesworth. The Ashover Light Railway, economically constructed with war surplus materials, was sufficiently indirect for its trains to start their journeys pointing away from Clay Cross, the eventual destination. Ironically, this service was so successful that it stimulated a competing bus service which siphoned off its passenger traffic; passenger services ended in 1936 although freight traffic survived until 1950. The Bideford Westward Ho & Appledore Railway linked the former place with the latter but by a circuitous route and had no connection with the LSWR line to Barnstaple. It was one of the most shortlived of railways, lasting only from 1901 to 1917. On the other hand, some equally circuitous lines survived to the period of nationalisation. The Easingwold Railway, which with the development of road transport no longer represented the best route to York, lost its passenger service in 1948; while the North Devon & Cornwall Railway, which hoped that the people of Hatherleigh would walk 2 miles to their station and then journey 20 miles by rail to Okehampton when the direct journey by road was a mere 7 miles, survived until 1965.

The Southwold Railway, one of the first light railways and one of the first to close, was entirely independent. Its cries for help to its main line neighbour brought no response. Light railways closely associated with a main line company survived longer. At the other end of the LNER system, the North Sunderland Railway was kept in operation almost entirely through the support of its larger neighbour. From this it might be supposed that light railways owned or operated by a major railway had a better chance of survival. For some, such as the Welshpool & Llanfair Railway, control by a main line company was a mixed blessing. The GWR saw no future in the passenger service on the line and quickly and ruthlessly put an end to it. However, the GWR was happy to support the Vale of Rheidol Railway as a tourist attraction, unlike the Southern Railway which closed the Lynton & Barnstaple, authorised as a conventional not a light railway, but a line for which one would have expected a similar tourist potential. On the other hand, it was the Southern Railway which continued to operate the old North Devon & Cornwall Railway, pursuing its meandering course through some extremely empty countryside.

What mattered most in the survival of light railways was usually the existence of managers or owners who were interested in the lines and who somehow managed to find the money to keep them going. This had been so from the beginning for many of these lines: 'Without the generosity and enthusiasm of the Chairman it seems doubtful whether the railway would ever have opened at all'.[12] This was said of Colonel Archer Houblon, the chairman of the Lambourn Valley Railway, who purchased the rolling stock with which the line opened in 1895, including the locomotives *Aelfred* and *Eahlswith* that cost him £1,350 each. Plates had to be carried on the stock testifying to Houblon's ownership. The Golden Valley Railway in Herefordshire depended, according to the line's historian, upon the 'unselfish labours of the country gentry'.[13] The best known individual benefactor of light railways, though, was Colonel Stephens, who dipped deep into his pocket to keep his railways running.[14] Light railways provoked devotion as much among railway staff as with the owners. A. C. Pain was engineer and then chairman of the Southwold Railway during its entire period of operation. His son became a director in 1929 and was still on the Board of Directors when the company was wound up in 1960. The District Goods Manager at Newcastle went well beyond the call of duty in his efforts on behalf of the North Sunderland Railway. People like these kept lines open for far longer than they should have been, if viewed only on the grounds of economics. Once their control was removed, final closure followed rapidly.

Two issues which excited a great deal of interest at the beginning of the light railway story, cost of construction and gauge, appear to have had little influence on which lines closed early and which survived. The Corris Railway and the Southwold, both narrow gauge, date from the same period but cost £1,800 and £8,500 per mile respectively to build. The Corris survived the Second World War to be hit by floods in 1948, but the Southwold closed in 1929. The North Sunderland, the Mid Suffolk and the Golden Valley Railway closed within a year or so of each other, but construction costs per mile were £6,200, £9,600 and £18,000 respectively.

The survivors

If it is impossible to discern a pattern in the closure of light railways, in the nature of things it is also impossible to enunciate principles to explain which lines remained open. W. J. K. Davies, in his study of light railways, notes that by 1939 only sixteen independent companies continued in existence and by the early 1960s only one, the Derwent Valley Railway, remained in being performing its original function.[15] Some eighty light railways had come into being by 1939, of which 65 per cent were open for traffic.[16] By 1960 some 33 per cent remained operational, but if the preservation lines are excluded the figure drops to 20 per cent.

Miniature railways did well: the Ravenglass & Eskdale, Fairbourne, and Romney Hythe & Dymchurch all survived on the strength of tourist traffic. Conventional narrow gauge, providing it was Welsh, continued to work, revived by tourist traffic, although in the case of the Vale of Rheidol Railway no such artificial aids were necessary for holiday-makers had always provided the bulk of the revenue: in 1912 over 80 per cent had come from this traffic. Welsh narrow gauge, both light railways and conventional, have survived in the shape of the Ffestiniog, Fairbourne Talyllyn, Vale of Rheidol and Snowdon Mountain Railway, with the Welshpool & Llanfair being resuscitated. There were closures: the Corris Railway, the Welsh Highland Railway and the Glyn Valley Tramway. In England no narrow gauge railway survived.

Standard gauge survival equally confounds definition. The Kent & East Sussex Railway, part of the Colonel Stephens group of light railways, was taken into the Southern Region in 1948 and closed only in 1961 immediately to be preserved. The North Devon & Cornwall remained open until 1965 and the Derwent Valley line near York until 1968. Services continued on a number of GWR-controlled light railways: the Lambourn Valley line closed in 1960, while the Culm Valley Railway, opened in 1876, ended life in 1963. Among the last to close was the Lampeter & Aberaeron branch, part of which was in use, serving agriculture, until 1973. The Totton Hythe & Fawley took on a new lease on life when an oil refinery was opened at Fawley in 1962.

But light railways did not die out. The rescue from closure of the Talyllyn Railway by a group of enthusiasts in 1950 was to lead to a busy preservation movement. Members of the Talyllyn's preservation society will proudly point out that theirs is not a light railway, having been built under its own Act of Parliament in 1865. As railway preservation got under way, the simplest and cheapest way to authorise the preserved lines was by means of a Light Railway Order. For lines bought from British

Railways the procedure was that British Railways obtained a Light Railway Order to be transferred subsequently to the new operating company. It was by this means that the Kent & East Sussex Railway regained its independence, although considerably reduced in length. Among others of this new breed of light railway were the Keighley & Worth Valley Railway (authorised 1967–68), the Torbay Steam Railway (1972) and the North Yorkshire Moors Railway (1971–75). These railways were created almost entirely with the railway enthusiast and the holiday-maker in mind, but there have been some other new light railways of more conventional organisation as British Railways followed the practice (observed on a number of occasions in this book) of transferring existing railways to operation under the 1896 Light Railways Act in order to save costs. The Central Wales line, a long, entirely rural route from Swansea to Shrewsbury, was the principal object of this policy. Yet a further twist to the story of the light railway came with the construction of the Docklands Light Railway to the east of London, and opened in 1987. It, however, had its own Act of Parliament, and trains more akin to trams.

With tourist lines, and the tram-like trains of the Docklands Light Railway, it is clear the light railway now is not what it once was; but, then, it has already been seen that the light railway was never quite what it was intended to be. Even so, squeezed in amongst the tourists and the enthusiasts, out mainly for the ride along the Severn Valley Railway, the Kent & East Sussex and the others, may be found a few housewives going to town for their shopping or some children going to school. In their journeys the spirit of the country light railway lives on.

Notes

1   Described as the 'Magna Charta [sic] of automobilism' by E. A. Pratt in *History of Inland Transport*, p. 476.

2   President of the Local Government Board which reduced the maximum speed for road vehicles from the 14 mph indicated in the Act to 12 mph.

3   Cole, *op. cit.*, p. 145.

4   *Ibid.*, p. 146.

5   Sir David Salomns, although a director of the South Eastern Railway, was an early motoring enthusiast, and President of the Self Propelled Traffic Association. He referred to motor cars as 'toys'. Quoted by Bagwell, *op. cit.*, p. 200.

6   Cole, *op. cit.*, p. 151.

7   Pratt, *op. cit.*

8 Cole, *op. cit.*

9 *Modern Transport,* 1 November 1919.

10 *Ibid.,* 2 December 1923.

11 Bagwell, *op. cit.,* p. 211.

12 *Modern Transport,* 26 June 1920 and 31 July 1920.

13 RC 1919, Q 18,799.

14 *Modern Transport,* 27 September 1919.

15 PRO, RAIL, 1054–5.

16 *Farmer and Stockbreeder,* 3 January 1921.

17 C. Klapper, *The Golden Age of Buses,* p. 43. The buses used had originally been owned by the Lynton & Barnstaple Railway.

18 PRO, RAIL, 266–107.

19 Lewis Cozens, *Aberaeron Transport,* p. 72.

20 With fares based on 1 ½*d* and 1 ¾*d* per mile for short and through routes respectively, and with good springs and tyres (then lasting about 22,000 miles) minimising damage to roads there had been 'a very marked and definite effect on the prosperity of small country towns', S. E. Smith, Manager of Bristol Tramway and Carriage Company in the discussion of S. E. Garcke's paper 'Road passenger transport in rural areas', *Modern Transport,* 9 December 1922.

21 Aldcroft, *op. cit.,* p. 38.

22 Even the most efficient narrow gauge system had to make use of transporter wagons or transhipment sheds with parallel narrow and standard gauge sidings arranged at different levels to facilitate loading and unloading. Such operations brought criticims of delay, damage and increased cost which were estimated to be between 1½*d* and 3*d* a ton.

23 *Alton Mail,* 8 February 1902.

24 There were exceptions. The third-class rate on the Wisbech & Upwell Tramway was only ½*d* per mile. Cole, *op. cit.,* p. 259.

25 RC 1896, Q 30,950-1.

26 PRO, RAIL, 332–2, 7 November 1930.

27 A. R. Taylor and E. S. Tonks, *The Southwold Railway,* pp. 36–9.

28 Memo to Lord Cawdor, August 1900. PRO, RAIL, 1057–2916.

29 Cole, *op. cit.,* p. 262.

30 The other railways associated with Stephens were the Paddock Wood & Hawkhurst, the Rother Valley (later Kent & East Sussex), the Hundred of Manhood & Selsey Tramway, the Ashover Light, the Rye and Camber Tramway, the Edge Hill Light, the North Devon & Cornwall Junction, the Plymouth Devonport & South Western Junction, the Sheppey Light, the Ffestiniog, and the Welsh Highland Railway. In addition, as engineer, he had obtained the Light Railway Commissioners' support for the Gower, the Hadlow, the Central Essex, the Kelvedon & Coggleshall, the Hadleigh & Long Melford, the Orpington & Tatsfield, and the Maidstone & Faversham Junction Railways. He was unsuccessful with the St Just Lands End & Great Western Junction, and the Long Melford Railways.

31 David St John Thomas, *The Country Railway*, p. 135.

32 *Modern Transport*, 19 April 1919. These may have been 'Crewe' Ford tractors, a LNWR conversion of a Model T chassis which were not supplied with a reverse gear for rail use because of their portable turntable. Only partially successful, they were disappointing on bad trackwork and their convertibility was rarely used. Railway records suggest there were 132 of them: WD records suggest 138. W. J. K. Davies, *Light Railways in the First World War*, pp. 161–2.

33 *Modern Transport*, 26 April 1919.

34 *Ibid.*, 21 July 1919.

35 *Ibid.*, 12 April 1924. The motive power was apparently provided by William Beardmore of the Dalmuir Works in Scotland but, unfortunately, no more details have come to light.

36 PRO, RAIL, 1007–429. I.R.C. 1925. Report by H. Marriott on light railways.

37 Quoted by Davies, *Light Railways*, pp. 201–2.

38 Paul Decauville, 1846–1922, son of Armand Decauville, a noted agriculturalist, who founded in 1869 the Société des Agriculteurs de France, designed 'matériel agricole perfectionné, et des petit chemins de fer à voie étroit destinés surtout aux grandes exploitations agricoles qui bientôt furent connus sous le nom de chemin de fer Decauville'. *Dictionnaire de Biographie Française*.

39 J. Fowler and Company, *Descriptive Catalogue*, III, to 1880.

40 *Light Railway and Tramway Journal*, 10 March 1904.

41 *The Country Gentlemen's Estate Book*, 1910, p. 336.

42 PRO, RAIL, 265–255.

43 PRO, RAIL, 1023–26. I.R.C. 1910. J. C. Inglis's Report on Rail Cars.

44 PRO, RAIL, 250–736. GWR Report on the Working of Branch Lines, March 1926.

45 *Ibid.*

46 M. R. C. Price, *The Lambourn Valley Railway*, pp. 14–19.

47 PRO, RAIL, 250–736. GWR Report on the working of branch lines, 1926.

48 *Railway Magazine*, August 1927.

49 *Locomotive*, 15 February 1929.

50 R. Cartwright and R. T. Russell, *The Welshpool & Llanfair Railway*, pp. 85–6.

51 *Ibid.*, pp. 95–6.

52 M. R. C. Price, *The Lambourn Valley Railway*, p. 11.

53 C. L. Mowatt, *The Golden Valley Railway*, p. ix.

54 Numerous other country railways authorised under their own Acts could be added to the list of those dependent on individuals to keep them open. Two examples in Wales were the Mawddwy Railway, which owed its various incarnations first to the Buckley family, then to Lieutenant-Colonel David Davies, grandson of the railway contractor, and the Manchester & Milford Railway, which was effectively carried for most of its independent life by the

Barrow family, who even after the line passed to the GWR continued to pay pensions to retired staff.

55 Davies, *op.cit.*, p. 59.

56 R. J. Kidner, *Light Railway Handbook*, lists more than eighty but includes preserved lines re-opened as light railways, and some mineral railways.

Conclusion

To ask whether nineteenth-century light railway legislation was a success is perhaps to miss the point. In the absence of a definition of light railways, many railways were built which were light in character but which owed nothing to any legislation directly connected with light railways. In 1900, to take a year at random, in terms of freight tonnage per mile of track, the Manchester & Milford Railway was less intensively used than the Easingwold, the North Sunderland or the Southwold. As far as passenger density was concerned the Manchester & Milford was on a par with the North Sunderland, but was completely overshadowed by the Southwold Railway and the Easingwold Railway. Thus 'light' railways emerged which were entirely unconnected with the specific light railway legislation.

Did the light railway legislation produce light railways? Railways did emerge, albeit slowly and, as we have seen, although 'light' in name many were not 'light' in fact, with capital charges and operating costs beyond what was advisable. Can the Light Railways Act be blamed for the failure of many schemes, including a large number which obtained a Light Railway Order, to give rise to a completed railway? Despite the inclusion within the Act of provision for central and local government support, private investment was quite simply unavailable. Most landlords would go no further than to give their land in return for shares, and perhaps to purchase a token number of additional shares. The small, local investor was a very rare bird. Of the Welsh farmer, for example, D. W. Howell observes 'they had an obsession with hoarding money for its own sake rather than investing it',' and it is clear that many such farmers feared that should an investment become known their landlords would seek to increase their rents. The 1896 Act encouraged a rash of promotions but local people were happy to have improved transport only on the understanding that they would not have to pay for it, either directly, or indirectly through the rates.

Did the Light Railways Act produce light railways? A criticism of the legislation was not that it failed to improve transport facilities in the shape of railway tracks and rolling stock, but that the majority of companies which took advantage of its terms were interested in building urban tramways rather than rural railways. There is no doubt that this was true, but equally there is little likelihood that the spread of urban tramways was at the expense of light railways in country areas. The money set aside by the Treasury for light railway building was not diverted into tramway building; it was quite simply not used.

Did the Light Railways Act help agriculture? As we have seen, the relationship between farmers and the railways was ambivalent. On the one hand, there was a resentment that railways appeared to be discriminating against the home farmer by carrying imported grain and meat at rates lower than those charged for home-grown produce. On the other, if the farmer wished to fight back, his transport costs must be cut and, further, if he contemplated moving into a different form of agriculture, perhaps liquid milk, or vegetables, the time taken in the transport of his produce must be reduced; railway extension would achieve both these objectives, and no doubt light railways did. To illustrate this point one need look no further than the Wisbech & Upwell Tramway and the Kelvedon line. But to suggest that this alone ended the depression in agriculture would be to ascribe too much importance to one factor. Whether the changes that occurred in agricultural activity were a cause or a consequence of the building of a light railway has not yet been completely established.[2] But was the railway relevent? Contemporaries were happy to see improved weather and — finally — a greater sense of co-operation among farmers as crucial factors in a recovery which was confirmed by the peculiar circumstances of the First World War.[3] Lord Ernle considered parliamentary action as trivial and, listing such legislation as the Market Gardeners Compensation Act of 1895 and the Agricultural Rates Act of 1896, ignored the Light Railways Act, clearly seeing it as playing no part in resolving agriculture's problems.[4]

Who, then, benefited from light railways? C. E. R. Sherington observed that much of the railway construction of the 1890s was unprofitable and believed that the Light Railways Act 'must have resulted in severe losses to the railway investor'.[5] However, heartless though it may seem, the campaign which culminated in the Light Railways Act had never expected that investors would become rich from their shares in light railways. The light railways that owed their origin to the Act, as was indeed the case with all rural light railways, did benefit the areas they served. The direct benefits to agriculture may be difficult to quantify but rural communities gained inestimably from improved transport. The hoteliers and apartment keepers at Southwold depended upon the railway; it was the railway that facilitated the expansion of the Seahouses fishing and fish processing industries. The railway diminished the isolation of Aberaeron and Newquay and put Easingwold into closer communion with York. The price of essential commodities such as coal fell and the supply problem was eased. Those people selling had larger and better markets opened up to them and those buying had a wider range of products from which to choose. For entertainment, too, the railway was of incalculable value: whether it was a day at the races from Seahouses or North Sunderland, or a Sunday School excursion from Aberaeron. Only when the motor car, lorry or bus had achieved a state of effectiveness after the First World War did the significance of the rural railway diminish. Paradoxically the main line railway companies, so few of which had taken advantage of the light railway legislation, continued to draw advantage from the 'contributary' value of their depressed neighbour.

As we have seen, it was road competition, coming as it did when problems of maintenance and renewal were beginning to bite, which brought the demise of some light railways or the reduction in services offered by others. When walking was often the only alternative, an average speed of under 20 miles per hour was satisfactory and the light railway was secure. Unfortunately, however, even a light railway in the best of condition (and few were by the 1920s) could offer little compared with a motor bus which was routed through villages and past houses, or a motor car which offered complete freedom of travel. For light railways which remained independent in the inter-war period the legacy of wartime control, the limitation on employees' hours, the increases in wages and the inevitable dilapidation of rolling stock and other equipment meant that this was a one-sided contest. Such railways serving widely dispersed communites and generating very limited traffic were perhaps worse placed than any other type of railway. Thus light railways, often including some of the most recently built, were among the first railway lines to succumb.

The Light Railways Act was intended to create better transport facilities in areas hard hit by the agricultural depression, to propagate the best features of those light railways already in being. This it did. It is probably true to say, however, that although such railways brought significant benefits locally, light railways cannot be said to have solved the problems of agriculture. Agriculture healed its own wounds and light railways which had been referred to slightingly as a 'ridiculous sticking plaster' remedy faced their own imminent demise.[6] However, although many light railway companies had a short working life (the Leek & Manifold Railway surviving for thirty-one years and the Lynton & Barnstaple for thirty-eight years), the age of preservation has resuscitated some of the original light railways and elsewhere seen the conversion of parts of the main line companies' systems to light railway operation. For a few, such as the Vale of Rheidol Railway and the Romney Hyth & Dymchurch Railway, this commitment to holiday-makers has not constituted a change of purpose; for the others, however, their strictly utilitarian purpose has given place to pleasure.

Notes

1   D. W. Howell, 'The impact of railways on agricultural development in nineteenth century Wales', *Welsh History Review*, VII (1974), p. 61.

2   Although railways brought Carmarthenshire farmers into close contact with the industrial centres of south and east Wales the response was poor. Fat cattle and dairy products were eschewed in favour of the continued production of store cattle. D. W. Howell, 'Rural society in nineteenth century Carmarthenshire', *Carmarthen Antiquary*, XIII (1977).

3   Interestingly, farmers had been urged to aggregate their consignments on many occasions before 1914 by the main line railway companies to secure reduced rates. For details of such actions by GWR see PRO 1057 3007. Other examples include the Ackenham Dairy Company, the Eastern Counties Dairy Institute also at Ackenham which was founded in 1888 and which by 1895 was training 1,000 students each year, and the Framlingham Egg Society launched in 1903.

4   Lord Ernle in P. J. Perry (ed.), *British Agriculture 1875–1914*, p. 9.

5   C. E. R. Sherington, *Hundred Years of Inland Transport 1830–1933*, p. 266.

6   *Railway Times*, 27 April 1895.

Appendix A
Light Railway Orders: the first ten years

This appendix presents a list of the Light Railway Orders issued following the Light Railways Act until the end of March 1908.

Name of order	Date of confirmation	Mileage authorised
	1897	
1. Basingstoke and Alton	9 Dec.	13
2. East and West Yorkshire Union	14 Dec.	$1\frac{3}{4}$
3. Potteries	22 Dec.	12
4. Hadlow	24 Dec.	$11\frac{1}{2}$
	1898	
5. Wrington Vale	18 March	7
6. Flamborough and Bridlington	21 March	7
7. Crowland and District	21 April	9
8. Lizard	21 April	$11\frac{1}{4}$
9. Lauder	30 June	10
10. Forsinard Melvich and Port Skerra	13 July	15
11. Gifford and Garvald	14 July	13
12. West Highland Railway (Loch Fyne)	14 July	$18\frac{3}{4}$
13. Bridlington and North Frodingham	14 July	$9\frac{1}{2}$
14. Caledonian Railway (Leadhills and Wanlockhead)	5 Aug.	$7\frac{3}{4}$
15. Carmyllie	6 Aug.	–
16. Great Western Railway (Pewsey and Salisbury)	6 Aug.	$20\frac{3}{4}$
17. West Hartlepool	11 Aug.	$2\frac{3}{4}$
18. Isle of Thanet	13 Aug.	$8\frac{3}{4}$
19. Dornoch	13 Aug.	$7\frac{1}{2}$
20. North Sunderland	13 Aug.	$1\frac{1}{2}$
21. Vale of Rheidol (Aberaeron Extension)	13 Aug.	$16\frac{1}{4}$
22. Goole and Marshland	16 Aug.	$13\frac{3}{4}$

Name of order	Date of confirmation	Mileage authorised
23. Pewsey and Salisbury (Devizes Branch)	31 Aug.	$\frac{1}{4}$
24. Amesbury and Military Camp (London and South Western Railway)	24 Sept.	$10\frac{3}{4}$
25. North Holderness	27 Sept.	$12\frac{1}{2}$
26. Gower	4 Oct.	$12\frac{3}{4}$
27. Dudley and District	1 Nov.	$8\frac{3}{4}$
28. Bankfoot	19 Nov.	3
29. St George and Hanham	28 Nov.	$1\frac{1}{2}$
30. Middleton	15 Dec.	$8\frac{3}{4}$
	1899	
31. Tanat Valley	4 Jan.	$16\frac{1}{2}$
32. Flamborough and Bridlington (Amendment)	9 Jan.	–
33. Barking and Beckton	13 Feb.	$1\frac{1}{4}$
34. South Norfolk	13 Feb.	$17\frac{3}{4}$
35. Didcot and Watlington	22 Feb.	$12\frac{3}{4}$
36. Grimsby and Saltfleetby	27 Feb.	$19\frac{1}{2}$
37. Leek Caldon Low and Martington	6 March	18
38. North Shields Tynemouth and District	6 March	2
39. Kinver	7 March	4
40. Ventnor Inclined	10 March	$\frac{1}{4}$
41. Liverpool and Prescot	10 March	3
42. Isle of Axholme	11 March	22
43. Sheppey	3 May	$8\frac{1}{2}$
44. London United	9 May	$7\frac{1}{4}$
45. Merthyr Tydfil	16 May	$3\frac{1}{2}$
46. West Manchester	2 June	3
47. Llandudno and Colwyn Bay	2 June	$8\frac{1}{4}$
48. Axminster and Lyme Regis	15 June	$6\frac{1}{2}$
49. Corringham	10 July	$2\frac{3}{4}$
50. Chatham and District	17 Aug.	$8\frac{1}{2}$
51. Poole and District	17 Aug.	$3\frac{3}{4}$
52. Penzance Newlyn and West Cornwall	19 Aug.	21
53. Trent Valley	23 Aug.	6
54. Portsdown and Horndean	2 Sept.	6
55. Fraserburgh and St Combs	8 Sept.	$4\frac{1}{2}$
56. Welshpool and Llanfair	8 Sept.	9
57. Southend-on-Sea and District	8 Sept.	6
58. Glasgow and South Western Railway (Maidens and Dunure)	30 Sept.	$19\frac{1}{2}$

Name of order	Date of confirmation	Mileage authorised
59. Didcot and Watlington (Extensions)	7 Oct.	$2\frac{3}{4}$
60. Coggleshall	20 Nov.	$2\frac{1}{2}$
61. Bradford and Leeds	23 Nov.	$1\frac{1}{2}$
62. Doncaster Corporation	27 Nov.	$7\frac{1}{2}$
63. Wick and Lybster	27 Nov.	$13\frac{1}{2}$
64. Cranbrook and Tenterden	8 Dec.	10
65. Glasgow and South Western Railway (Cairn Valley)	29 Dec.	$15\frac{3}{4}$
	1900	
66. Basingstoke and Alton (Amendment)	11 Jan.	–
67. North Lincolnshire	12 Jan.	$21\frac{3}{4}$
68. North Lindsey	29 Jan.	$14\frac{1}{2}$
69. Essington and Ashmore	29 Jan.	$4\frac{3}{4}$
70. Redditch and District	30 Jan.	4
71. Isle of Thanet (Extensions)	23 Feb.	2
72. Dudley and District (Extensions)	3 April	3
73. Rhyl and Prestatyn	3 April	$3\frac{1}{2}$
74. Mid Suffolk	5 April	$42\frac{1}{2}$
75. Callington	1 May	11
76. Bexhill and St Leonards	6 June	$5\frac{1}{4}$
77. Cheltenham and District	8 June	$3\frac{1}{2}$
78. Cheltenham and District (Extension)	8 June	$2\frac{1}{4}$
79. Robertsbridge and Pevensey	12 June	15
80. Highbridge Wedmore and Cheddar	29 June	$12\frac{1}{2}$
81. Bere Alston and Calstock	13 July	4
82. Lastingham and Rosedale	31 July	8
83. North Wales Narrow Gauge Railways (Beddgelert Light Railway Extension)	3 Aug.	$4\frac{1}{2}$
84. Barnsley and District	11 Aug.	3
85. South Staffordshire	11 Aug.	$4\frac{1}{4}$
86. Gateshead and District	22 Aug.	$2\frac{1}{2}$
87. South Staffordshire (Extensions)	1 Sept.	$2\frac{3}{4}$
88. Bromsgrove	1 Sept.	3
89. Peterborough and District	1 Sept.	$5\frac{1}{2}$
90. Bourne Valley	26 Oct.	$11\frac{1}{4}$
91. Bishop's Waltham	26 Oct.	$4\frac{1}{4}$
92. Gorsforth and Ponteland	5 Nov.	7
93. Wootton under Edge	3 Dec.	$3\frac{1}{4}$
94. Rhyl and Prestatyn (Extensions)	7 Dec.	2

Name of order		Date of confirmation	Mileage authorised
		1901	
95.	Oakington and Cottenham	25 Jan.	4
96.	Long Melford and Hadleigh	8 Feb.	15
97.	Sheerness and District	12 Feb.	$2\frac{1}{2}$
98.	West Hartlepool (Deviation & c)	19 Feb.	–
99.	Ormskirk and Southport	21 Feb.	6
100.	Kelvedon Tiptree and Tollesbury	27 Feb.	$9\frac{3}{4}$
101.	Morley and District	4 March	$8\frac{3}{4}$
102.	Maidstone and Faversham Junction	8 March	12
103.	Brackenhill	19 March	5
104.	Cleobury Mortimer and Ditton Priors	23 March	12
105.	Nidd Valley	30 March	$6\frac{1}{4}$
106.	Spen Valley	22 April	$7\frac{1}{2}$
107.	Spen Valley (Extensions)	22 April	$11\frac{3}{4}$
108.	Nuneaton and District	26 April	$8\frac{3}{4}$
109.	Mansfield and District	13 May	10
110.	Mid Suffolk (Amendment)	1 June	–
111.	Isle of Thanet (Amendment)	7 June	–
112.	East and West Yorkshire Union	7 June	$1\frac{1}{4}$
113.	Blackpool and Garstang	14 June	$14\frac{1}{2}$
114.	Nelson	17 June	$1\frac{3}{4}$
115.	Barrowford	17 June	1
116.	Colne and Trawden	17 June	$5\frac{1}{4}$
117.	Central Essex	3 July	$21\frac{1}{2}$
118.	Pewsey and Salisbury (Extension of Time)	5 July	–
119.	Lizard (Extension of Time)	16 July	–
120.	Wales and Laughton	16 July	$5\frac{1}{4}$
121.	Bridlington and North Frodingham (Extension of Time)	16 July	–
122.	Tickhill	7 Aug.	$12\frac{1}{2}$
123.	Wakefield and District	13 Sept.	10
124.	Bury and Diss	19 Sept.	$27\frac{1}{4}$
125.	Welshpool and Llanfair (Amendment)	22 Sept.	–
126.	Kidderminster and Bewdley	2 Oct.	$4\frac{1}{4}$
127.	Blackburn Whalley and Padiham	2 Oct.	14
128.	Durham and District	4 Oct.	$2\frac{3}{4}$
129.	Hadlow (Amendment)	4 Oct.	–
130.	Derby and Ashbourne	10 Oct.	13
131.	Tanat Valley (Amendment)	25 Oct.	–

Name of order	Date of confirmation	Mileage authorised
132. Bath and District	2 Nov.	$13\frac{3}{4}$
133. Mitcham	6 Nov.	3
134. Amesbury and Military Camp (Amendment)	16 Nov.	–
135. Bardsfield and Sible Hedingham	18 Nov.	$7\frac{3}{4}$
136. Halesowen	18 Nov.	9
137. Bridgewater Stowey and Stogursey	22 Nov.	11
138. Harrow and South Shields	17 Dec.	$3\frac{1}{4}$
139. Worcester and District	17 Dec.	$4\frac{1}{4}$
140. East Sussex	19 Dec.	7
141. County of Middlesex	19 Dec.	$15\frac{3}{4}$
142. Loughborough and District	21 Dec.	$6\frac{1}{2}$
143. Barton-upon-Irwell	21 Dec.	$1\frac{1}{4}$
	1902	
144. Essington and Ashmore (Amendment and Extension)	9 Jan.	$1\frac{1}{2}$
145. Aldershot and Farnborough	16 Jan.	$5\frac{1}{2}$
146. Lyndhurst	23 Jan.	$2\frac{1}{2}$
147. Middleton (Deviation, &c)	27 Jan.	–
148. East Anglian	30 Jan.	$3\frac{1}{2}$
149. Wigan	30 Jan.	4
150. Worcester (Extension)	3 Feb.	4
151. Dartford	6 Feb.	$5\frac{1}{4}$
152. Potteries (Extensions)	6 Feb.	6
153. Rother Valley (Extensions)	13 March	8
154. Lizard (Amendment)	4 April	–
155. Southwold	4 April	9
156. Deanhead	16 April	$5\frac{1}{4}$
157. Gower (Amendment)	23 April	–
158. Swansea and District	28 May	$7\frac{3}{4}$
159. Grimsby and Saltfleetby (Amendment)	31 May	–
160. Orpington, Cudham and Tatsfield	10 June	$7\frac{1}{2}$
161. Holmfield and Southowram	23 June	$4\frac{1}{2}$
162. Halesowen (Extensions)	14 July	$1\frac{3}{4}$
163. Darlington	24 July	$5\frac{1}{2}$
164. Barnsley and District (Extensions)	24 July	$4\frac{1}{4}$
165. Colne and Trawden (Capital and Further Powers Amendment)	25 July	–
166. Doncaster Corporation (Deviation, &c)	31 July	$\frac{1}{4}$
167. Llanelly and District	31 July	$7\frac{3}{4}$

Name of order	Date of confirmation	Mileage authorised
168. Derwent Valley	31 July	$16\frac{1}{4}$
169. Vale of Rheidol (Amendment)	1 Aug.	–
170. Cromarty and Dingwall	1 Aug.	$18\frac{3}{4}$
171. Wakefield and District (Extensions)	19 Aug.	$12\frac{1}{4}$
172. South Norfolk (Extension of Time)	21 Aug.	–
173. Spen Valley and Morley (Extensions)	23 Aug.	$3\frac{1}{4}$
174. Bentley and Bordon	6 Oct.	$4\frac{3}{4}$
175. Crowland and District (Amendment)	13 Oct.	–
176. North Shields Tynemouth and District (Extension)	20 Dec.	$\frac{1}{2}$
	1903	
177. Cheltenham and District (Extensions No. 2)	8 Jan.	$6\frac{3}{4}$
178. Amesbury and Military Camp (Bulford Extension)	10 Jan.	$2\frac{3}{4}$
179. Padstow Bedruthan and Mawgan	14 Jan.	12
180. Poole and District (Extension)	5 Feb.	$1\frac{3}{4}$
181. Walthamstow and District	12 Feb.	$9\frac{1}{2}$
182. Glamorgan County Council (Morriston to Pontardawe)	19 March	$5\frac{3}{4}$
183. Barking (Extensions)	26 March	$1\frac{1}{2}$
184. Leighton Buzzard and Hitchin	6 April	19
185. Mid Suffolk (Deviation and Amendment)	23 April	–
186. Doncaster Corporation (Extensions)	24 April	$1\frac{1}{2}$
187. Amesbury and Military Camp (Newton Toney Curve)	28 April	$\frac{1}{2}$
188. Colne and Trawden (Aquisition of Lands Amendment)	6 May	–
189. Canterbury and Herne Bay	6 May	$9\frac{1}{2}$
190. Warrington Corporation	11 May	$1\frac{1}{2}$
191. Warrington and Northwich	11 May	$19\frac{1}{2}$
192. County of Middlesex (Lands)	9 June	–
193. West Manchester (Extensions and Amendment)	23 June	$1\frac{1}{2}$
194. Callington (Extension of Time)	24 June	–
195. Gloucester Corporation	7 Aug.	7
196. County of Gloucester (Gloucester and Brockworth)	7 Aug.	$3\frac{1}{2}$
197. Bath Electric Tramways (Light Railway Extensions)	18 Sept.	$\frac{1}{2}$
198. Llandudno and Colwyn Bay (Deviation and Amendment	26 Sept.	$\frac{1}{2}$

Name of order	Date of confirmation	Mileage authorised
199. Dartford District	30 Sept.	$23\frac{1}{2}$
200. Lastingham and Rosedale (Extension of Time)	30 Sept.	–
201. Bankfoot (Extension of Time)	10 Oct.	–
202. Burton and Ashby	10 Oct.	$11\frac{1}{2}$
203. Dover and River	12 Oct.	$1\frac{1}{4}$
204. Bere Alston and Calstock (Extension of Time)	10 Nov.	–
205. Totton Hythe and Fawley	10 Nov.	$8\frac{3}{4}$
206. Dartford (Extension)	13 Nov.	1
207. Barrowford Light Railway Order, 1901 (Transfer, &c)	19 Nov.	–
208. Avonmouth	1 Dec.	2
209. Maidstone Corporation	9 Dec.	2
210. Robertsbridge and Pevensey (Extension of Time)	23 Dec.	–
211. Quarry Bank Brierley Hill and Rowley Regis	23 Dec.	2
212. County of Middlesex	30 Dec.	$21\frac{3}{4}$
213. Watford and District	31 Dec.	$1\frac{1}{2}$
	1904	
214. County of Hertford (No. 1)	26 Feb.	$3\frac{1}{2}$
215. Bradford Corporation (Nidd Valley Transfer)	1 March	–
216. Rugby and District	2 April	$4\frac{1}{2}$
217. Clacton-on-Sea and St Osyth	2 April	$4\frac{1}{4}$
218. Leicester and District	2 April	$6\frac{3}{4}$
219. Kent and East Sussex (General Powers)	20 April	–
220. Aldershot and Farnborough (Amendement)	25 April	–
221. Lowestoft Corporation (East Anglian Transfer)	6 June	–
222. Ripon and District	22 June	3
223. Leek Caldon Low and Hartington (Extension of Time &c)	23 June	–
224. Witney, Burford and Andoversford	23 June	$23\frac{3}{4}$
225. Southend-on-Sea and District (Extensions)	4 July	$3\frac{1}{2}$
226. Woodbridge and Bawdsey	26 July	$9\frac{3}{4}$
227. Bideford Westward Ho! and Appledore	27 July	$1\frac{1}{2}$
228. Maidstone and Faversham Junction (Extension of Time)	19 Aug.	–
229. Cheltenham and District (Extension No. 3)	19 Aug.	$\frac{1}{10}$
230. Axminster and Lyme Regis (Further Capital Powers)	24 Aug.	–
231. Brackenhill (Extension of Time)	22 Sept.	–
232. Tickhill (Extension of Time)	22 Sept.	–

Name of order	Date of confirmation	Mileage authorised
233. Southend and Colchester	29 Sept.	27½
234. London United Tramways (Light Railway Extensions)	4 Nov.	9
	1905	
235. Blackpool and Fylde (Change of Name &c)	14 Jan.	–
236. North Lindsey (Amendment)	20 Jan.	–
237. Hope Bradwell and Castleton	13 Feb.	3
238. Mid Suffolk (Halesworth Deviation)	23 Feb.	–
239. Basingstoke and Alton (Speed Amendment)	22 March	–
240. Portsmouth and Hayling	29 March	3¾
241. Welshpool and Llanfair (Further Borrowing Powers)	1 May	–
242. Guildford	4 May	2¼
243. Campbeltown and Machrihanish	8 May	6¼
244. North Wales (Narrow Gauge Railways Light Railway)	6 June	–
245. County of Middlesex (Extension of Time)	17 June	–
246. Bath Electric Tramways (Light Railway Extensions)	18 July	1¾
247. Homfield and Southowram (Amendment and Extension of Time)	25 July	–
248. Devon South Hams	31 July	13¾
249. Axholme Joint Railway Hatfield Moor Extension)	5 Aug.	5
250. East Sussex (Amendment)	14 Aug.	–
251. Central Essex (Amendment)	4 Sept.	–
252. Priston	5 Sept.	3
253. Bere Alston and Calstock (Amendment)	12 Oct.	–
254. Padstow Bedruthan and Mawgan (Extension of Time)	13 Oct.	–
255. Devonport	7 Dec.	4 chains
	1906	
256. Grimsby District	15 Jan.	6½
257. Newark and District	15 Jan.	3½
258. Bideford Clovelly and Hartland	24 Jan.	13½
259. Tarporley	6 Feb.	7¼
260. Ryhope Seaham Murton and South Hetton	16 Feb.	6½
261. Blyton and Frodingham	26 Feb.	15¼
262. North Staffordshire Railway (Light Railway)	2 March	–
263. County of Middlesex (Waltham Cross and Enfield)	16 March	4¾

Name of order	Date of confirmation	Mileage authorised
264. County of Hertford	16 March	$3\frac{1}{2}$
265. Blagdon and Pensford	20 March	$12\frac{1}{4}$
266. Burton and Ashby (Amendment)	30 March	–
267. Headcorn and Maidstone Junction	10 May	10
268. Woking and Bagshot	18 May	$12\frac{1}{2}$
269. Stretford	15 June	1
270. West Manchester (New Lines, &c)	15 June	$1\frac{1}{2}$
271. Canterbury and Herne Bay (Extension of Time)	4 July	–
272. Barking (Lands)	10 July	–
273. North Lindsey (Extensions)	10 July	$8\frac{3}{4}$
274. Bath and Landsdown	9 Aug.	$1\frac{1}{2}$
275. Tottenham Walthamstow	9 Aug.	$1\frac{1}{2}$
276. Bath Electric Tramways (Light Railway Extensions)	18 Aug.	$1\frac{1}{2}$
277. Clayton West and Darton	22 Sept.	$3\frac{3}{4}$
278. Falkland	2 Oct.	$2\frac{3}{4}$
279. Lampeter Aberaeron and Newquay	9 Oct.	$21\frac{1}{2}$
280. Bere Alston and Calstock (Extension of Time, &c)	16 Oct.	–
281. Portmadoc Beddgelert and South Snowdon Railway (Beddgelert Light Railway Extension)	24 Oct.	$\frac{3}{4}$
282. Leek Caldon Low and Hartington (Borrowing and Further Powers Amendment)	17 Dec.	–
	1907	
283. Maidstone Corporation (Extensions)	5 Jan.	$3\frac{1}{4}$
284. Warrington and Northwich (Extension of Time)	24 Jan.	–
285. County of Middlesex (Extension and Lands)	7 Feb.	1
286. Robertsbridge and Pevensey (Extension of Time)	26 Feb.	–
287. Mansfield and District (Extensions)	9 April	$6\frac{1}{2}$
288. Leicester and District (Extension of Time)	16 April	–
289. Brackenhill (Extension of Time)	16 April	–
290. Ackworth	23 April	$5\frac{1}{2}$
291. Llanelly and District	23 April	$6\frac{1}{4}$
292. Dudley and District (Amendment)	6 May	–
293. Kirkby Malzeard	6 May	6
294. Central Essex (Extension of Time)	5 June	–
295. Wolverhampton and Cannock Chase Railway (Light Railway)	11 June	$8\frac{1}{4}$
296. East Sussex (Extension of Time and Amendment)	21 June	–

Name of order	Date of confirmation	Mileage authorised
297. Dartford District (Amendment and Extension of Time)	3 Aug.	–
298. Derwent Valley Light Railway (Transfer, &c)	26 Aug.	–
299. Callington (Amendment and Transfer)	28 Aug.	–
300. Kent and East Sussex (Further Borrowing Powers)	10 Sept.	–
301. Southwold (Borrowing Powers, &c)	27 Sept.	–
302. Llandudno and Colwyn Bay (Extension and	30 Sept.	$1\frac{1}{2}$
303. Headcorn and Maidstone Junction (Amendment)	10 Oct.	–
304. Holmfield and Southowram (Extension of Time)	10 Oct.	–
305. Cromarty and Dingwall (Extension of Time, Deviation and Amendment)	4 Nov.	–
306. East and West Yorkshire Union (Borrowing Powers)	4 Nov.	–
307. Maidstone Corporation (Extensions No. 2)	9 Dec.	$1\frac{1}{4}$
	1908	
308. London and North Western Railway (Dyserth and Newmarket Light Railway)	17 Jan.	$1\frac{1}{2}$
309. Stottesdon Kinlet and Billingsley	13 Feb.	$5\frac{1}{4}$
310. Portsdown and Horndean (Extension, &c)	13 Feb.	$\frac{3}{8}$
311. London United Tramways Light Railways (Extension of Time)	23 March	–

Source: Appendix to Board of Trade Report

Appendix B
Light Railway and Tramway Journal
questionnaire

In May and June 1901 the *Light Railway and Tramway Journal* published the results of a questionnaire which had been distributed to many people actively involved in building and operating light railways. The questions and one of the responses — from Mr H. L. Godden, C.E. (Messrs Jeyes and Godden), London — are given below.

1. Are you of opinion that Light Railways are of real service in suitable Districts?

We do not think that there can be the least doubt as to the utility of and service rendered by light railways in country districts. Sufficient evidence of this is afforded by the use made by farmers, stock raisers, and others of those already in whole or in part constructed, such as the Goole and Marshlands, Haxey and Crowle, etc., light railways. Beyond giving the agriculturalists an easy and cheap outlet to and from their markets, they must tend, we believe, to keep the labour on the land by doing away with the present isolation. The resources of a very large area in our rural districts are not by any means fully developed in their agricultural, mineral, or manufacturing capabilities, and this is chiefly, if not entirely, owing to lack of transport facilities. Large beds of coal, ironstone, brick-earth, limes, and other natural deposits are lying unworked from this cause. On the development of home production largely depends our commercial prosperity, and it forms the *raison d'être* of the Light Railways Act. Light railways open a fresh field for commercial travellers and tradesmen in the principal villages and help in every way the progressive spirit of the age, and are, we consider, a necessity for our country's well-being.

2. Kindly give any actual experience which you may have had of Light Railway promotion and working.

As engineers for several projected light railways we have had considerable experience of the promotion of the schemes. By the great bulk of all classes of the population the proposal has been invariably warmly welcomed, and opposition has only come from (a) individual landowners or occupiers; (b) from public bodies, councils etc., generally only restricted to certain minor points; and (c) occasionally from existing railway companies on the ground of competition. With reasonable care in choice of route and in matters of local interest the promotion of light railway Orders under the Act is not made unduly difficult, nor is it unreasonably expensive. The crucial point comes in the promotion of the company when the capital has to be raised, and, practically, the Act gives us no assistance here. As an investment for capital, light railways do not appeal to the public because they have no well-known established successes to go upon. The district immediately interested is unable in almost every case to find any appreciable proportion of the money requisite. Yet, as progress goes on, it will be seen that these lines can be made very profitable, and once this is realised there is a brilliant future opened. Landowners, except in a few individual cases have not realised how closely their interests run in line with railway development. They both can and should do a great deal more to help the promotion of lines than they have done so far.

3. Do you think the Light Railway Commissioners should be a paid body? (At present only one is paid £1,000 a year.)

The duties of the Light Railway Commissioners are so onerous and responsible that it is only reasonable that they should be paid for their trouble. At the same time, the fact of their being a paid body would not increase their efficiency, at all events with the present excellent *personnel.*

4. Is it your view that the number of Commissioners should be increased from the present number of three, so as to facilitate enquiries, etc.?

The present number of the Commissioners is, and will be, ample, so long as the present difficulties with regard to finances blocks the progress of the Light railway development.

5. Do you advocate the creation of a special Light Railway Department at the Board of Trade, so that the existing delays in the confirmation of Orders may be obviated, and Light Railway projects pushed through whilst local interest in them is strong and fresh?

Not under present conditions. The Light Railway Commission is now practically a special Board of Trade department.

6. Please state your views as to the free use of the ordinary roads by Light Railways, provided the ordinary traffic is not hampered.

In certain districts in the country where there are very wide roads, free use may be made of them with advantage, and no detriment is found in practice. For instance, the Wisbech and Upwell Tramway of the Great Eastern Railway is a typical light railway on the road, and works quite smoothly. Of course there is a great saving of prime cost for acquiring land, etc. Nevertheless, there are few places in this country in which the roads lend themselves readily for this plan. Such roads should be at least 30 ft wide.

7. What advantages do you see in Light Railways being promoted and worked by County Councils rather than by private persons or Companies?

County councils have greater facilities and a stronger position in promoting Orders than private persons or companies, and a better chance for raising capital for construction. But in working the line afterwards they do not have the same advantages, and, except in some cases of town tramways which do not cater for goods traffic, have neither the experience necessary nor the opportunity for acquiring it. Moreover, their time and attention as a body is always too fully occupied with other matters, and the exigencies of a constantly varying traffic demands a freedom from the binding routine necessary to them as a public official body.

8. Would you favour a special rate being levied for Light Railway purposes, and, if so, would you limit the area of its application to the district served by such Light Railway?

Not unless they were state, county council, or municipal lines, or the like.

9. Do you favour the proposition that the ordinary Railway Companies should be deprived of any locus standi *as regards opposition to Light Railways, on the ground that the latter proposes to do what the ordinary railway has not done?*

No. This would not be fair in view of the large capital sunk in, and the wide scope of, ordinary railway companies. At the same time the allowable grounds of their opposition should be more strictly defined, and a limit put to the expenditure incurred in urging their case. Some greater freedom might be allowed light railways in obtaining powers to form junctions with, and use stations of, existing lines subject to payments to be settled by arbitration.

10. Would you favour the idea of Treasury assistance being given on easier terms, and more freely, where good cause can be shown for the construction of a Light Railway in poor districts?

Most certainly. This is one of the points in which the Act of 1896 is almost a failure. Many of the districts that can least afford the expense are those most in need of transport facilities to develop their resources, and are those from which the best commercial returns would eventually ensue.

11. Do you approve of the proposal that land should be purchasable compulsorily at average local prices under ordinary conditions in all cases where it is clearly shown that a Light Railway would greatly benefit any given area?

Certainly; due compensation being allowed for specific, not sentimental, damage. But does not the betterment clause, No. 13 (1), in the Act already cover this?

12. Would you support the adoption of the Belgian system, under which Light or Local Railways are constructed at the joint expense of the district, the Province or County, and the State? (In Belgium, under this system, the mileage of Light Railways amounts to 54 per cent of that of the ordinary railways, and is quite successful.)

Not as compulsory. Private enterprise is too prominently the basis of our commercial development, and has always achieved the greatest results. The Belgian system is a compulsory pseudo-co-operative one, and it would be almost impossible to get the respective bodies to work in harmony in this country.

13. Have you any preference for electrical over steam working?

For town tramways, especially when combined with lighting, electrical traction is undoubtedly the better, but the cost of power stations and production of current renders it unsuitable for intermittent longer-distance traffic at present. Were all our main lines converted to electricity the case might be different.

14. What are your views as to the promotion of Tramways under the Light Railways Act?
They should not be taken under the Light Railways Act as it stands. If, however, this is allowed, they should be treated as distinct. Their conditions and objects are widely different from railways proper. In this case an addition to the constitution of the Light Railway Commission is necessary and would facilitate the work of both branches.

15. Do you favour the existence of a purchase clause enabling the local authority to acquire the undertaking at the end of a fixed period? If so, in how many years?
Only in the case of tramways and then not under 10 but preferably 14 years.

16. Is it not most desirable that the period for the repayment of loans should be greatly extended, so as to lessen a burden which now weighs seriously upon these undertakings?
It would be decidely advantageous.

17. Should not the Treasury rate of interest on loans be reduced from the $3\frac{1}{2}$ per cent specified in the Act to $2\frac{1}{2}$ or even 2 per cent?
Certainly, if possible.

18. Kindly express your views fully on any point not raised in the foregoing queries.
Generally speaking the Light Railways Act of 1896 would be made more beneficial and workable by the amendment of Sections 1(1), 4, 5, 8, 9, 10, 11(1), and 23. Practically the Act has resulted in giving a sufficiently rapid and inexpensive means of obtaining the necessary statutory powers, but it has lamentably failed so far in assisting the construction of the lines. In facilitating the obtaining of Orders it has perhaps opened a door for a form of speculation detrimental to good results — while in not giving real help towards construction it has almost precluded any results at all. These are to be commercial undertakings, and if the public are to be induced to invest in them they must see a fair prospect of dividends in return. At present they have practically no precedent to go upon. It is quite impossible for those formulating a scheme to set forth a sound basis of figures showing definite returns in £ s d. A great deal of the necessary evidence is not even open for their inspection. Now there are two elements in this that have to be considered: First, the traffic awaiting quicker or cheaper transport; and, secondly, the traffic that will arise from the better development of the district. For the first it may be possible to obtain some very incomplete figures, partly over and partly under estimated, while for the second only a very rough guess can be hazarded. Not even a true analogy can be adopted, so far, in this country. It is with a view to lightening this obscurity that I venture to suggest the amendment of the Act in the clauses mentioned and the formation of a special Light Railway Department of the Board of Trade headed by an augmented Light Railway Commission. This special department should go a great deal further than do either the Commissioners or the Board of Trade at present into the merits of the applications. Its work in addition to that already entailed would be chiefly connected with the financial prospects of the lines. It

would have to consider the two elements above mentioned, and in doing this would have to have placed at its disposal all the tabulated information of the Board of Trade, Board of Agriculture, Railway Clearing houses, Census returns, Geological Surveys, and of all the various Chambers of Commerce, County Mining, Manufacturing, Industrial, and Trade Associations of the country. This knowledge being once centralised, the department could thereon base a sound estimate of the immediate and future prospects of the line as a paying proposition.

Appendix C
The Association of Smaller Railway Companies

The Association was formed in 1919 with the establishment of the Ministry of Transport and by October 1920 represented the following railway companies: Brecon & Merthyr; Bridgewater; Didcot Newbury & Southampton; East & West Yorkshire Union; Ffestiniog; Freshwater Yarmouth & Newport; Harborne; Isle of Wight Central Railway; Mansfield; Mawddwy; Mold & Denbigh; North Lindsay; North Sunderland; Sheffield District; South Yorkshire Junction; and the Stratford on Avon & Midland Junction.

The Association was particularly concerned to prevent a downward revision of the percentage of gross receipts payable by operating companies to owning companies, and on this issue it was regarded by the Ministry of Transport as the companies' spokesman. A reduction in the percentage payable would hit owning companies as it would reduce the likelihood of them paying a dividend and would reduce the value of the lines in the event of a proposed amalgamation. The Association led a campaign to obtain suitable compensation anticipating the absorption of most of the minor railways by the 1921 Act. It must not be assumed, however, that all owning companies were keen to join the Association. The Teign Valley Railway Company, approached in November 1920, responded with hostility, demanding details of membership levels and funding: would it have to pay a year's subscription (£20) for the period between November and 31 March? The final chapter to this story is that by the Act of 1921 each of the worked companies submitted a claim for compensation and were awarded a sum apparently set at 73 per cent from the 500,000 set aside for that purpose.

The postscript is that the Teign Valley Railway, having joined the Association, was sent a bill for 2½ per cent of the award, a sum generally agreed, to meet costs.

Compensation claims and awards under the 1921 Act (£)

Railway company	Sum claimed	Sum awarded
Lampeter & Aberaeron	539	395
Welshpool & Llanfair	3,636	2,667
Teign Valley Railway	15,366	11,271

Source: PRO, RAIL 1057–219

Appendix D
Branch line economies

The problems of operating rural branch lines were well illustrated in March 1926 when the GWR issued a report analysing the predicament of fifty-three branch lines operated by the company and investigated ways in which savings could be made. Inevitably few of the branch lines in question were light railways, but the report shows that proposed methods of reducing expenditure ignored what was then almost an arbitrary division. Indeed, on the subject of applying to the Ministry of Transport to convert lines to light railway operation the major advantages were summed up as merely withdrawal of gatekeepers, which would save £202 per annum on the Golden Valley Railway, gates and signalling equipment, and the institution of cattle guards. On the other hand, disadvantages attendant upon conversion to light railway status, such as reduction in speed and the obligation to illuminate signs at cattle crossings, were also mentioned. More methods of saving money included the following.

Reduction in fencing
Kerry and Vale of Rheidol lines: the cost of fencing on the latter line was £1,090 in the six months to 31 December 1924, nearly 20 per cent of total receipts for the year.

Reduction in staff
The Lambourn Valley line has been controlled by a single station master at Lambourn and on the Clevedon line rail motors have been run without guards.

Reduction in Sunday services
The winter Sunday service on the Clevedon branch was discontinued with a saving of 210 per annum.

Use of Tilley lamps instead of oil lamps
Six Tilley lamps could replace twenty oil lamps with a saving of £2 17s 0d per annum in oil.

Withdrawal of first-class accommodation
This would reduce the dead weight on trains.

Reduction in electrical signalling equipment
On ten named branches this was expected to save over £1,300 annually.

Centralised control of branch lines
The system of concentrating accounts, clerical work and supervision of Branches would be extended to save £3,259 per annum. Examples of savings on individual lines include: Aberaeron & Lampeter, £327; Pontrilas & Hay, 739; Tanat Valley, £477; and Wrington Vale, £245.

However, the major source of saving money was the closure of branch lines. Of the fifty-three lines under consideration six were singled out for possible closure: Yealmpton, saving £13,881; Llantrisant & Aberthaw, £4,827; Titley & Eardisley, £4,808; Pontrilas & Hat, £11,631; Dinas Mawddwy £4,653; and Welshpool & Llanfair, £6,502.

Other serious methods of saving money were confining services to a single eight-hour shift (£4,222); the transfer of passenger services to road but leaving freight to be dealt with by an eight-hour shift (£5,673).

Estimated savings from branch-line closure

Branch	Estimated annual savings (£)
1. Abbotsbury	30
2. Aberaeron & Lampeter	522
3. Abermule & Kerry	674
4. Abingdon	—
5. Alcester	—
6. Ashburton	—
7. Blenheim	324
8. Brentford	2,135
9. Bridport	115
10. Brixham	—
11. Calne	—
12. Chard	20
13. Cirencester	—
14. Clevedon	210
15. Cleobury Mortimer & Ditton Priors	490
16. Clynderwen & Letterston	1,313
17. Dinas Mawddwy	4,653[a]

cont.

18.	Eardisley	4,808[a]
19.	Exe Valley	114
20.	Falmouth	–
21.	Faringdon	–
22.	Hemyock	810
23.	Highworth	240
24.	Lambourne	540
25.	Lauceston	–
26.	Llantrisant & Aberthaw	4,827[a]
27.	Llanymynech & Llanfyllin	53
28.	Leominster & New Radnor	345
29.	Liskeard & Looe	130
30.	Malmesbury	389
31.	Minehead	336
32.	Moretonhampstead	76
33.	Moss Valley	2,044
34.	Newcastle Emlyn	5
35.	Pembroke & Whitland	27
36.	Pontrilas & Hay	11,631[a]
37.	Presteigne	–
38.	Princetown	–
39.	St Ives	–
40.	Shipston-on-Stour	212
41.	Tanat Valley Line	1,724
42.	Teign Valley	–
43.	Tetbury	353
44.	Vale of Rheidol	1,290
45.	Wadebridge	–
46.	Wallingford	–
47.	Watlington	8
48.	Welshpool & Llanfair	6,502[a]
49.	Wrexham Brymbo & Minera	1,663
50.	Wrexham & Rhos	385
51.	Whitland & Cardigan	1,084
52.	Wrington Vale	245
53.	Yealmpton	13,881[a]
	TOTAL	64,208

[a] These figures represent the total cost of working and maintaining the Branches and do not take account of the traffic which would be lost if the lines are closed.

Source: GWR Report on Branch Lines; PRO, RAIL 250–736

Bibliography

Parliamentary Papers

1879 Royal Commission on Agriculture
1893 Royal Commission on Agriculture
1896 Royal Commission on Land Use in Wales and Monmouthshire
1919 Royal Commission on Agriculture

Public Record Office: company records

RAIL 167/ff.	Easingwold Railway
RAIL 236/719/19	Sir Henry Oakley on Light Railways
RAIL 250/736	GWR Report on Branch Line Economies
RAIL 258/305	GWR Secretarial Papers, Local Development & Light Railway Company Ltd
RAIL 258/309/3	GWR Secretarial Papers Salisbury to Pewsey Light Railway
RAIL 258/309/6	Miscellaneous GWR papers
RAIL 266/45	GWR Station Statistics
RAIL 266/107	GWR Road Passenger Statistics
RAIL 267/255	Special Report. Steam Rail motors in the Stroud Valley
RAIL 332/1 ff.	Kent & East Sussex Railway
RAIL 338/1 ff.	Lambourn Valley Railway
RAIL 339/1 ff.	Lampeter & Aberaeron Railway
RAIL 390/386	Absorption of Mid Suffolk by LNER
RAIL 456/1 ff.	Manchester & Milford Railway
RAIL 479/1 ff.	Mid Suffolk Light Railway
RAIL 523/1 ff.	North Devon & Cornwall Light Railway
RAIL 533/1 ff.	North Sunderland Railway
RAIL 1007/429	Light Railway Investigation Committee 1921
RAIL 1021/63	Light Railway Association of Great Britain
RAIL 1023/18	Comments on Light Railways Act
RAIL 1053/212	Street and Road Tramway Returns

RAIL 1053/228	Report to Board of Trade by Lieutenant-Colonel H. A. Yorke, 1912
RAIL 1054/1 ff.	Light Railway Commission. Particularly 1054/5, Light Railway Investigation Committee Report and Appendices
RAIL 1057/219	Miscellaneous Correspondence on Association of Minor Railways
RAIL 1057/229	Teign Valley Railway
RAIL 1057/230	Teign Valley Railway Station Statistics
RAIL 1057/475/6–8	Miscellaneous correspondence relating to the Lampeter & Aberaeron Railway
RAIL 1057/827	Proposed Lambourne Wantage & Didcot Light Railway
RAIL 1057/2903	Proposed Painswick Light Railway
RAIL 1057/2916	Lambourn Valley Railway
RAIL 1057/3007	Miscellaneous papers on Railways and Agriculture
RAIL 1075/89	Prospectus Manchester & Milford Railway
RAIL 1075/91	Prospectus Axminster & Lyme Regis Light Railway
RAIL 1075/122	Prospectus Golden Valley Railway
RAIL 1075/140	Prospectus Lampeter & Aberaeron Railway
RAIL 1075/197	Prospectus South Hams railway
RAIL 1075/2711	Prospectus Kent and East Sussex Railway
RAIL 1110/56	Reports and Accounts Vale of Rheidol Railway
RAIL 1110/71	Reports and Accounts Cleobury Mortimer & Ditton Priors Railway
RAIL 1110/93	Reports and Accounts Culm Valley Railway
RAIL 1110/235	Reports and Accounts Lambourn Valley Railway
RAIL 1110/236	Reports and Accounts Lampeter & Aberaeron Railway
RAIL 1110/357	Reports and Accounts North Devon & Cornwall Railway
RAIL 1110/443	Reports and Accounts Swindon & Highworth Light Railway
MAF 48/581	The Wissington Railway
MT 58/20	Miscellaneous Documents on the North Sunderland Railway
MT 58/280	Miscellaneous Documents on the Lampeter & Aberaeron Railway
Z LIB 4/277	G. A. Brown, 'Lynton and Barnstaple Railway' (typescript)
Z LIB 15/32/14	A. Ross, *Light Railways*, Liverpool Engineering Society

National Library of Wales
Dolau Cothi Documents. Miscellaneous Correspondence on the Lampeter & Llandilo Light Railway.

14807C	J. Rees, 'The Manchester and Milford Railway', 1944 (typescript)

Suffolk Record Office
150.10.14.1   Southwold & Halesworth Tramway
150.2.5.77.B   Blyth Valley Railway
150/2/5/78.B   Mid Suffolk Light Railway

Theses

Atkins, P. J., 'The Milk Trade of London 1870–1914', Ph.D., University of
    Cambridge, 1977.
Bosley, P. B., 'The Manchester and Milford Railway 1860–1906', M.A.,
    University of Wales, 1977.
Fisher, J. R., 'Public Opinion and Agriculture', Ph.D., University of Hull, 1972.
Howell, D. W., 'Welsh Agriculture', Ph.D., University of London, 1969.
Mason, N. M., 'Unprofitable Railway Companies in England and Wales 1845–
    1923', Ph.D., University of London, 1982.
Parris, H. W., 'Railways in the Northern Pennines to 1880', M.A., Leeds, 1954.

Newspapers and journals

The Times
Alnwick and County Gazette
Cambrian News
Carmarthen Weekly Journal
Halesworth Times
Haverfordwest and Milford Haven Telegraph
Wilts and Gloucestershire Standard
Board of Trade Journal
Country Gentlemen's Estate Book
Engineer
Herapath's Journal
Light Railway and Tramway Journal
LNER Magazine
Modern Transport
Railway Magazine
Railway Times

Books

Acworth, W. M., *The Elements of Railway Economics*, 1924.
Adams, W. B., *Roads and Rails*, 1862.
Aldcroft, D. H., *British Railways in Transition*, 1968.
Bagwell, P. S., *The Transport Revolution Since 1770*, 1974.
Ballard, S., *Cheap Railways for Rural Districts*, 1884.

Barker, T. C. and Savage, C. I., *An Economic History of Transport in Britain*, 1959.
Baughan, P., *Regional History of the Railways of Great Britain: North and Mid Wales*, 1980.
Bett, W. H. and Gillham, J. C., *The Great British Tramway Network*, 1957.
Boyd, J. I. C., *Narrow Gauge Railways in Mid Wales*, 1965.
Calthorp, E. R., *The Economics of Light Railway Transport*, 1896.
Cartwright, R. and Russell, R. T., *The Welshpool and Llanfair Railway*, 1981.
Clinker, C. R., *Light Railway Orders*, 1977.
Colyer, R. J., *The Welsh Cattle Drovers*, 1976.
Comfort, N. A., *The Mid Suffolk Railway*, 1963.
Course, E., *Independent and Light Railways in Southern England*, 1976.
Cozens, L., *Aberaeron Transport*, 1957.
Cole, W. H., *Light Railways at Home and Abroad*, 1899.
Darsley, R., *The Wissington Railway*, 1984.
Davies, W. J. K., *Light Railways*, 1964.
——, *Light Railways in the First World War*, 1967.
Ellis, C. H., *British Railway History*, 1959.
Gordon, D. I., *Regional History of the Railways of Great Britain: Eastern Counties*, 1977.
Gourvish, T. R., *Railways and the British Economy 1830–1914*, 1980.
Hartley, K. E., *The Easingwold Railway*, 1970.
Hawke, G. R., *Railways and Economic Growth in England and Wales*, 1970.
Heywood, A. P., *Minimum Gauge Railways*, 1898.
Higgins, S. H. P., *The Wantage Tramway*, 1958.
Howell, D. W., *Land and People in Nineteenth Century Wales*, 1977.
Ingram, A. and Baldwin, L., *Light Vans and Trucks*, 1977.
Irving, R. J., *The North Eastern Railway Company 1870–1914*, 1976.
Jenkins, A. B., *Memories of the Southwold Railway*, 1973.
Kidner, R. W., *Light Railway Handbook*, 1950.
Kirkaldy, A. W. and Evans, A. D., *The History and Economics of Transport*, 1920.
Klapper, C., *The Golden Age of Buses*, 1961.
——, *The Golden Age of Trams*, 1978.
Lewis, H. G., *The Railway Mania and its Aftermath* (reprint), 1968.
Lewis, W. J., *An Illustrated History of Cardiganshire*, 1970.
Mackay, J. C., *Light Railways for the United Kingdom, India and the Colonies*, 1896.
Mawson, E. O. and Calthorp, E. R., *Pioneer Irrigation and Light Railways*, 1904.
Morgan, J. S., *The Colonel Stephens Railways, A Pictorial History*, 1978.
Mowatt, C. L., *The Golden Valley Railway*, 1964.
Ottley, G., *A Bibliography of British Railway History*, 1965.
Oxley, J. S., *Light Railways*, 1901.
Padfield, R. and Burgess, B., *The Teifi Valley Railway*, 1974.
Paish, G., *The British Railways' Position*, 1902.
Parkinson, R. M., *Light Railway Construction*, 1902.
Perry, P. J., *British Farming in the Great Depression 1870–1914*, 1974.

Pratt, E. A., *A History of Inland Transport and Communication*, (reprint), 1970.
—— *The Organisation of Agriculture*, 1904.
—— *The Transition in Agriculture*, 1906.
Price, M. R. C., *The Lambourn Valley Railway*, 1964.
—— *The Whitland and Cardigan Railway*, 1976.
Pollins, H., *Britain's Railways: An Industrial History*, 1971.
Sherington, C. E. R., *A Hundred Years of Inland Transport 1830–1933*, 1934.
Simmonds, E. J., *Memoirs of a Station Master* (reprint), 1974.
Simmons, J., *The Railway in Town and Country 1830–1914*, 1986.
Taylor, A. R. and Tonks, E. S., *The Southwold Railway*, 1979.
Thomas, D. St J., *The Country Railway*, 1979.
—— *Regional History of the Railways of Great Britain: The West of England*, 1981.
Thomas, G., *Calm Weather*, 1930.
Williams, D., *The Rebecca Riots: A Study in Agrarian Discontent*, 1955.
Wright, A., *The North Sunderland Railway*, 1967.

Articles

Acworth, W. M., 'Light railways', *JRASE* (1894).
—— 'Light railways', *Journal of the Society of Arts*, XLIII (1895).
Baxter, R. D., 'Railway extension and its results', *Journal of the Statistical Society*, XXXIX (1866).
Burns, G. Frank, 'Railways of the 2′ 6″ gauge', *Railway Magazine*, December (1927).
Cain, P. J., 'Traders versus railways: the genesis of the Railways and Canal Traffic Act', *Journal of Transport History*, September (1973).
—— 'Railways and price discrimination: the case of agriculture 1880–1914', *Business History Review* (1978).
—— 'British railway rates problem 1894–1913', *Business History Review* (1978).
Calthorp, E. R., 'On some aspects of the light railway problem', *The Land Agents' Record*, 2 March and 16 March 1895.
Davies, J. Llefelys, 'Livestock trade in west Wales in the nineteenth century', *Aberystwyth Studies*, XIII (1934), and XIV (1936).
Delano, W. H., 'Secondary or narrow gauge railways for agricultural purposes', *JRASE* (1881).
Denton, J. B., 'The future extension of the railway system', *Transactions of the Institute of Surveyors* (1869).
Grantham, R. B., 'Private agricultural railways', *Transactions of the Institute of Surveyors* (1873).
Hind, J. R., 'Light railways for potato traffic in S. E. Lincolnshire', *Railway Magazine*, December 1927.
Howell, D. W., 'Impact of railways on agricultural development in nineteenth century Wales', *Welsh History Review* (1974).

—— 'Rural society in nineteenth century Carmarthenshire', *Carmarthen Antiquary*, XIII (1977).

Jones, J. E., 'Fairs in Cardiganshire', *Transactions of the Cardiganshire Antiquarian Society* (1930).

Kellett, J. R., 'Writing on Victorian railways: essay in nostalgia', *Victorian Studies* (1964).

Lawford, W. and Haughton, S. W., 'On the Wotton Light Railway', *Transactions of the Institute of Civil Engineers of Ireland* (1875).

Pain, A. C., 'Light railways and tramways', *The Field* (1873).

—— 'True and false economy in light railway construction', *Min. Proc. Inst. Civil Engineers*, CXXIX.

Parris, H. W., 'Northallerton to Hawes, a study in branch line history', *Journal of Transport History*, iv, 2 (1956).

Rodwell, J. K., 'Agricultural tramways', *Transactions of the West Suffolk Chamber of Agriculture*, March 1882.

Sellon, T. S. P. W. D'A., 'A few arguments in favour of light or road railways', *Journal of the British Association* (1888).

Veevers, H., 'Light railways', *Railway Magazine*, October and November 1915.

Whetham, E. H., 'The London milk trade 1860–1900', *English Historical Review* (1961).

Whigham, G. R., 'Light railways', *Min. Proc. Inst. Civil Engineers*, CXLVIIX.

Wilkinson, R., 'Railwayman's days at Wantage Road Station', *Berks. and Bucks. Countryside*, January 1975.

Wilkinson, R., 'Remembering Wantage's successful tramway', *Berks. and Bucks. Countryside*, October 1975.

Technical Correspondence Agency: *Light Railways for Agricultural Districts,* 1895.

Index